Social Consciousness

Social Consciousness

VOLUME 3 OF REMOVING
THE MIDDLEMAN

Rashed Hasan

© 2019 Rashed Hasan
Published by Rashed Hasan

Cover design by Aziz Hasan and Nyla Hasan
Book design by Rashed Hasan and Aziz Hasan

All rights reserved. No part of this publication may be reproduced, stored in a retrieval system, or transmitted in any form or by any means without the prior written permission of the author, with the exception of brief quotations in printed reviews.

ISBN 10: 0-9909811-2-6
ISBN 13: 978-0-9909811-2-1
Library of Congress Control Number: 2019903034
LCCN Imprint Name: Rashed Hasan, Alexandria, Virginia

Removing the Middleman is a book that Muslims and non-Muslims alike will find of interest. Bypassing a reliance on traditional religious scholars (*ulama*), Rashed Hasan affirms the right of Muslims to go straight to the text of the Qur'an, tackling the issue of Islamic reform head on, reading and reinterpreting the text of the Qur'an within the context of the contemporary world.

—*John Esposito*, *university professor and founding director, Center for Christian Muslim Understanding, Georgetown University, Washington, DC*

This is a contemporary English translation of the Qur'an. It has been thoughtfully and painstakingly translated. Following each set of verses is a thoughtful reflection and action statement designed to give further insight into the verses and help put them in to a positive way of living. To do this has required great fluency in multiple languages to avoid missteps in translation. I have three other English translations of the Qur'an but find this one the most readable, and, as a result, most meaningful. I look forward to further enlightenment as Mr. Hasan translates more chapters in the future. Once completed, this will be the contemporary English translation against which others will be measured.

—*Dr. John Power*, *cardiologist, Pittsburgh, Pennsylvania*

For young Muslims living in the United States or other parts of the Western world, this book bridges the divide between our traditional understanding of the Qur'an and applying it to the modern world. Rashed states plainly that "religion in its purest form was meant to forge a global alliance of goodwill and common humanity by encouraging diverse tribes to work together." When I read this book, I feel as if there's a stronger bond between Muslims and our Christian and Jewish brethren in the sense that we're all competing for goodness on this planet, and we should lift up others who are seeking to become better people in this world.

—*Siraj Hashmi*, *news anchor and journalist, McLean, Virginia*

A thoughtfully written analysis that encourages you to look into religious text through a pragmatic lens. A standout from other books on the Qur'an; an academic yet practical take on understanding religion.

—*B. Shah*, editor of Sandstorm:
A Leaderless Revolution in the Digital Age, *New York City*

Removing the Middleman is a really accessible and thought-provoking translation of the Quran. The commentary provided by Rashed Hasan as well as the definition of key terminology using nonacademic, modern language has made this translation both refreshing and practical in terms of how to apply these concepts to my day-to-day life. This book highlights the universal and inclusive nature of Islam, a concept that is rarely emphasized today.

—*Sadia Sayeed* MD, *resident pathologist,*
Virginia Commonwealth University Health Systems, Richmond, Virginia

As a Christian person of faith, I try to learn and understand other cultures, religions, and beliefs. Reading and understanding the Qur'an has been challenging. *Removing the Middleman* was exactly the help I needed. It is written in language that makes it easier to understand Islam and the Muslim faith. It is obvious that Mr. Rashed Hasan is a man of exceedingly spiritual faith and knowledge and has studied the Qur'an in depth. I am grateful to, and applaud, him for writing *Removing the Middleman*, and I'm waiting for volume 2.

—*Sincerria Elliott*, *physical trainer, Alexandria, Virginia*

As a young professional in my late twenties, I grew up on conflicting and confusing values that mixed culture and religion. The latest book in my collection to help decrypt the true message, *Removing the Middleman, Volume 1: Deciphering Faith without Ritual*, has provided me solid, credible, and well-articulated knowledge. I applaud the author's ability to focus on a small passage and really explain it in detail with real-world examples that are both relevant and relatable. I would recommend this book to readers of any age, regardless of religion, who want to truly understand context from Islam.

—*Anonymous (by request)*, *accountant, Arlington, Virginia*

As a young professional, I have been focused on my education and my career and have not devoted much time to learning about my faith. I had read the Qur'an as a child but in Arabic, and the translation was also in a secondary language. As a parent, I wanted to learn more about my faith so that I could guide my son to the best of my ability. I appreciate that *Removing the Middleman* is written in modern English and with thought-provoking insights that go beyond just a translation.

—*Aamer Shah*, *MBA, financial analyst, Alexandria, Virginia*

Rashed Hasan offers the reader a deeply informed understanding and appreciation of the Qur'an in all its richness and beauty. Through its combination of scrupulous translation and thoughtful analysis and reflection, the book invites both those new to Islam as well as those raised in the faith to fully explore and comprehend the Qur'an's universal message. The suggested actions accompanying each set of verses bring this message to life in today's context, offering inspiration and guidance for living a life of faith and service.

—*Fred Mills*, *Government Contractor, Vienna, Virginia*

Books by the Same Author

Removing the Middleman Series

    Volume 1: Deciphering Faith without Ritual (published in 2015)

    Volume 2: Free to Choose (published in 2017)

    Volume 3: Social Consciousness (current volume)

    Volume 4: Personal Accountability (to be published in 2020)

Dedication

In the middle of writing this book, Shagufta and I were blessed with our first grandchild, Celina, who was born in June 2017, in New York City. Her arrival brought so much joy, and it also provoked intense reflection about the cycle of life. Holding her in my arms reminded me of the moment that I held her father, Aziz, our firstborn, some thirty-four years ago.

Each life is precious, sacred, and blessed with unlimited possibilities to establish its presence on this planet and in our universe as well as to improve the richness of our world. Each of us adds to human knowledge, enriches our collective human experience, and contributes to our constant and persistent aspiration to understand our Creator and to improve our connection with God and fellow human beings.

This is not an easy task, and it is fraught with failure, as we can attest by our current observation of the world, where we have created a knowledge economy, unprecedented wealth for nations and individuals, and an enormous volume of human knowledge easily accessible to the masses through electronic media. In the presence of such huge gains, we also see half of humanity living in abject poverty; the rise of political corruption across many nations, including a vast majority of Muslim countries; unconscionable atrocities and mischief by terrorists and nation states against innocent citizens and civilians; and man-made pollution of our environment, which threatens the very essence of our health and economy and the purposefulness of our existence on this planet.

As God said in the Qur'an, *"We [God] created human beings with the best of attributes (i.e., the attributes of God), yet some of them render themselves to the lowest of the lows, but with the exception of those who are faithful and strive to do good."* (95:4–6). This challenge to affirm our goodness over evil, to overcome our temporary lapses that deny the grace of God, and to rise again and again in the face of frequent failures to remain true to our human purpose is what life is all about and how we will measure our success and how we will be judged by our Creator in this life and in the life to come.

God endowed Adam and Eve with knowledge and choices and endowed every human child at the beginning of his or her life to know God, to acknowledge God, and to be mindful of the purposefulness of life as an innate part of our consciousness and our day-to-day existence. *[Consider the truth] when your Sustainer God brings forth the offspring of the children of Adam, from themselves, He makes them confirm the truth about themselves: "Am I not your Sustainer God?" They say: "Yes, we do confirm." [Such is the truth], lest you say on the Day of Resurrection: "we were unaware of this" or you complain: "It was our forefathers who invented polytheism (or atheism), and we are but their descendants after them. Would You then make us face the consequence of their untrue conjectures?" This is how We [God] make the guidance explicit so that you may return [to the truth].* (7:172–174)

The challenge today for our generations is to affirm the truth and rise to the occasion to establish truth and justice in our world as God continues to urge us: *"(Let there be) from among Our creations a group that guides (itself and others) to truth and pursue justice thereby"* (7:181). It is to this pursuit that this volume is dedicated, and this can only happen by deepening our social consciousness as individual human beings and collectively, as the stewards of our planet.

With God is the knowledge of what is unknown—none knows but He. He knows what is in the land and what is in the sea. Not a leaf falls but He knows, nor is there a grain in the deep darkness of the earth or a thing green or dry; all are clearly defined and documented. He is the One Who takes your soul away as you sleep at night, and He knows what you accomplish during the day. He lets you rise each day so that your appointed term for life can be completed. Eventually all of you will gather back to God, and He will inform you the end results of your lifelong pursuits.

— "The Cattle," 6:6

Say: "How can I seek out a Sustainer other than God Himself, since He is the Cherisher of all things?" No soul bears but what it earns, and no soul will be made to face the consequence of what someone else did. At the end of your life, you return to your Cherisher God so that He can inform you on matters that you differed on (while alive). He is the One Who made you (the current generation) the successor on earth and made some of you excel over others (in matters of intelligence, leadership, wealth, spirituality, morals, ethics, kindness, freedom, etc.) so that He may ascertain your worth with respect to His gift He had given you. God is prompt in requiting (your actions), and He is ever the Forgiver, the Merciful!

— "The Cattle," 6:164–165

[Let be reminded] when the earth will shake with an upheaval [that you have not experience before] and all that the earth is burdened with will come forth; [at that juncture] people will say: "What is the matter with this earth?" On that [tumultuous] occasion, the earth will inform as inspired by its Sustainer God. Human beings will come forth, alone, so that they may be shown what they have accomplished in their lives [on the earth]; anyone who had done even an atom's weight of good work will see it; and anyone who has done even an atom's weight of evil work will see it (as well).

— "The Upheaval," 99:1–8

Table of Contents

Preface · xxi
Introduction · xxvii

Chapter 5 Surah Al-Maidah (The Repast) · 1
Chapter 5 Verses 1–3 · 4
Chapter 5 Verses 4–6 · 7
Chapter 5 Verses 7–11 · 10
Chapter 5 Verses 12–16 · 13
Chapter 5 Verses 17–19 · 15
Chapter 5 Verses 20–32 · 17
Chapter 5 Verses 33–37 · 21
Chapter 5 Verses 38–43 · 24
Chapter 5 Verses 44–50 · 28
Chapter 5 Verses 51–58 · 31
Chapter 5 Verses 59–66 · 34
Chapter 5 Verses 67–71 · 37
Chapter 5 Verses 72–82 · 39
Chapter 5 Verses 83–86 · 42
Chapter 5 Verses 87–93 · 44
Chapter 5 Verses 94–100 · 48
Chapter 5 Verses 101–108 · 51
Chapter 5 Verses 109–120 · 55
           Key Concepts in Surah Maidah (The Repast) · · · · · · · · · 58

Chapter 6 Al-Anam (The Cattle)	96
Chapter 6 Verses 1–11	99
Chapter 6 Verses 12–24	103
Chapter 6 Verses 25–32	106
Chapter 6 Verses 33–41	108
Chapter 6 Verses 42–50	111
Chapter 6 Verses 51–60	114
Chapter 6 Verses 61–70	118
Chapter 6 Verses 71–83	122
Chapter 6 Verses 84–93	126
Chapter 6 Verses 94–99	129
Chapter 6 Verses 100–111	132
Chapter 6 Verses 112–121	135
Chapter 6 Verses 122–135	138
Chapter 6 Verses 136–144	141
Chapter 6 Verses 145–153	145
Chapter 6 Verses 154–160	149
Chapter 6 Verses 161–165	152
Key Concepts in Surah Al-Anam (The Cattle)	155
Chapter 7 Surah Al-Araf (The Elevation)	197
Chapter 7 Verses 1–18	200
Chapter 7 Verses 19–31	203
Chapter 7 Verses 32–41	207
Chapter 7 Verses 42–53	210
Chapter 7 Verses 54–58	214
Chapter 7 Verses 59–72	217
Chapter 7 Verses 73–93	221
Chapter 7 Verses 94–102	226
Chapter 7 Verses 103–129	229
Chapter 7 Verses 130–137	233
Chapter 7 Verses 138–147	236
Chapter 7 Verses 148–156	239
Chapter 7 Verses 157–158	243

Chapter 7 Verses 159–171 · 247
Chapter 7 Verses 172–181 · 251
Chapter 7 Verses 182—188 · 255
Chapter 7 Verses 189—198 · 258
Chapter 7 Verses 199–206· 261
          Key Concepts from Surah Al-Araf (The Elevation) · · · · 264

Glossary of Key Arabic Terms ·299
Appendix A: Five Pillars of Faith · 325

Preface

The external history of a religious tradition often seems divorced from the raison d'etre of faith. The spiritual quest is an interior journey; it is psychic rather than a political drama. It is preoccupied with liturgy, doctrine, contemplative discipline, and an exploration of the heart, not with the clash of current events…Very often priests, rabbis, imams and shamans are just as consumed by worldly ambition as regular politicians. But all this is generally seen as an abuse of sacred ideal. In Islam, Muslims have looked for God in history. Their sacred scripture, the Quran, gave them a historical mission. Their chief duty was to create a just community in which all members, even the most weak and vulnerable, was treated with absolute respect…A Muslim would meditate upon the current events of his time and upon past history as a Christian would contemplate an icon, using the creative imagination of the external history to discover the hidden divine kernel.

—Karen Armstrong, *Islam: A Short History*

THIS CONTINUED JOURNEY INTO the Qur'an (volumes 1 through 3 to date) is intended for two audiences: (1) Muslims, especially the young and the restless who cannot seem to obtain reliable, discussion-oriented, context-driven, and actionable sources of information for understanding the essence of Islam in the context of their language, time, and environment and (2) others who want to increase their understanding of Islam and are willing to forge a global alliance of goodwill and common humanity. It is my firm belief that until we can bring the world of diverse faiths and ethnicities into a common framework where we can uncover our common ground from our diversities and can celebrate and appreciate our shared values and cherished differences so that every person can exercise his or her free will and express his or her uniqueness, we will not succeed as a species, and we will not fulfill God's will as His representatives on this earth.

I am truly fortunate to be able to complete this volume 3 as I continue the journey into the Qur'an and continue to evolve in my faith in God and to understand His message to humanity. To those who have already read volumes 1 and 2, I welcome you to this volume, which covers chapters (*surah*) 5, 6, and 7 of the Qur'an. Volume 1 covered chapters 1 and 2. Volume 2 covered chapters 3 and 4. I welcome your comments, observations, and suggestions; you can email me at rashed@rashedhasan.com and/or visit the book website at www.rashedhasan.com to share your thoughts, ideas, and questions.

In selecting *Social Consciousness* as the title for this volume, I wanted to establish a basic framework of how faith and goodness evolve in human societies and certainly in the minds of people as we progress through our lives. In volume 1, *Deciphering Faith without Ritual*, in the context of the first two chapters (surah) of the Qur'an, I was trying to drive at the important notion that in all our rituals and religious practices, as well as our social, political, and corporate activities, intentionality and purposefulness have to dominate and be sustained while one performs those rituals and activities. Too often the process and the ritual become the focal point and soon degenerate into a set of mindless activities, and we derive satisfaction from a job done but fail to achieve the results that motivated the acts. This is like getting consumed in the act of driving and failing to arrive at the destination. In volume 2, *Free to Choose*, in the context of chapters 3 and 4 of the Qur'an, I wanted to convey the universal truth and basis for human creation and human dignity in one's ability to make informed choices through knowledge and wisdom. Our individual and collective responsibility to create social norms and environments requires unfettered freedom to make such choices, in all areas of human endeavors, wants and aspirations, faith and its expression, livelihood, and political systems within the framework of truth and justice. In choosing the tile for this current volume, *Social Consciousness*, I wanted to highlight the constant theme in the Qur'an of social consciousness, without which we can neither make the right choices nor devise the right mechanisms to achieve the intended results of those choices.

Why Initiate This Conversation?

Please refer to the prefaces in volumes 1 and 2 to find an exposition as to why I have been driven to undertake this work and continue to this day as an explorer into the world of the Qur'an, a gift to mankind from God, our Creator, as He gifted previous generations with the Bible, the Torah, and other Books of Revelations, many of which no longer exist in their original form yet contain wisdom and divine connections that a set of discerning eyes can easily see.

Volume 1 (published in 2015), volume 2 (published in 2017), and this current volume are a continued representation of my modest attempts to initiate a vigorous conversation and offer a contextual commentary on (as opposed to a pure translation of) one of the greatest books on earth for the benefit of Muslims, whose faith is centered around the guidance from the Qur'an and the examples of great prophets such as Mohammad, Jesus, Moses, and Abraham. But this endeavor is also for people of other faith groups and people without faith but aspiring to human goodness so that we can reestablish our common faith and the human goodness in all of us.

This series is intended for all of us, since the Qur'an is for all humanity, and it has been commented on with that goal in mind. One of the earliest revelations in the Qur'an declares, *"Truly, this is nothing but a reminder for all of mankind!"* ("The Pen," 68:52). The Prophet of Islam delegated every person of faith to convey the message of God and His teachings and values to the next generation. I believe that the Qur'an needs to be commented on and explained for every generation by every generation to facilitate better and more accurate understanding of Islam's teachings and values in the contemporary language and in the context of contemporary culture, politics, and social norms; failure to do so will only reflect our own inability and lack of commitment as people of faith to make a difference in our world. It is a generational responsibility that we cannot and should not rely solely on previous generations to achieve, nor can it be delayed for the next generation.

The first two volumes have generated interesting conversations among people of different faiths and among neighbors. These have afforded Muslims in particular opportunities to attempt to understand their faith through a new prism—a prism of contemporary world affairs and the current state of human knowledge and social norms. It has enabled our Christian and Jewish neighbors and friends to reinvent the deep connection that exists in our faiths and in the contents of our revealed texts—The Torah, The Bible and the Qur'an, that each group tried to lay claim as their own, instead of acknowledging that each of these revelations has helped advance the cause of our ever-expanding understanding of our purpose and connection to our Creator.

The successions of these revelations are no different than perhaps the way physics evolved through Galileo, Newton, and Einstein's writings and experiments. While revealed texts have been inspired directly by God to His designated prophets, human beings of extraordinary spiritual, social, and intellectual prowess and endowments, so have human sciences as God inspired gifted human minds from all generations and from all ethnicities to contribute to collective human knowledge and experience. Accepting Einstein's theory of relativity in no way negates Newton's theory of motion or his contribution to gravity, nor does it diminish Galileo's attempt to infer that the earth is round and rotates around the sun. On the contrary, it magnifies the enormous challenges that previous scientists had faced and the awesomeness of their discoveries and understanding of the natural world with limited tools in the face of intense and life-threatening opposition, especially from Christian churches, not to mention from fellow scientists. The constant friction between Christian churches and the scientific community led to an adversarial relationship between science and religion—a blanket mindset that is not true in the context of Islam in particular and in many other world religions that are deeply rooted in exploring the natural world as one of the ways to understand and appreciate God's work and His presence.

The reading of the Qur'an is in many ways an advancement and confirmation of what is already in the Torah and the Bible—without taking anything away from these Books of Revelations, as they are all inspired by the same God.

When my Christian neighbor asks me whom I worship, my answer is simple—I worship the same God that Jesus and his apostles worshipped. When my Jewish colleague asked me whom I worship, my answer is similarly simple—I worship that same God Who spoke to Moses.

Muslims in general should have a better understanding and appreciation of other faiths, especially if that faith is grounded in One God and better appreciation of human sciences, since the Qur'an constantly calls for unity of faith and unity of Godhead and calls for deeper attention to the natural world and human societies, including other creatures that cohabitate the earth with us. In our contemporary world, there is plenty of evidence to the contrary, though, where corrupt political leaders and misguided religious clerics have inspired some people to violate the basic tenets of Islamic faith regarding the sanctity of life and property and commit horrifying injustices in the name of God and faith. Unfortunately, so has been the case in other faith groups and the atheists (a.k.a. communists) that manifested in Holocaust, the carnage of two world wars, and untold human atrocities by communists in Russia and China, to cite a few examples. There has been a genocide against Muslim minorities in Myanmar by the otherwise pacifist Buddhist majority, and there are confirmed UN reports of over a million minority Uighur Muslims thrown into concentration-style camps in China as I write this volume.

As I quoted at the beginning of the preface from Karen Armstrong, someone I personally admire, valuing her thoughtful exposition of the world of faith as it is and not how it is presented by some members of each faith group, is something that we all need to endeavor to rise to, as we discuss our own faith and the faith of others, since all faiths originated from the same God, and we will all go back to the same God on our death. *"It is to Us [God] is your return, and it is on Us [God] to ensure your accountability"* ("The Overwhelming Event," 88:25–26).

I encourage you to continue to make this journey with me into the Qur'an and let your inner conscience be a party to the journey—use not only your physical self and your outer senses but develop a mindful intimacy and a conversation with God and His message so that you can have an inner discourse with yourself and reassess your current understanding of faith and human purpose.

Part of the proceeds from this Qur'anic commentary will be directed to a nonprofit organization, MyLLife Inc., (www.myllife.org) which is dedicated to bringing people of all faiths together for our common vision of human dignity and peace for all. We hope that you will contribute to this cause as well as benefit from this commentary. If you would like to make contributions to MyLLife Inc., please go to our website at www.myllife.org or send contributions to the following address:

MyLLife Inc.
PO Box 22460
Alexandria, VA 22304
USA

May God help us in our sincere endeavors to be better human beings and to help our fellow beings achieve a higher platform of performance and position, as was intended by God when He asked the Angels to bow before Adam, the first person to receive the gift of knowledge from God, a gift that continues for every generation of human beings. I pray and sincerely hope that each one of us strives hard to achieve that goal and remembers God's call: *"Mankind, you have to engage in a deliberate and sustained effort [for goodness] toward your Sustainer [God] until you meet Him"* ("The Sundering," 84:6).

Introduction

The Structure of the Book

This book (volume 3), as well as volumes 1 and 2, is presented as a series of discussions in a conversational style. It takes one or several verses from each chapter (surah) in sequence and attempts to provide meaning, context, and deeper insight as I see it. It is also intended to encourage discourse among readers in the spirit of understanding the last revelation of God and to engage such understanding to better our lives in all their various dimensions. Too often, a verse is taken in isolation or without context, sometimes by well-meaning (or not-so-well-meaning) Muslims or other religious or political adversaries, often distorting the true essence of the verses in question, both intentionally and unintentionally.

Please refer to volumes 1 and 2 for more detail discussion on the structure of the book.

Understanding Common Terms such as Islam, Muslim, and Qur'an

In volumes 1 and 2, I have provided simple but pertinent definitions and exposition on these common words so that those who are Muslims can take a step back and ponder the meaning and significance of these terms, perhaps divorced from their own cultural or superficial understanding of these important concepts and terms that over the years have been distorted or have taken on a common vernacular without proper perspective and intentional meanings. It is also beneficial for people of other faiths—especially those who come from Abrahamic faiths—to try to understand the deeper and contextual meaning of these terms rather than what is being pushed in the media and sometimes, unfortunately, preached to them from their respective pulpits and in social discourse.

As I have maintained throughout my discourse in this series, faith in God is central to Abrahamic faith and many other faiths, although we have created religious differences based on how we interpret this singularity of Godhead and how we assign divinity to others, if at all, and create religious practices not necessarily mandated by the prophets in whose name such religious distinctions are created, established, and perpetuated. Qur'an is the final book in the continuation of God's guidance to mankind. It builds on the previous revelations and teachings from all prophets, including Moses, Jesus, and Abraham, and calls for unity of faith while respecting the desires of each group to maintain its distinctiveness and calling for goodness in our conduct with respect to one another regardless of such religious affiliation. This fundamental notion of religious plurality is central to Islamic teachings and has been a time-honored practice for many generations of Muslims. The recent aberrant behavior of fringe groups of terrorist organizations, self-serving imams, and political leaders who exploit religion to perpetuate their rule over people in our contemporary world has given pretext to media pundits and so-called experts to blame the Islamic faith rather than the Muslims who behave contrary to what faith teaches them. It is important to understand such basic tenets of faith and in particular of Islam so that as you read this volume and continue your journey into the Qur'an, we are able to frame the questions and reflect on what the Qur'an teaches.

I want to mention the use of the word "Muslim" in my books. While the conventional English dictionary does not allow the use of the word "Muslim" without a capital M, there are times I have forced the use of the word as "muslim" as I believe the Qur'an had also done to make a distinction between one who professes to be Muslims by acknowledging Prophet Mohammad as the final Messenger and the Qur'an as the final revelation vs. one who is a muslim by attributes of true submission to One God and alignment with God's teaching brought forth by prophets of all ages. It is in this vein, that the Qur'an declares Abraham to be a muslim and the disciples of Jesus called themselves muslims. This distinction is fundamentally important for everyone of faith to understand

Introduction

and is particularly crucial for Muslims, some of whom will claim to be a Muslim but will never fully develop the true attributes of a muslim, one who is genuinely faithful to God and works consistently and persistently for human goodness.

SUGGESTIONS FOR THE READING OF THIS BOOK

In the previous volumes I provide some thoughts and suggestions on how to read the Qur'an as presented in these volumes. It would be good to refresh your memory or read them for the first time before you delve into this volume.

The Qur'an should be studied on a regular basis, with reasonable time included for reflecting and making correlations. Life is the real expression of the Qur'an, and one cannot benefit from the Qur'an unless one becomes attentive to the details of life and the universe we live in. The Qur'an will offer different levels of understanding and insights to different people based on our intellectual and commonsense capabilities and willingness to discuss and practice the various aspects of our personal, social, business, and political lives. If we are unwilling or unable to refer to the Qur'an on a day-to-day basis, it will become an intellectual luxury or a ritualistic recipe rather than a tool to enhance the value of life for us or others around us.

Several points are outlined again (as was done in previous volumes) on how to read this commentary on the Qur'an. First, realize that this book is more a commentary and less a translation and that it will not be able to convey the power of the language and the style of the Qur'an, which was well suited to serve the time and the place in which it was revealed. Since you are reading this commentary, your native language may not be Arabic, or you may be seeking additional perspective on the Qur'an beyond what you get by reading directly in the Arabic language, if that is your mother tongue, or you are unsatisfied with many of the existing translations of the Qur'an. I have used simple, colloquial American English so that readers who are either English speaking or have a decent command of the English language can benefit from this book. I have also cited limited but pertinent contemporary world events and views to bring some of the insights of the Qur'an to reality, as we learn better when we can see the reflection of a principle in action. I hope others who share my views in this commentary will cooperate with me in the future to translate this commentary of the Qur'an into their native languages.

As stated earlier in this commentary, instead of keeping each sentence in the Qur'an separate, I have made it part of a paragraph, as the sentences become part of a continuous thought and topic. I felt that this way, the information would become more meaningful and coherent. Arabic terms in each section that require explanation to provide deeper and more accurate meaning of the Qur'an's content can be found at the end of the section under "Key Arabic Terms." These terms and their explanations are also included in a glossary toward the end of the book and can be referred to as necessary. Certain words or phrases are also included in brackets ( ) throughout this commentary in order to make explicit hidden intents or meanings and to complete sentences that otherwise may be confusing or misleading, as each language has its unique structures, styles, and word positioning to convey a meaning to the reader. Though this volume only covers chapters (*surahs*) 5, 6, and 7, from time to time I make references to other chapters that can easily be found in any Qur'an translation. My hope is to provide such a commentary and conversation for the remainder of the Qur'an in the near future as this personal journey into the Qur'an continues.

I have also used footnotes where I felt issues, ideas, or directives needed to be discussed. These are my personal understandings based on my readings of the Qur'an, the Prophet's traditions (*hadith*), and books by scholars—both Muslim and non-Muslim; on my education in the East and the West in science, technology, business, and the human origin and condition; and on reflections of our lives. I encourage readers to read, reflect on, and adopt or challenge as necessary the views expressed here, but do try to come to a conclusion in your mind so that you are comfortable with your understanding of Islam and how to be a person of faith and a dignified human being.

It is also important that one should develop the courage and humility to agree to disagree with me or others in our mutual discourse (this book being part of this continuous discourse), as long as it does not make us divisive or disunited. Also, one has to recognize that even though we may disagree on certain positions at an individual level, we may have to take a unified stand as a community based on consensus and majority opinion, and we need to respect that, even if we personally disagree. By the same token, where individual differences are expected, the community should not insist on conformity just for the sake of conformity. For example, the topic of wearing a veil or *hijab* creates strong emotions in the Muslim community as well as in the West. Muslims should be tolerant of people who wear the hijab or veil as well as of those who choose not to wear either one, since a hijab is not fundamental to our faith nor our ability to be good people. My personal position is that it is NOT required under Islam, though some Muslim clerics would insist on it based on misreading certain verses of the Qur'an and unreliable hadiths to impose their dogmatic views and practices on women. The majority of the Islamic centers that I am familiar with and have visited in the United States are also very restrictive when it comes to women who do not wear a hijab. The majority of Muslim women around the world, with the exception of the Middle East, do not consider the hijab a religious requirement, and such a cultural norm puts undue social pressure on Muslim communities around the world, even in the West. I would just remind us to be extremely cautious when it comes to restricting human freedom and choices and to be extra vigilant when it comes to women's rights, which have been violated on a large scale throughout human history, including Muslim history. As God said in the Qur'an, *"Do not let your tongue deliver a lie when you say, 'This is lawful [halal], and this is forbidden [haram],' thereby inventing a lie in the name of God. Those who impose such lies in the name of God will not prosper"* ("The Bee," 16:116).

I suggest that, at a minimum, one continuous topic be read in one sitting and that you, the reader, spend some time reflecting on what you have read and try to make a personal commitment to follow through with its implications, whether it means adjusting your paradigm of thinking, your position on certain issues, or how you act and do certain things with regard to yourself, your livelihood, your fellow humans, the natural world, and God. As you read through the commentary, try to draw meaning and relevance from lessons in your own life and from lessons that come from observing nature or people, including your parents, your spouse, your children, and people of other faiths and cultures.

The Qur'an should be a source of lifelong learning and guidance for devotion to God and service to humanity. As God said in the Qur'an, *"Say [to people], 'Truth has indeed been revealed to you from your Cherisher God; so whoever makes the right choices does that for his own benefit, and whoever makes the wrong choices does it to the detriment of his own soul, and I [Prophet Mohammad] am not a custodian on your behalf'"* ("Jonah," 10:108). This statement is God's gentle way of reminding us that we have an obligation to Him and to our fellow humans that we have been given the freedom and conscience to choose the response we deem appropriate, for each one of us is responsible for not only what we do but also what we choose not to do. This is why the Qur'an is very emphatic that it is not good enough for us to only believe but that we also have to remove evil from our lives and societies and establish truth and justice: *"You are the best community, evolved for the benefit of mankind because you encourage what is good, you discourage what is evil, and you believe in God"* ("The Family of Amran," 3:110). Our responsibility cannot be made clearer than this!

It is critically important that we read, understand, and interpret the Qur'an in the light of our current condition and global matters and not dwell too much on the conditions that prevailed at the time of its revelation. The Qur'an is not time bound and was revealed for all generations of humanity. There are great similarities between the conditions of Muslims today and those of the Muslim community that first emerged in Medina with the Prophet's migration. A large majority of Muslims feel that their communities are under a competitive threat economically, socially, politically, and perhaps militarily, just as the small community of Muslims was at the time of its creation and the creation of its religious, political, and economic infrastructure.

Today's Muslims are many, scattered around in a large number of sovereign countries with a Muslim-majority population as well as being ever present in many other countries as the second-largest religious community. We should strive to organize for the betterment of all people, including ourselves, through education, God consciousness, and constant contribution to human enlightenment. All Muslims, irrespective of where they are from and where they live, should strive to contribute to the Muslim community and the larger society in a positive and substantive way.

As I have done in the previous volumes, I have added an appendix, this time on the Five Pillars of Faith—*Shahada* (declaration of faith), *Salat* (daily and weekly prayers), *Sawm* (fasting during the month of Ramadan), *Zakat* (2.5

percent mandated charity each year from your assets), and *Hajj* (annual pilgrimage, mandated once in a lifetime). Too often these are called Pillars of Islam in classical Islamic literature, and they are frequently mentioned in conversations among the Muslims and referred to in the media. But I prefer to call them the Pillars of Faith, since Islam is based on the duality of faith and good work, just as our existence has a spiritual and a physical dimension. This duality should be on equal footing, and maintaining proper balance is the middle ground the Prophet of Islam has always emphasized and strived to reflect in his own life and in the lives of the community he aspired to build. Overemphasis on rituals at the cost of social consciousness and social justice leads to creating bad names for faith and the failure of such people to lead their communities and their nations.

One final note about the use of pronouns about God in the Qur'an, specially for those who might not be unfamiliar with the Qur'an. Islam is strictly a monotheistic religion and Oneness of Godhead is central to Islamic faith. There are places in the Qur'an where God refers to Himself as I or Me or He and in many other places God refers to Himself as We or Us, which might confuse non-readers of the Qur'an. Here are two examples: *"When My servants (faithful) inquire you (prophet) about Me, I am (always) near! I answer the calls of those who seek Me; they should then hear My call and believe in Me so that they can secure the right way"* ("The Cow," 2:186); *"It is to Us [God] is your return, and it is on Us [God] to ensure your accountability"* ("The Overwhelming Event," 88:25–26).

The use of singular implies a level of intimacy and directedness between God and his creations, including those who are faithful and devoted to God and His guidance. In the first example, it is God who is the object of worship and God is the only One who defines when and how to respond, letting the person know that He is always near and He hears. With respect to the second verse, we all go back to God and to all those who are with God already, namely the angels, the spirits and other hosts that we have no knowledge of but nonetheless is part of God's team to manage the affairs as God intends and directs. In the second part of the second verse, accountability is taken not only God but also by fellow human beings, for example, as God wills and as we witness on this earth in our current life.

In our day to day conversation, there are times when we take a thing personally and say, "I will take care of it or I will help you". Other times we say: "We will take care of or We will get it done" meaning me or my family, my group or my organization will take care of this matter. It is a matter of tone, emphasis and an acknowledgment of others who are involved in the execution of the task at hand. This in NO way implies that others included in the "We", if any at all, have any divinity in them or a share in God's sovereignty – an area that causes lots of controversy and cognitive dissonance when one tries to explain the concept of Trinity in Christianity or the godhead of Jesus Christ, while at the same time reaffirming the concept of monotheism in Christianity.

CHAPTER 5

Surah Al-Maidah (The Repast)

(120 verses in total; revealed in Madinah)

THIS SURAH TAKES ITS NAME from a special supplication that the disciples of Jesus requested him to make to God to provide them with repast from Heaven (5:112–114) to comfort their souls and to reinforce their conviction in the faith and truth as taught by Jesus Christ. This surah continues to reinforce the unity of faith as taught by Moses, Jesus and Mohammad and emphasize the need to remain true to the teachings of prophets and the teaching in this Qur'an and not to fall prey to selective interpretation or denial of some aspects of faith in favor of others. God also proclaims in a special verse (5:3) revealed before the death of Prophet Mohammad that God has perfected the teaching of monotheism with this Prophet and with Qur'an as the last direct call from God for our faith and goodness. Now all people of faith, especially those who submit to God, the God Who spoke to Moses on Mount Sinai and the God about Whom Jesus spoke in his Sermon on the Mount as recorded in the Bible and as corroborated in the Qur'an, should uphold the truth regarding the unity of Godhead and the unity of faith and guidance from the same God. We owe it ourselves and to our common humanity to sustain and to generate momentum in our continuous march of human progress toward God and goodness.

This surah deals with a diverse set of topics of human and social contracts with God and with fellow human beings, the nature of Jesus and Christian faith revisited, lessons to be learned from stories of Abel and Cain and other prior generations, the encouragement of rational thinking and avoidance of all forms of superstitions, fortune-telling, and game of chance. Respect for human lives and social justice has been repeated here as a reminder, basic dietary rules are reemphasized, and physical aspects of worship are made an important part of being in God's presence during daily and weekly worship. One critical aspect that we need to be mindful of and pay particular attention to is to be vigilant against excesses of clerical interpretations in detailing guidance where such interpretations are overly constraining and impinging on human freedom to think rationally and choose for ourselves as we see it.

Finally this surah calls for each one of us to have a sense of purpose and be willing to face adversity and difficulties in achieving such purpose. Only such commitment and sacrifice demonstrate our true understanding of our existence and our purpose in this life and the life to come.

Following are key concepts in this surah; they are listed here and further explained at the end of the surah:

1. Dietary rules explained (5:1, 3, 4–5, 87–88, 93)
2. Honoring the signs of God (5:2)
3. Avoiding transgressions and maintaining justice at all times (5:2, 8–10)
4. The perfection of faith and guidance (5:3, 11)
5. Marriage to people of faith (from other religions) (5:5)
6. Ablution for prayer detailed (5:6–7)
7. Lessons to be learned from people of previous revelations (5:12–26, 41–47)
8. Lessons from Abel and Cain (5:27–31)
9. The killing of human beings and corruption on land is forbidden (5:32)
10. Success requires sacrifice and a sense of purpose (5:35)
11. The punishment for disrupting social order (mischief, loss of life and property) (5:33, 38–40)
12. The Torah, the Bible, and the Qur'an all lead to the same God and goodness (5:44–48, 69)
13. God's warning about failing to remain true to His guidance (5:54–56)
14. Warning against the excesses of clerics (5:59, 62–66, 68)

15. The nature of Jesus explained (5:72–77, 109–118)
16. Christian priests and monks are praised for humility (8:82–85,66)
17. The importance of keeping oaths and promises (5:89)
18. Injunction against intoxicants, gambling, and fortune-telling (5:90–92)
19. Good and bad are distinct (5:100)
20. The desire for over-clarification is discouraged (5:101)
21. God's protection (5:67,105)
22. The need to draw up a will and protect it with witnesses (5:106–108)

CHAPTER 5

Verses 1–3

In the name of God, the most Merciful and the Instiller of Mercy (to His creatures).

O People of Faith, be faithful to your covenants. Lawful to you are all beasts similar to cattle, except any specific mentions (as unacceptable), and do not hunt when you are in the state of pilgrimage. God prescribes according to His will. Do not violate the symbols set up by God (or of God), or the Sacred Month, or the offerings for sacrifice marked as such, or those who flocks to the Sacred Mosque seeking God's pleasure and grace. Only after your pilgrimage, you can hunt.

Never let your hatred of a people who may hinder you from the Inviolable House of Worship lead you to act of aggression. Rather, help one another to advance virtue and increase your (collective) sense of responsibility (to God and to fellow humans). And do not help one another to further evil and enmity. Be conscious of God and know that God is severe in retribution (of evils)![295]

Forbidden to you is carrion, blood, flesh of swine, one on which any name other than God's has been invoked, a strangled animal, an animal beaten to death, one killed due to a fall, one gored to death or savaged by beast of prey but not what you have slaughtered. Forbidden also is anything sacrificed on altars for idols. (You are also forbidden to) seek to learn by divination about the future—this is sinful.

On this day, those who have persisted in denying the truth have lost all hope (of destroying) your way of life. So fear them no longer, but continue to *be conscious of Me (God). On this day, I have perfected your Guidance (Way of Life) and completed My blessings on you and willed wholesome submission to Me [Islam] as your way of life. Now, if anyone is driven by dire necessity (to what is forbidden) and not inclined to sin, then he will find God to be much Forgiving and a Dispenser of Grace.*²⁹⁶

²⁹⁵ The dietary rules are laid out here with respect to lawful meat to be eaten and what is unlawful. The exceptions are minimal and kept very simple compared to dietary rules in other religions, which have been made more complicated by their followers, such as dietary rules in Jewish and Orthodox Hindu traditions. Respecting symbols of God such as the house of worship or the Sacred Month is described in the same vein as how to lawfully partake of meat from cattle and other animals, since all creatures of God are also His symbols, and we have to mindful of His blessing that we derive benefits from such animals (e.g., cattle).

²⁹⁶ This is the last revelation that was given to the Prophet on his last pilgrimage during his stay at Mount Arafat, after which he lived for less than three months. By this time the Qur'an had been fully revealed; all laws and regulations of the Islamic way of life had been enunciated, communicated, and firmly established in the lives of the followers; and the last remaining threat from the people of Makkah had been eliminated. Now the first generation of followers of the Prophet was fully established. The show of their unparalleled dedication to the Message and the Messenger and their subsequent success in attracting people throughout the world to Islam and its way of life is nothing short of spectacular in the history of mankind.

REFLECTION

Islam and the Qur'an are the culmination of all the messages and the messengers who contributed to the reality of One God and One Message of universal goodness. The focus of people of faith has to be to unite under this common framework of belief in One God and our common yearning for human dignity, well-being, and unity.

ACTION

The key challenge for Muslims, as we understand from the Qur'anic teaching and the legacy of the Prophet, is to unite all human beings to advance the cause of peace, prosperity, and happiness for all of humanity. In this regard, we need to work closely with people of other faiths, build a shared vison, and work toward a common outcome.

Key Arabic Term
91. *aqd* (covenant)

CHAPTER 5

Verses 4–6

They ask you about what is lawful. Say: "All things good and pure are lawful." With respect to hunting animals that you teach how to hunt with knowledge that God has imparted on you, eat what they hunt for you, but do mention God's name over them and be mindful of your responsibility and remain conscious of God. Surely God is swift in taking accounts. Today all things pure and good are made lawful for you. The food of those who have received revelations before (e.g., Jews, Christians, and others) are lawful to you, and so is your food to them. (It is lawful also) to marry women who are faithful and women from faiths that have received revelations before, provided you offer dowry, intending to marry them and not fornicate or engage in secret love (e.g., a mistress). Whoever denies faith (after such broad guidance) will render his work vain, and he will be among the losers in the Afterlife.[297]

O People of Faith: When you get ready to pray, wash your face and your hands and arms up to the elbows, wipe your head, and wash your feet up to the ankles. If you have an obligation for shower, then do so (rather than just ablution). But if you are sick, or on a journey, or have satisfied a call of nature, or have sexual intimacy but cannot find water, then take advantage of pure dust, lightly passing over your hands and face. God intends no hardship on you but wishes to purify you and to bestow His full grace on you so that you have reasons to be grateful.[298]

---

[297] This verse is of fundamental importance as far as the broadness of Islamic principles goes and the amount of latitude and freedom given to human societies

and individuals within Islam and among all people of faith and good conscience. All things in nature, including each member of humanity, are created to benefit us and one another, and we are free to partake of these gifts and treasures of God as long as they are pure and good and do not go contrary to any specific prohibitions. Too many clerics, imams, rabbis, fundamentalists, and people with a narrow view of faith and human potential want to impose too many restrictions in our lives, whereas God gives us the broadest possible freedom of choices with very limited restrictions. Islam accepts food from all people of faith, allows marriage with people of faith, and collaborates in all acts and rituals that are good and pure. God wants us to remain ever conscious of our purpose and goal in life and to interact, partake in all good things, and engage in all good activities in collaboration with all with shared values and visions.

[298] Physical purity in spiritual acts is a fundamental teaching of Islam and reflects the recognition and enhancement of the duality of our existence in the physical domain and the spiritual domain. While we need to perform physical cleanliness in order to achieve spiritual closeness to God and one another, the same is true in terms of all our activities that need to be cleansed with good intention. Two of the famous quotations from the Prophet go as follows: (1) cleanliness is 50 percent of your faith, and (2) each and every action will be judged by its intention. Also, in the matter of our mandate to clean ourselves before prayer, God lightens the burden in the event we can't find water and allows the token use of pure dust, which is as abundant as air and water on this planet. Here lies another fundamental principle: Every rule has an exception, and such exceptions should be granted based on our good and collective judgment. Another famous quotation from the Prophet: when it comes to social rules and regulations, if I have multiple options, I always choose the one that is easy for people to follow.

REFLECTION

These verses point out the awesome elegance, beauty, simplicity, and comprehensiveness of God's guidance for mankind. We are encouraged to engage in all that is good and pure; impose no burden beyond one's capacity and availability; and keep faith, goodness, and our sense of responsibility and accountability to God and fellow human beings in the forefront of our consciousness. God means our life on this earth not to be a burden but to be a spontaneous expression of free will, seeking knowledge, practicing love and peace, and helping one another reach our highest human potential.

ACTION
Going beyond reflection but with appropriate reflections, thoughtfulness, knowledge, and practical wisdom, we need to implement simple, commonsense, fair, and just remedies for our ailments and solutions to our common failures in the world today.

CHAPTER 5

Verses 7–11

Remind yourself of God's (constant) favors and blessings on you and of the pledge with which He commits you when you said: "We hear and we commit." (Therefore) Keep your duty to God (and to fellow human beings). God is ever aware of what you intend to do and what you keep in your heart. O People of Faith: Be constant in your devotion to God, and bear witness with justice and truth; Do not let hatred of a people incite you to acts of injustice and inequity. Be just—this is the closest to the observance of your responsibility (to God and to fellow human beings). Remain God Conscious and be true to your sense of duty—surely God is fully Aware of all that you do.[299]

God has promised to those who believe and do good work that they will have forgiveness and a reward from Him that is grand, whereas, those who persistently deny, disbelieve, and reject God's messages are destined for Hellfire. O People of Faith: Remind yourself of God's favor when a group of people have tried to displace you but God restrained their hands (and helped you establish yourself as a community). Therefore, be conscious of God, and on God every person of faith should establish true reliance.[300]

[299] We need to be mindful of God's blessings on us to sustain our lives, such as the simple act of breathing, the ability to ingest and digest food, the abundance of natural resources to sustain our lives on this planet, the gifts of having parents, children, friends, and neighbors at a physical level, and having a brain to think and calculate, a mind to analyze and form intent, and a soul to guide and persist on truth and justice—all examples of the innumerable gifts and blessings that

God has given to us. In return God wants us to use our faculties, our physical strength, and our commitments to do good, to be just, and to be truthful in dealing with one another. God's guidance to us and our innate desires and abilities are truly aligned—so how can we do wrong or be unjust? This is a question that we need to ask each one of us with true consciousness and humility.

³⁰⁰ God rewards and punishes on a very simple formula that we all can relate to: God will forgive the shortcomings and mistakes of those who believe in His grace and are committed to do good and justice on this earth, and He will make them inhabitants of Paradise. Those who deny His graces and rebel against His guidance to truth and justice and as a result cause harm and disharmony in this world will have to face the consequent punishment from fellow humans and ultimately from Hellfire, a place they will inhabit as a consequence of their own conduct.

REFLECTION

In our world today where we are beset with acts of terrorism and then reactive counterterrorism that sometimes causes more harm; staggering income disparities; unprecedented environmental pollution; a prevalence of corrupt practices by government and special-interest groups; an enormous amount of weapons of mass destruction in the hands of nations, rebel groups, terrorists, and gangsters—while at the same time, we have seen the proliferation of knowledge and information across the globe; the rise of technology that brings unprecedented creature comfort and health treatment; the rise of instant communication among people across national and communal boundaries; and son on—one wonders why we have NOT been able to improve dialogue among nations and communities, why more than half of the world's population has not seen the benefit of technology, why gender inequality continues to persist, why profitable companies fail to provide living wages to its employees, and why fewer people control increasingly more of the wealth of the planet. There are fundamental challenges we will continue to face until we bring a sense of fairness and justice into our day-to-day and strategic dialogues, until we recognize that our resources are gifts from God and that we need to share and distribute them in true proportion to effort and justified basis and not purely on entitlement or intellectual merit alone, until democratic institutions are driven by people and not by moneyed individuals or institutions, until we try to genuinely understand human concerns, especially those who are violated and oppressed. In this regard, paying real attention to the message from the Creator and His guidance can truly transform our societies and nations.

ACTION

As we read this Qur'an and other Books of Revelations, the people of faith have to put into practice the practical teachings and guidance found in these books and be true to our reality that we are a transient people on this planet for a fixed term and that the quality of our life on this planet and our life after death will all be determined by how we conduct ourselves, how we treat one another as human beings (beyond national and ethnic identities), and how we help one another grow and become true human beings as God intends.

CHAPTER 5
Verses 12–16

God made a similar covenant with the Children of Israel, and He caused twelve of their leaders to be sent (to search the land of Canaan). God said to them: "I am with you. If you sustain your worship (of Me), share your wealth with the poor, believe in My Messengers and assist them, and offer up to God a loan of goodwill; then God will efface your evil deeds and let you enter Paradise (of peace and plenty) wherein rivers flow. But whoever denies the grace of God after this, he will have moved far from the right path." It is on account of their failure to stay true to the covenant that We rejected them and made their hearts to harden. (As a result) they distort the meaning of God's revelations by taking them out of context and became unmindful of a certain portion of their reminders (revelations). You will experience treachery from them all except a few; yet pardon them and forbear since God loves those who do good (to others).

As for those who say: "We are Christians," We (God) also took a solemn pledge (covenant), but they became similarly unmindful of a certain portion of the reminders (revelations); As a result, We let enmity and hatred to stir up among them, until the Day of Resurrection. God will soon make them understand what they contrived (against one another).

O People of the Previous Revelations: Surely Our Messenger has come to you who makes it clear much of which you had concealed from the book (Bible and Torah) and forgives much. Now indeed, a Light and a Clear Book has come to you from God, Who by His will brings those who is so inclined to the path of peace and brings them out of darkness (Ignorance) to Light (Knowledge and Wisdom), thereby guiding them to the Straight Path.[301]

³⁰¹ God here cites the cases of both Jews and Christians who were party to the same solemn pledge as Muslims pledged (5:7)—to remain true to God, to worship Him, to help the poor, and to work with the Messengers. Failure to keep their solemn pledge resulted in their losing their path, the hardening of their hearts, and the inability to fully subscribe to all the tenets of the revealed books. Christians suffered a fate of enmity and hatred among their various and numerous sects and communities (nations), for example, during the two World Wars in Europe and the persistent animosity between Catholics and Protestants. Nonetheless, God asks the Prophet and his followers to forgive and to forbear despite such neglect and hostility by previous followers of revelations. It is appropriate to reflect in this context, the current hostility between Shia and Sunni Muslims, specially in Middle East, is also due to violations of Muslim Pledge to God.

REFLECTION
God deals with all people—Jews, Christians, and Muslims—with the same set of criteria. If we follow His guidance and remain true to the covenants we made with God, then we will be rewarded in this life and in Paradise in the Afterlife. Most Muslims feel that such consequence is only for the Jews and Christians as described here, but it must be understood that Muslims are subject to the same set of rules, and our current failures are a testimony to the truth that God's disfavor is reserved for anyone who ignores His guidance and denies His grace.

ACTION
In our private and public lives, we need to accept all Books of Revelations and the universal message contained in these revelations as truth. The Qur'an reconfirms and augments these truths, and we should make a commitment to follow God's guidance and join with anyone who has this shared vison and objective.

CHAPTER 5
Verses 17–19

Those who say God is the Christ, Son of Mary are indeed deniers of God. Say (to them): "Who will prevail against God in any matter if He wishes to destroy Christ, Son of Mary, his mother, and all who live on this earth?" Remember that God's dominion covers the earth, the heavens, and all in between. He creates what He wills, and God has power over all things. The Jews and the Christians say: "We are sons of God and His beloved." Say (to them): "Why does He then make you suffer for your sins? You are nothing but mortals from His creations. He forgives whom He wills, and He causes to suffer whom He wills. God's dominion extends over heavens, earth, and all in between. (Your) journeys (and pursuits) are destined to come to Him (for resolution)."[302]

O People of the Previous Revelations: Surely a Messenger has come, after a long cessation when no prophets came, to explain the truths; lest you say: "No bearer of good news or warning came to us. Now a bearer of good news and a warner came to you (as God willed); God is ever powerful to will anything."

---

[302] The message regarding purity of faith continues in this section as well. Christ as God is unacceptable to God, and also unacceptable is the notion that some people (in this case Jews and Christians) are entitled to be favored by God to the exclusion of others. God's presence encompasses everyone, and closeness to Him is not based on self-claimed entitlement but on being true to His message and

being responsible, as the last Prophet, who came for all humanity, reiterated the same guidance as was given to Jesus, Moses, and Abraham.

REFLECTION

Claims of entitlement and closeness to God is not a monopoly of the Jews or Christians; some conservative Muslims and many terrorists, falsely attesting to their Islamic identity, claim that they are better than other Muslims, Jews, and Christians. On such false pretense, they commit and encourage heinous crimes against innocent people in the name of respect to the Prophet or to God. The killing of twelve journalists at Charlie Hebdo in Paris in 2015 is a stark reminder that some of these terrorists desecrate innocent lives to show their pretentious affinity to the Prophet's image or God's name.

ACTION

The life and property of any human being are sacred, and hatred of any people is not a justification for transgressing norms of justice, morality, and human dignity. The Qur'an is very emphatic about this, and all people, especially those who claim to be Muslims, should be mindful of their conduct in light of such a clear injunction against unlawful killing and acts of injustice against unarmed innocent civilians.

CHAPTER 5

Verses 20–32

(Remember when) Moses said to His people: "O my people, remind yourself of the favors of God Who raised prophets from among you and who gave you control over yourselves and (blessings) that were not given to any other nation. O my people, enter this Holy Land which God has promised you, and do not turn your backs—if you do, then you will be lost." The people replied: "O Moses, there are powerful people in this Land, and we shall not go in until they depart, and if they do, we will surely enter in it." Two people (Joshua and Caleb, according to the Old Testament) who were God-conscious and who were blessed by God said: "We should enter through the front gate, and if we (have the courage to) do that, we will surely be victorious. As people of faith, we should put our trust in God (Almighty)." But the people refused: "O Moses, we will not make such an attempt as long as these powerful people are there. (Perhaps) you and your God should go and fight while we sit (and wait)." He (Moses) prayed (to God): "My Sustainer, I have no control over these people except me and my brother (Aaron). Separate us from these people who transgress (often)." He (God) replied: "This Land is forbidden for them for forty years (a lifetime); they will wander about on this earth without aim. Do not grieve, for people transgress as such." [303]

Now relate to them with truth the story of the two sons (Abel and Cain) of Adam—they both made offers to God, but God accepted only from one of them (whose offer was genuine). So the one (whose offer was not accepted) said to the other: "I will kill you." Said the one (whose offer was accepted): "God only accepts from those who are mindful and responsible.

If you attempt to kill me, I will not do the same. I am afraid of (the consequence of my action, if I do so, from) God, who is the Cherisher of the Universe. I would rather that you bear the burden of my sins and your sins and such of your action will put you into the Hellfire, which is the suffering for those who are unjust." At last his blind envy and disregard of his own soul drove him to kill his brother, and he became one of the lost. Then God sent a raven, which scratched the ground to show how he could cover the body of his dead brother. This put him into deep remorse, and he cried out: "Am I not able to do what this raven did and cover my brother's dead body?"

In light of this did We (God) prescribe to the Children of Israel (and by implication to all): Whoever kills a person, unless for committing murder or for spreading corruption in the land, it is as if he has killed all of humanity; and whoever saves a life, it is as if he has saved all of humanity. Surely our Messengers came with clear teachings and arguments; yet, after this many people go on committing all sorts of (evil) excess on earth.[304]

---

[303] God's grace and blessings to followers of Moses were numerous, starting in Exodus with the Ten Commandments and including heavenly provisions and showing them the land of plenty and opportunity, just to name a few. Yet time and again they refused to make an effort on their own to follow and secure those benefits. This condition is not unique to the people addressed here but is a common human condition that one can overcome only with genuine consciousness and positive determination. Throughout the world today, enormous developments in agricultural production, new technology, fast transportation, and extraction of natural resources could result in unprecedented human well-being and improve human welfare beyond what was possible even a century ago—these are God's gifts and blessings; yet the human race is caught in widespread corruption around mineral exploration, the new technology is widening the gap of haves and have-nots, irresponsible methods of production and consumption are creating havoc in the environment, irresponsible terrorism and counterterrorism are splitting the world apart, and human rights and freedom of expression are being trampled in the name of politics and homeland security.

³⁰⁴ The story of Abel and Cain is the first instance of violence of one human being against another human being without any justifiable reason and Cain's failure to comprehend the enormity of the crime involved. This enormity of crime and injustice is reflected in God's command that the unjustifiable killing of a human being is like killing all of humanity, and in the same vein, saving a human being like saving all of humanity. Despite such a clear prescription and our own innate sense of justice and fairness, we see large-scale killing and the oppression of human beings all over the globe by terrorists, by nation states in the name of counterterrorism, political oppression by autocratic leaders, the denial of living wages to workers by profitable corporations and business owners, wanton disregard of the health and well-being of all creatures on this planet from environmental pollution, and exploitation of natural resources for the benefit of the few, causing direct harm to average citizens in many parts of the world.

REFLECTION

The causes of human suffering and oppression are many, but it boils down to some simple truths: Do we value human life and property as sacred and inviolable? Are we committed to safeguarding human dignity? Do we believe in a just society? Do we consider freedom of expression as a God-given right? Do we believe that natural resources are a gift to the entire human race and not to a select few? Do we believe that our fortune should be shared among all people irrespective of national, ethnic, or religious identities? Do we believe that each one us is responsible to God to do what is right, to remove what is wrong and evil, and to be true to his or her soul and the teachings of God?

ACTION

We need to deepen our conviction in all these truths and increase our resolve to individually and collectively harness our God-given intellect, knowledge, wisdom, emotional maturity, compassion, empathy, and passion for justice to change our condition, one by one. Each of us must find one way to make his or her mark, wherever it may be and in whatever increment we can make it happen, but we have to make our contribution to better our collective lives with patience, empathy, and truthfulness.

CHAPTER 5

Verses 33–37

The only punishment befitting those who engage in war against God and His apostles (against truth and justice) and make mischief and widespread corruption on earth (i.e., killing, oppression, destruction of environment, financial inequality, etc., in a persistent manner) is that they be murdered, crucified, hands and feet cut off, or vanished from earth (i.e., in a manner and with deterrent that is most effective and lawful in contemporary world). This is their (deserved) disgrace on this earth and in their Afterlife, (God will bring just and) grievous punishment to them. But if any of them repent before they are overpowered, then God is Ever Forgiving and Merciful.[305]

O People of Faith: Be mindful of your responsibility to God (and to fellow humans) and always seeks ways to get close to God (and fellow humans) and strive diligently on the path toward God (and goodness to others), that you may find and achieve success.[306]

Those who deny the grace of God (and oppose goodness), they will be willing to offer all that they had on earth and more than that on the Day of Resurrection, to avoid the consequence of their evil deeds; but such bargain will not be accepted and they will face an awful chastisement. They will desire to come out of the Fire but will not (be able to) come out of it; their chastisement will be long lasting.

[305] There should be zero tolerance toward abuse of human rights, corruption of social justice, torture, oppression, and denial of freedom to human beings by anyone in any society at any time. The human condition had led us from time to

time to observe large-scale violations of human rights and persistent oppression against people and what is good. Unfortunately, in our recent history, we have seen evidence of gross violations of human dignity such as the Holocaust, slavery on the American continent, colonial rule in large parts of the world, atrocities during various wars fought in Europe and Asia by different powers, the excess of communists in Russia and China, apartheid in South Africa, abuse and large-scale corruption, and abuse of national wealth by leaders such as Gaddafi and others in Middle East and Africa. These types of situations call for extraordinary measures to face force with force to prevent the spread of such abuse and to put in place measures to contain and eliminate such possibilities, while leaving room for cessation of hostilities, if the party responsible amends their behavior and commits to peace; overpowering force should not inflict injustice in the name of justice either.

[306] In the face of injustice, people of faith have a serious responsibility to strive for justice and sustain a just society. Their faith should make them ever conscious of social justice, which manifests itself in the form of building social cohesiveness and closeness among human beings, just as their faith should make them come closer to God. This parallel endeavor to be close to God and to bring people closer is a fundamental obligation and striving for it is the primary criteria by which God will judge people of faith and define their success in this life and also in the Afterlife.

REFLECTION

Denial of justice and peace in a society is a serious crime and a serious disruption to the human condition on this planet. Such a situation calls for active engagement against the forces of evil and injustice by people of faith, whose stance on such situations will deter the forces of evil. Such a stance will always leave room for forgiveness and a sense of humility when victory is achieved, and peace is restored.

ACTION

Our faith in God and in goodness demands that we be ever vigilant against oppression and injustice in society. A lack of social consciousness will lead to anarchy, oppression, and denial of social justice, as we are witnessing around the world and in many Muslim countries.

CHAPTER 5
Verses 38–43

As for those men and women who persist in theft (of common good or public good), cut off their hands as a punishment and as an exemplary punishment from God (as a deterrent—only after proper judgment and proof beyond doubt). God is Mighty and Wise. But if they repent their wrongdoing and make correction in their conduct, then God will accept such repentance (so should you). God is Forgiving and Merciful (to mankind). Do you not comprehend Who God is—His dominion is over all of heavens and earth. He chastises whom He will, and He forgives whom He will. He is ever powerful over all things.[307]

O Messenger: Do not grieve for those who persist in denial of the truth, those who say outwardly "We believe" but in their hearts believe not; and some among Jews (or any people who claim faith in today's context) who eagerly listen for a lie or listen to people instead of coming to you (the source). They alter the meanings of words, take them out of context, and presuppose the outcome by advising others: If you are told such, then accept, and if you are told something other than this, then be cautious.

You cannot save someone (all the time) who is tempted to do evil. For such as these, God intends not to purify their souls (as they themselves desire). For such is a disgrace in this world, and in the Afterlife they will face awful consequence. They eagerly listen for lies and devour forbidden things; yet if they come to you to seek judgment (or guidance), you can offer judgment or stay aloof, as they can do you no harm; but if you do render judgment, then do so with justice and equity because God loves those who deal with justice and equity. How is it that they seek judgment from you while they have such judgment (guidance) already from God in the Torah, which they refuse after all of these? They have no faith! [308]

[307] The punishment for theft by cutting off hands physically should be a matter of last resort and is meant to show the seriousness with which theft is disliked in society. The real intent is to develop a mechanism, relevant to every generation, to limit the ability to commit future theft by individuals and by the ringleaders of large-scale thefts, which have become commonplace in our world today by corrupt political establishments; financial and corporate policies that provide uncontrolled profiteering rights to shareholders at the cost of employees and consumers; and exclusive ownership of, exploitation of, and profiteering from natural resources by individuals, corporations, and corrupt leaders. For individual cases, this is a deterrent and applies under strict conditions of justice and equity, with due process of law, if the pattern of behavior is clearly established and not due to a genuine need for safety, food, and security that society has failed to provide for that individual. I have several comments on this:

1. Theft is commonly believed to be shoplifting or common criminals stealing goods from people's houses or stores, yet there are other forms of grand theft, as I alluded to earlier (white-color theft, as it's known in America), being committed by corrupt political leaders, kings, and powerful community leaders directing national wealth to personal use; wealthy individuals using insider trading to siphon off other shareholders' wealth; business owners and corporate leaders collaborating with financial institutions (e.g., Wall Street) to manipulate share prices or commodity prices; and financially savvy individuals using derivatives and options to gamble on financial markets. Such efforts and practices can and should also fall under grand theft, and corresponding deterrents need to be in place and enforced by society. There is an English saying—when a common person steals a handkerchief, he goes to jail, but when a rich man steals a county, he becomes the duke. This is very appropriate to keep in mind when we think about this verse. Capitalism, the way it is practiced

today around the world—focusing only on consumerism and benefits for the capital owners; favoring corporate leaders and shareholders without concern for employee welfare, living wages, environmental pollution, and social justice; usurping mineral rights under corrupt practices or legal framework that does not provide equitable benefit to all; and so on—is an area that should demand the attention of corporate governance, corporate laws and practices, and our policy makers. While focusing on bad practices of capitalism, one should not forget that the competing ideology of Communism has done worse in term of accumulating money and power to select political elites and one party apparatus while destroying human and religious rights, freedom of expressions, rule of law and faith in God.

2. The temptation to seek instant gratification and to accumulate excessive wealth is part of human nature. Each society that imposes duty on citizens—for example, not to steal—should have a corresponding responsibility to ensure that the temptation to steal does not exist, through equitable distribution of wealth, social security, and a minimum standard for food, shelter, and health for every citizen. To stem the accumulation of excessive wealth, we need to define guiding principles and laws on how we practice capitalism—balance shareholder wealth with employee wealth, modulate profit margins to balance corporate benefit vs. benefits to consumers, protect employee rights and privileges, regulate instruments such as options and derivatives, remove the presence of monopoly and oligopoly in the free-market systems, and so on. Abject poverty in society can lead to great evil, and when it is accompanied by huge income disparities, this is a cause for major concern. The Prophet's guidance on this is worth paying attention to: He once said: *"Poverty may well turn into a denial of truth (leading to social chasm)."* He also said: *"Take care of your poor people who lift the burden of the society."* And He also said: *"Pay a just due (wager) to the laborer before his sweat dries out."*

3. We need to shape our spiritual and physical development in a way that brings people together and creates goodwill among all people—rich and poor, intellectual and common man; civic, political, religious and business leaders - all guided by a common vision stemming from faith and goodwill or goodwill alone to make sure we encompass as many people

to foster goodwill in our human societies across national, religious, and ethnic boundaries. Our laws, commercial rules and policies, societal norms, sense of fairness, goodwill, and so on all must be consonant to drive us to a higher form of human existence.

³⁰⁸ The rule of judgment has to be based on fairness and equity, irrespective of the condition of the plaintiff or the defendant. Too often our rules are flawed and framed by the influence of wealthy individuals or wealthy corporations, to the detriment of the common good and welfare of the citizens. The challenge to people of faith, people of goodwill, and people who believe and support democratic principles and institutions is to create harmony and fairness in social conduct and community rules and regulations.

REFLECTION

The Qur'an has touched on many social issues affecting human conduct, including prevention of theft, abuse of human life, gender equality, caring for the underprivileged, and rendering fair judgment to everyone as foundational principles that we need to reflect on, create a workable framework for, and put into practice.

ACTION

Certainly, those of us who claim to have faith and wish to do good, irrespective of our religious or ideological affiliation, have to engender a system of moral, ethical, societal, and commercial principles and guidance that can overcome any temptation, lies, and unfairness that are part of our human construct. All of us have to act on these principles and this guidance individually and collectively to create a sustainable and resilient system to govern our lives and our conduct. God's guidance is here, and we need to act on these—we have no excuse in this world, and in the Afterlife, we sure will have no defense in front of God, the Ultimate Judge.

CHAPTER 5

Verses 44–50

We (God) indeed revealed the Torah containing guidance and light (knowledge), by which prophets, who submitted (to God), rendered judgment for the followers of Jewish faith; as did the rabbis and the scholars—(they were all) entrusted to preserve what God had revealed of the Book of God and they were to bear witness over it. Therefore, do not fear people but fear Me (God), and do not misinterpret the message for earthly gains. Deniers of truth are those who fail to judge (act) according to what God had revealed. We (God) prescribed for them: life for life, eye for eye, nose for nose, ear for ear, tooth for tooth, and similar to the wound inflicted (Exodus 21:23, Jewish law of retaliation). But for anyone who forgives and forgoes, such act will atone his sins. And whoever does not judge (act) according to God's revelations, he is deemed an unbeliever.

We made Jesus, the son of Mary, to come after them, confirming that which was in the Torah, and revealed to him the Gospel (Bible), which also contained guidance and light (knowledge). It verified what remained of the Torah and served as a guidance and as an admonition for those who were mindful and responsible. So let the people of the Gospel judge (and act) according to what God had revealed in it. Those who do not do so are deemed oppressors.[309]

We have revealed to you (Prophet Mohammad) the book (the Qur'an) establishing the truth, verifying all books that came before it, and making it a guardian (preserving and encompassing this truth). So, (as we commanded other prophets before), judge (and act) between and among these people (of the book and your own followers) based on what God has revealed, not deviating from it, which is their desire. For every group (of people) We (God) have allowed different rules and different ways of life (as they opted for). If God had willed, He could have made all into a single community, but He wanted to test each group in what they find themselves. Therefore, compete for goodness (no matter who you are or what faith you subscribe to). Since to God all of you will return, He will then inform you in all that you were differing (on earth, so that you will at last see and agree on the truth, though it is in front of you even now and you still could not come to terms).

It is imperative that you judge among people based on what God has conveyed in revelation and not be swayed by the errant views of some of them. Be cautious, lest some of them tempt you to deviate from parts of what God has conveyed in revelations. If (at the end) they do move away from the truth, then it is because God desires to afflict them with their own sins, since many of them have already transgressed. What is it they want—judgment of ignorance? Who is better than God as a judge for those who have firm faith and conviction in truth?[310]

[309] Just as Muslims, Jews and Christians have been gifted by God with revelations in the Torah and the Bible. The Qur'an came to confirm all previous Books of Revelations and to preserve an enduring collection of guidance and light (knowledge) for all generations to come—this guidance and light has been the main message in all revealed books. All people who have received revelations are required to study, deliberate, comprehend, and implement these ideas and laws in their personal, social, and spiritual existence on this planet and in this life. Failure to do so or to somehow corrupt these ideas and rules with one's errant views deliberately is tantamount to lack of faith, lack of justice, lack of civility, and lack of conviction in truth.

[310] Even though the guidance and the light that shines in these Books of Revelations, the respective followers (including the Muslims) created their own narrow interpretations and injected their own cultural norms, historical biases,

personal temptations, and errant views to limit the full and honest exploration, implementation, and ongoing adaptations of this foundational guidance and these laws. God could have made us all adhere to the truth message but gave us our freedom of choice, allowing us to explore and find our own ways of life. The prudent choice for us is not to fight, not to blame one another, but to compete in doing good for one another despite our differences so that we can build a global society of peace and harmony. God, to Whom we all belong and to Whom we will be eventually gathered, will enlighten us on our differences. Until then, God wants us to do good however we express our faith and be just and peacefully coexist.

REFLECTION

In our world today, where there is so much misunderstanding, hate, and violence against people within the same faith and across different faiths or ideologies, it is critical that we use our common sense, our innate desire to love one another, our capacity for compassion, and our aspiration for life, freedom, and happiness to build a peaceful world. As the Qur'an says, we need to accept our differences as the will of God and converge on our common goal of goodness for all as our major challenge and opportunity to prove our worth to one another and to our Creator.

ACTION

Muslims in particular need to rise above the superficial differences between Sunnis and Shias and the national and ethnic diversity among the 1.6 billion Muslims and accept, as God has asked them to accept, the way Jews and Christians exercise their faith as a God-given right and God's allowance for our human freedom of choice, so that Muslims can unite and work hand in hand with people of other faiths (especially those who follows the ways of Abraham—Jews and Christians) in making this world a better place where every human being has dignity, safety, and freedom to choose.

CHAPTER 5
Verses 51–58

O People of Faith: Do not take Jews and Christians (as relevant to Prophet's generation) into your confidence; they are friends of each other. If you do that, then you become like them, and God does not guide people who are unjust. You can see people who have doubts (about faith) incline toward them and say: "We fear that a misfortune will fall on us." Perhaps God will bring victory (for the faithful) or any other outcome that will become a source of regrets for those who harbor such thoughts (against faith and the faithful) in their souls. Those who are firm in their faith (will reflect on the outcome) and wonder: "Are these the same people who took a strong oath to align themselves with the adversaries?" Their action bore no positive results, and they suffered losses.[311]

O People of Faith: If you abandon your Way of Life (and your commitment to goodness), God will bring another generation who will love Him, and He will love them. These people will be humble with the faithful and resolute against those who deny faith (and goodness in people), strive their utmost to follow God's guidance and persist in the face of all obstacles. This (disposition and resolve) is a grace from God, who is Infinite and All Knowing. Your friends are God, His Messenger, and those who have firm faith—those who maintain their worship of God, take care of the needy, and humble themselves (in their day-to-day conduct). If you nurture such fellowships with God, with His Messenger, and with those who are firm in their faith, then you are aligned with God, who will ensure your eventual triumph (in life).[312]

> *O People of Faith: Do not align yourself with those who mock your faith and take it as a sport, be they from the people who received revelations before or people who deny God and the truth. Be mindful of your responsibility if you claim to have faith. When people are called to prayer (to worship God and to humble themselves), they mock and take it as a sport because they fail to comprehend (its true significance).*

[311] Here advice is given with respect to forming alliances with people who espouse a common framework for life and the pursuit of happiness and perfection. If there are people who are not aligned and in active opposition, irrespective of whether they are Jews, Christians, or people who claim faith on the surface but in their hearts harbor doubts and mischief, one needs to be careful, especially at times of open hostility and armed conflicts. This not a blanket statement against Jews or Christians, as some conservative Muslims or terrorists who terrorize people in the name of religion would like us to believe. In a similar vein, there are many verses in the Bible that caution followers of Jesus against the Jews. Again, these are not blanket statements against Jews, as some conservative Christians would like us to believe, but against specific groups of people, be they Jews or Romans, who were bent on denying Jesus a proper hearing of his message and to put him on the cross to end his life and his emergent call to faith and goodness. We also know that the people of the Pharaoh were against the Children of Israel, who were enslaved, and the Torah is full of caution against them and their lifestyle. But even there we see that a certain member of the Pharaoh's family was giving shelter to Moses and supporting his call to God and goodness.

[312] God is infinite in his capacity to make people believe in Him or to punish them for lack of faith, if He wills. The key challenge for us as individuals and as a community is to fulfill our commitment to God and to fellow humans if we truly claim our genuine faith. Irrespective of whether we call ourselves Muslims, Jews, or Christians, if we fail to fulfill our commit to God and our fellow human beings, then God will bring another generation of people (as history is full of such events and outcomes) who will be truer to faith and human goodness. The rise of the Children of Israel against the Pharaoh, the rise of Christians against Roman and Jewish priesthood, the rise of Muslims against the excess of the Byzantine and

Persian Empires, and the rise of the Ottomans against the Arabs are examples of the past. In our more recent memories, the rise of the Americas against British and Spanish colonial oppression, the rise of the Allies against Hitler, the collapse of the Soviet communism by the Afghans and the Easter Europeans, the emergence of Arab Spring, and so on are also evidence of the same truth that God will bring a different group of people who will be more attuned to truth and human dignity than the prevailing power. We all can take lessons from such consistent turns of events.

REFLECTION
We need to understand that God is looking for real commitment to truth and justice for all people and by all people and not just a mere claim or token gesture by one group or another. In the same vein, calling ourselves Muslims or Jews or Christians (or any other group) does not mean that we are committed to fulfill our bond with God and to follow the guidance contained in Books of Revelations such as the Torah, the Gospel, and the Qur'an. When the Qur'an calls to People of Faith as we read it 1,450 years after its revelation, we have to recognize that it is a call to all people who claim to have faith, not just to Muslims. The Prophet Mohammad came to all of humanity, and the Qur'an is the final revelation for all of humanity.

ACTION
We have to interpret the call of the Qur'an as a call to each and every human being, and its calls, its injunctions, and its guidance need to be deliberated in the context of our specific needs, social norms, human conditions, and collective knowledge to derive the true meaning and to apply it in the most efficient and effective ways, ensuring justice, equality, and compassion.

Key Arabic Term
92. *hujuan wa layiban* (mockery and sport)

CHAPTER 5

Verses 59–66

O People of the Book (Jews, Christians and other people of faith): What fault do you find with us other than that we believe in God, in what has been revealed to us, and in what has been revealed before (to you all), while most of you are transgressing. Say (to them, O Prophet): "Shall I inform you who is in worse shape before God to face His retribution? It is those whom God has rejected and condemned and who have earned attributes of apes and swine as they follow the evil ways. These people are in worse position and farther away from the right path." When these people come to you (the Prophet), they say they believe, but they come in a state of denial and go away in the same state. God knows best what they hide (from you). You can see many of them competing with one another for sinfulness and transgression and amassing illegal gains (to themselves, depriving others). Certainly it is evil what they practice. Why do not their men of God [rabbis] and their scholars (legal experts) discourage them from sinful conduct and amassing wealth with unlawful means? Certainly, it is evil what they strive for.[313]

The Jews say: "God's hands are tied (not generous)." In reality, it is their hands that are shackled, and they are condemned for what they say. The truth is that God's hand is ever spread out, and He dispenses what He will. What God has revealed to you will cause many of them to increase in their rebellion and denial of truth. Therefore, we ordained enmity and hatred among them to continue till Resurrection Day. Every time they light up the fire of conflict, God puts it out. They strive continuously to make mischief on earth, and God has no love for mischief makers. Only if the People of the

Book have confirmed their faith and become mindful of their responsibility to God and to people, We (God) would remove them from their sins and welcome them to the paradise of bliss. Only if they have been faithful to the Torah and the Bible and acted according to what has been revealed from God to them, they will be blessed with the gifts from Heaven and earth. There is a group among them that pursues the right course, but most others are engaged in evil.[314]

[313] Historically, every group that has received revelations from God has been tempted to deny future revelations out of envy or for earthly gains—not all of them, but a majority of them. This happened with Moses even in his own lifetime when the Children of Israel, whom he had saved from the yoke of slavery, refused to follow many of the instructions of Moses. Similarly, when Jesus came and challenged some of the prevailing practices that were contrary to what is in the Torah, there was widespread opposition from Jewish priests about the teachings of Jesus. Jesus's teachings have also been tampered with by his followers over the years. When the Prophet Mohammad came to confirm the truth in the Torah and the Bible and continued with the revelations of the Qur'an, a sequel to God's continued guidance to mankind, as God promised to Adam and Eve, there was widespread opposition and active enmity demonstrated. Nowadays there are groups of Muslims who are committing acts of violence, spreading corruption, and creating the means for amassing wealth at the expense of the general public contrary to the teachings contained in the Qur'an. This is to caution some Muslims who feel that it is only the Jews and Christians who have deviated from their Books of Revelations. The reality is that we all have fallen short of our commitment to God and to fellow humans in our time in the world today.

[314] The reality that if we all commit to faith and goodness, God's blessing will be for all of us is something that is lost among all people of faith—Jews, Christians, and Muslims are no exception, however vehemently each group might deny such a statement. A recent Oxfam report shows that by 2016, the eighty richest individuals will have more wealth than 50 percent (3.5 billion) of the world's population from the bottom up—should this not be a moral issue where wealth is being

accumulated in ways that might may not be moral or ethical though our prevailing systems of commerce, finance, and brokering might allow it to occur? How is it that a racial minority in United States (African American) and a religious minority in France (Muslims) are the majorities in the jails of these two countries—is this not violating the tenets of the Torah and the Bible? How is it that all Muslim countries have fewer universities than one country in the developed world—is this not violating the tenet of the Qur'an that started out with the words *"Read and know that your God is most Generous; who taught by the pen; taught man what he did not know"* (96:3–5). How are we a good steward of this planet and have faith in God when we have polluted this planet's air, water, and land on a scale that was unimaginable even a century ago?

REFLECTION

Jews, Muslims, and Christians—all of us who claim to have faith and an alliance with goodness—should question whether our actions, prevailing systems of governance and finance, social norms, and so on truly reflect our commitment to God and to His creation.

ACTION

The Qur'an's uncompromising posture on our role and responsibilities to God, to fellow creatures, and to the natural world is something that we need to take seriously—individually and collectively—if we are to create a better world for ourselves and have lasting peace in the Afterlife.

Key Arabic terms
93. *esmi wal wudwan* (sin and tyranny)
94. *kaulihimul esmi wa aklihimus suhta* (uttering sinful things and amassing wealth and power through illegal means)
95. *al-adawat wal baghdhaa* (enmity and hatred)

CHAPTER 5
Verses 67–71

O Apostle: Convey the message that has been revealed to you by your Sustainer. If you do not do so (in its totality), then you have not delivered the message. (Rest assured that) God will protect you from people (who are hostile to the message); God does not guide people who deny the truth.

Say to the People of the Book: "You cannot claim to faith until you accept what is in the Torah and in the Gospel and what is being revealed from your Sustainer." Surely what is being revealed to you (Prophet Mohammad) will make many of them (People of the Book) grow in arrogance and denial of truth; therefore, do not grieve for them. Indeed, anyone who has faith, and those from the Jews, the Sabians, and the Christians—whoever establishes (and demonstrates) faith in God and the Day of Judgment and does good (to others)—they will have no reason to grieve or fear (see also 2:64).[315]

We (God) took a solemn pledge from the Children of Israel, and We (God) sent Messengers to them. But whenever a Messenger came to them whose message did not fit their earthly desires, they would call some of the Messengers liars, and some they would seek to kill, thinking that there would be harm in it. As a result they became blind and deaf (lost their ability to see and comprehend God's message). But God turned to them (with mercy and forgiveness), but they again acted as blind and deaf. God sees all that they (we) do.

---

[315] God's message has to accepted in its totality—we cannot pick and choose as we please, as has been done by the people of Book in accepting certain parts and

distorting other parts of the Torah and the Bible and opposing the message from the Prophet Mohammad that did not fit with their earthly desires. The Prophet Mohammad has been cautioned against such tendencies of the followers of the book and his own followers and has been assured that God will protect him and the message. At the end of the day, God assures us that any people who believe in God and do good things to others, irrespective of whether they call themselves Muslims, Jews, Christians, or followers of another faith, will be successful and rewarded by God. Such is the universality of the message from God contained in the Qur'an. People of all faiths should do the same!

REFLECTION

God's message for faith and good work is consistent in every Book of Revelations, and all who follow such guidance are on the right path. There is one God and one set of guidance for the human race, no matter how differently we might label ourselves and claim to follow it. Respecting all prophets, accepting all Books of Revelations, and learning and living the teachings from these Messengers of God will enable us to be the human beings that God wants us to be, and it is consistent with our innate predisposition, pure thoughts, and just conduct.

ACTION

We need to broaden our perspective on faith and good work beyond the narrowness of the clerics and the fundamentalists, and it can happen only if we endeavor to know the truth and secure the truth in our societies.

CHAPTER 5

Verses 72–82

It is a confirmation of disbelief (in God) for those who say: "God is the Christ, Son of Mary," whereas Christ himself said: "O Children of Israel, Serve God, who is my Sustainer and your Sustainer." Whoever associates anybody (or anything) with God, he is forbidden entry to Paradise, and his residence will be in Hellfire. Those who propagate evil (false beliefs), there are no helpers for them. It is also a confirmation of disbelief (in God) for those who say: "God is one of the three, whereas there is no god but One God." If they do not desist from such false assertions, grievous consequences will fall on them due to their persistent denial (of truth). Why do they not then turn to God and ask for forgiveness? God is Ever Forgiving and Merciful.

Christ, son of Mary, was an Apostle (of God), and many apostles have passed away before him. His mother was a woman of great virtue and truthfulness. They both ate food (like other creatures of God). See how We make the matters clear to them; yet see how they continue to deny (the truth). Say (to them): "Do you worship besides God such an entity that cannot control any good or harm for you? God is All Hearing and All Knowing." Say: "O People of the Book, do not extend the boundary of your faith without justification, and refrain from the errant views of people who have themselves gone astray, led many people astray, and continue to stray from the right path (even to this day)."

Those who disbelieve from among the Children of Israel, they have already been chastised by David and Jesus, Son of Mary (Psalms 78:21–22, 31–33 and Matthew 12:34, 23:33–35, for example), for their rebellion and persistent transgressions against God's guidance. They did not discourage and prohibit one another against evil (in the society). Evil was indeed what they did (evil acts and not removing evil from society). You see many of them more aligned with those who disbelieve (than with those who aspire to belief), and their minds (and earthly desires) push them toward evil so that God is displeased with them, and they earn chastisement as a result. If they truly believed in God and abided by the revelations, then they would not befriend those (who deny the truth), and many of them do transgress. You will find the people most hostile to those who have faith are the Jews and those who worship idols, whereas nearest to the faithful are those who say: "We are Christians." They have priests and monks among them and they are not arrogant.[316]

[316] Attention is being drawn here from a historical perspective to the new followers of faith. Each group that was given revelations before—Jews and Christians alike—had confounded their faith in God by either trivializing such faith or corrupting it by adding partners to God. Beyond tampering with faith, they have also introduced corrupt practices and evil ways in their respective societies, leading to further deviation from the guidance of God. After 1,500 years of the revelation of the Qur'an, it is very appropriate to look inside the Muslim communities themselves and see if we have also trivialized our faith in God and persist in social norms and practices that goes against the guidance of God. It is fundamentally important that each individual, community, and nation do such analysis and retrospection to find that the sort of issues that God warned the early Muslim about Jews and Christian, have already afflicted the later generations of Muslims, including the current generation. A new generation of clerics and so-called scholars has come into the picture telling the faithful to do things that are contrary to true faith. Muslims in general have given up on the personal responsibility to understand faith and the guidance from the Qur'an and the Prophet's traditions, instead opting to follow these clerics and scholars in blind allegiance. Political leadership has been usurped by corrupt and inept leaders due to people's apathy to actively engage in guiding one another and their leaders. Worldly gains and immoral pursuits have gained widespread prevalence in

societies, as corruption has taken deep root in many Muslim countries. I do not think it would be inaccurate to say that God's displeasure is as acute with respect to Muslims of today as it was with Jews and Christians of yesterday.

REFLECTION

For people of faith, the Qur'an provides windows of insight and guidance through which we need to see ourselves and others and not dwell on the past conduct of our adversaries—it will only perpetuate our current mistrust of one another and delay any hope for creating a better world where faith and goodwill prevail, irrespective of our affiliations with specific labels of Muslims, Jews, or Christians.

ACTION

We all need to get back to our common root of faith in God and commitment to uphold human dignity for all. We need to use the teachings of the prophets to analyze our conduct, reaffirm our common origin as children of Adam and Eve, and put in practice our equal obligations and rights to serve from each other and from the resources of the world, a gift from God given to all of humanity.

Key Arabic Term

96. *siddiqat* (a woman of great virtue and truthfulness—in reference to Mary, Mother of Jesus)

CHAPTER 5

Verses 83–86

When they (the Christians mentioned in the previous verse) come to understand what has been revealed to the Messenger (Prophet Mohammad), they are overwhelmed (with emotion and) tears in their eyes as they fully comprehend the truth. They say: "Our Sustainer, we reaffirm our faith and include ourselves among those who bear witness (to the truth). What reasons do we have not to believe in God and the truth that has come to us while we truly aspire to be among the people of faith and truth?" So God rewards them with Paradise (of peace and plenty) wherein the river flows to reside as a fitting recognition for those who do good. But those who continue to deny God and reject the messages are destined for the evil of flaming fire.[317]

[317] This is a beautiful and universal recognition of the fact that whoever (in this case Christians), irrespective of his or her previous beliefs, comes to recognize the message of God as truth and commits to doing good will be counted as a person of faith and truth and will be amply rewarded. This is a good reminder for the Muslims that they have no monopoly on God's favor, which is reserved for any human being who believes in God and is committed to do good. Another implication is to stay open minded and be cognizant of the fact that people who are open to truth and justice in any part of the world (especially Christians) will always be impressed by the elegance and truth contained in the Qur'an and its unequivocal confirmation of the truth in earlier revelations (the Torah and the Bible) and acceptance of all prophets (Abraham, Moses, Jesus, and others) as

God's prophets propagating the same and consistent message of peace and prosperity for human beings.

REFLECTION
Many Muslims today fail to recognize goodness in other people, while the Qur'an consistently praises people, no matter what their professed label might be, when they do good and establish faith in God. The Prophet Mohammad, during the days when the hostility between the emerging group of Muslims and their adversaries from the Arab tribes was at its peak, used to lament that he missed those days when he could work together with everyone to serve the common interests of the community. Islam, as all statistics show, is the fastest-growing religion in the world even today after commanding 1.6 billion followers, and most of the people coming to this universal faith are Christians, confirming the truth contained in these verses.

ACTION
Muslim should focus on perfecting our faith and conduct in our daily and collective lives and let our neighbors and community members see Islam as exemplified by thoughtful and humble people at a time when some deviant Muslims (such as ISIS, Al-Qaeda, the Taliban, Boko Haram, and so on, as well as autocratic Muslim leaders in some countries) are igniting a different image of Islam and Muslims in the world.

CHAPTER 5
Verses 87–93

O People of Faith: Do not deprive yourself of all that God has gifted you of good things, but stay within limits of its use (consumption, extraction, accumulation, etc.). Surely God loves not those who exceed limits. Benefit from all that is lawful and pure that God has blessed you with, and be conscious of your role and responsibility, if you believe in God. God will not hold you accountable for minor and casual oaths you might make, but He will call you to account for deliberate oaths that you make, in which case you can expiate such oath (1) by feeding ten needy people in the same measure that you feed your family or (2) by clothing them or (3) by freeing a person from bondage, and if you do not have the means or access to such remedy, then fast for three days. This is the expiation for oaths that you take (but can't keep or should not keep). Be faithful to your oaths when you make them. This is how God makes His message clear to you so that you can give thanks.[318]

O People of Faith: Intoxicants, games of chance, the practice of idolatry, fortune-telling, etc., are loathsome and the Devil's work. Stay clear of these, that you may be successful. The Devil only desires to keep you from remembrance of God and your worship of God by such means as intoxicants and games of chance. Will you not then refrain from such? Attend to God's message and His Messenger and be ever cautious against evils; but if you fail to heed, then know that the Messenger is only trusted to convey the message (and not to make you pay attention—that is your job). Those who believe and do good, they incur no blame to eat (take advantage of what they are gifted with) as long as they are mindful of their responsibilities, have faith, and do good and continue to increase in their commitment to their responsibilities, faith and good work. God certainly loves those who do good.[319]

[318] Islam makes broad allowances for all that is good and pure to be lawful, and one should seek benefit from such without committing excess or depriving others. Whether it is a matter of eating what is lawful, conducting business and making a profit, or extracting natural resources for the benefit of society—one should engage in all these activities, which bring about good for individuals and societies, but ensure that one does not overconsume, make excessive profit, or transfer natural resources to benefit one party at the expense of all other stakeholders. An equitable and just basis for all resource allocation and consumption is a cornerstone of Islamic tradition and laws—both at a personal level, where a personal sense of responsibility is the main gatekeeper, and in social norms and socials laws that ensure that everyone's interest is adequately protected and not harmed by individuals or groups through abuse of power or wealth or even by legal means that may have unfairly been put into the law.

[319] This verse clearly prohibits a broad set of practices and consumption that is harmful at individual level as well for societies. Any kind of mind-altering drug, chemical, drink, and so on is forbidden if it may affect immediately our level of consciousness and might have similar longer-term implications. In a similar vein, chemicals that are being produced, consumed, and dumped into our land and air, causing serious environmental pollution and contaminating our food supply, need to be examined for this prohibition. Genetic manipulations that are altering the character of naturally evolving organisms, plants, animals, and so on also need to be scrutinized. Games of chance and gaming on foretelling such gambling, financial tools such as derivatives and options, which rely on chance and future speculation, many of risk insurance industry practices and provisions need to be examined, especially when the burden is shifted to consumers from the providers by design and by law and creates incentives for manipulation and excessive

control. The proliferation of media and social adoration for fashion icons, movie stars, media personalities, singers, political figures, business tycoons, and even some clerics is distorting social values and leading to practices that are unhealthy for social consciousness, human development, and societal priorities. As repeated in these verses, our sense of human responsibilities, faith in God, and social good has to override all other trends if we want to be successful as a human race and as individual human beings.

REFLECTION

If we truly reflect on these verses and extract the underlying principles to apply them to our current societal and legal norms, rules and regulations, and social practices, then we will have to reexamine our business roles, industrial and political practices, societal values, and priorities. In a consumer-focused world driven by industrial greed and inept political leadership fed by special interests, average citizens are being left behind, as evidenced by ever-increasing income inequality, a diminishing middle class, environmental degradation, pollution of our food supply, drugs that are more harmful than beneficial, man-made financial crises that shift wealth to the wealthy, the rise in corruption around the world, the loss of human dignity and privacy in the name of security, the unending cycle of terror and counterterror, and so on are putting a heavy burden on human consciousness and making it increasingly difficult for new generations to prosper and live a healthy and dignified life.

ACTION

These trends are very alarming, and we all need to address the imploding situation with urgency, a sense of humility, consciousness of our common humanity, goodwill, and deepening faith in God. Particularly, the educated citizens, business owners and operators, and political leaders who share a common faith in God and in our humanity have a significant and urgent role to play in assessing and reversing these alarming trends that are compromising human dignity, equality, and human progress.

Key Arabic Term
97. *al-khamru, al-maisiru, al-ansabu, al-ajlamu* (intoxicant, gambling, idolatrous practices, and fortune-telling)

CHAPTER 5
Verses 94–100

O People of Faith: God will certainly try you with respect to game (of hunt during pilgrimage) that comes within your reach and your weapons so that God can ascertain who is conscious of Him unseen. Whoever goes outside the boundary of this guidance will face its due consequence. O People of Faith: do not kill game when you are on pilgrimage, and whoever does this intentionally, he will compensate (such an offense) by sacrificing the cattle equivalent as judged by two persons of good faith, to be brought to Kabah, or he can expiate by feeding the poor or fasting in an equivalent manner—this is such that he can face the gravity of his conduct (despite repeated guidance). God forgives any past misdeeds on this, but whoever returns to it (after clear guidance), God will make him suffer its consequence. God is ever Mighty, an Avenger against the unjust.

Beneficial to you is the game of the sea and what it provides, a provision for you and for travelers, and the game of the land is forbidden when you are in pilgrimage. Be mindful of your responsibility to God Who will gather you all to Him. He had made the Kabah, the Inviolable House, a symbol for benefit to mankind, with its sacred month, the offerings with embellishments to make you aware that God knows all that is in the heavens and on earth; He knows all that exists. Be cognizant that God avenges all evils while at the same time He is Ever Forgiving and Merciful. The Messenger is here only to deliver messages, and God knows what you do openly and what you hide (do in secret contrary to the message).[320]

Say: "Good (pure) and bad (unclean) are not the same, though the presence and abundance of bad may please you. So be mindful of your responsibilities to God (and to fellow humans) if you claim to be a person who understands, to ensure your success."[321]

[320] Conforming to moral and ethical norms, whether you are in the Kabah in a state of pilgrimage, in your home serving your family, in a courtroom rendering judgment or witnessing judgment, in a position of leadership informing and guiding people, an educator seeking and disseminating knowledge, or an explorer looking for God's gifts on this planet—no matter what your endeavor is and what your pursuit might be—being mindful of our responsibility and making proper choices to benefit one another and not to harm one another are fundamental tenets of human existence and the core of God's guidance. The Kabah, its precinct, its sacred months, the specials rules about games and sacrifice are just a way to illustrate the broader consciousness and commitment we need to develop in every sphere of our activities and conduct, in public and in private, as individuals and as communities.

[321] As if the example above were not adequate and explicit enough, a clear rendering is made that good and evil are never comparable or compatible. Also, the prevalence of evil or our temptation toward evil that we might experience in our lives and in our world should never be grounds to do evil and sustain evil instead of establishing good and justice. We are challenged to develop and validate our knowledge and wisdom to distinguish between good and evil and to conform to good if we wish to be successful as human beings on this planet and in the life to come (after death).

REFLECTION

As we read these words of revelations in the Qur'an or in other books such as the Bible, the Torah, or similar books, we have to be able to extract sublime and elegant truths about our lives and our existence and make sure such truths resonate with our innate feelings and core consciousness, however we define or experience these deeper meanings of life.

ACTION

True reflections, introspections, gathering knowledge, developing wisdom, and so on should lead to establishing and restoring a sense of responsibility in each of us toward God and to our fellow human beings to do good and to do no harm.

Key Arabic Term

98. *qiyam lin nas* (support or mainstay for mankind)

CHAPTER 5

Verses 101–108

O People of Faith: Do not ask for (undue details) of things (regarding rules or guidance), to prevent such details from becoming burdensome for you. If you ask such details while the Qur'an is being revealed (or afterward from Prophet), these might indeed be revealed. God forgives this (some of your eagerness). God is Forgiving, Forbearing. People before (followers of previous revelations) have asked such questions and then failed to fulfill, thus becoming deniers.[322]

God does not ordain or require any animal to be segregated (to reserve for God and deny the benefit to humans as practiced under idolatry for man-made gods). Such devices are a fabrication of lies against God due to their lack of understanding (by most of them). When they are told: "Attend to what God had revealed and align with the Messenger," they say: "We find sufficient the practices and ways of our forefathers." But what if their forefathers did not have the knowledge or the guidance? O People of Faith: Take care of your soul by being responsible. If you are on the right path, the endeavors of those who err will not harm you. To God you all will come back, and He will certainly inform you about your doings.

O People of Faith: When your death approaches you and you make a will, call witnesses from among you or from outside, if you happen to travel and death befalls you—two persons of integrity. You should ask them after performing a prayer; if you feel doubtful about their integrity, then ask each to swear by God: "We will not take any gains for the sake of any relatives or hide this testimony before God. Otherwise, we will be committing a sin." If it turns out (or is suspected) that these witnesses are guilty of such sin, then two others shall come forth whose rights have been violated, to witness against the first two and shall swear by God: "We consider our testimony truer than the testimony of these two, and we have not transgressed the boundary of what is right; for if we do, then we are committing an evil." Such arrangement makes it more probable that the first party will give true testimony or will fear that other oaths will be taken (if warranted) after theirs. Be mindful of responsibility and strive (to follow the guidance)—God does not guide people who transgress.[323]

[322] The directive here is profound and sweeping in terms of keeping rules and regulations at a level that has certain clarity of intent, is procedurally simple, and does not overburden the individual or society to the detriment of one group or another. It leaves room for different groups to formulate ways to follow the guidance without causing undue conflicts and confusion, and to continue to challenge the evolution of human societies under the broader set of principles, values, and guidance that ensure overall equity, justice, and human freedom. Many of the requirements in Jewish law are very cumbersome, such as kosher dietary requirements or Sabbath duties, which have made many Jewish people abandon such guidance, either found in the Torah or later detailed by Rabbis or Jewish scholars. Similarly, in Christianity, requirements such as celibacy, monastery, insistence on trinity, and papal supremacy (for Catholics) have made many Christians move away from Christianity or create numerous sects to find and follow doctrines and practices they find more meaningful or conducive.

Some similar trends have crept into practice among Muslims over the years—the way Shia and Sunni sects have emerged and fought, even today; the types of arrogance and dogma exhibited by some scholars, imams, and leaders who prescribe rules in their countries or communities under the banner of Islam but contrary to Islamic teachings and the so-called Sharia laws practiced by some countries or communities, which have not been reviewed for centuries and reflect tribal rules and cultural norms but have very little to do with Islam and the teachings of the Qur'an.

323 Here is a practical example of encouraging the instrument of Will when someone is approaching the end of his or her life journey, to create a smooth transition of property to the rightful heirs and other needy causes and encourage others to witness and facilitate such a process with truth, honesty, and human dignity. It offers wide latitude as to who a witness can be, how to minimize the risk of false witnesses in the future, and, in a different revelation, provides further guidance as to whom to include in inheritance and how allocation can be made for the time in question in the existing social construct. Some people will take those examples as firm guidance with literal interpretations and formulate rules that constrain people and society, causing serious injustice in man-woman relations and property ownership and destroying human freedom to follow God's guidance.

REFLECTION

The Qur'an has touched on so many legal and social issues and provided sometimes specific injunctions as examples and responses to the time, but mostly broad guidance for human beings to evolve in a just and compassionate society. It is for this reason that the Prophet Mohammad has been recognized as the best lawgiver for human society, and he has been declared as the most influential human being in human history—one can dispute such assertions, but facts and history document his enormous contribution above anyone else in all spheres of human activity and social laws. This is a triumph of faith, and all people of faith—Muslims, Jews, and Christians—should take solace that our faith and the revelations have given us guidance that is in reality the foundation of our social norms and legal system.

ACTION

This is an area of real work that Muslims need to embark on and implement in all our individual, community, and global affairs, in collaboration with people of other faiths. We need to engage in meaningful dialogue and take deep interest in understanding the revealed texts to extract fundamental values and principles to guide our societies and do so with humility, personal and intellectual integrity, and a sense of commitment to human dignity.

Key Arabic Term
99. *wasiaat* (will)

CHAPTER 5

Verses 109–120

When God will gather all the Messengers and ask: "How was the response (from your community to your messages)?" they will reply: "We have no knowledge (beyond our time), whereas You are the Knower of all that is hidden or unseen." God will (turn to Jesus and) say: "O Jesus, Son of Mary, do you remember My favor to you and to your mother—how I strengthened you with the Holy Spirit; how you spoke to people from childhood to grown age; how I taught you revelations, wisdom, the Torah, and the Gospel; how you shaped out of clay the form of a bird and breathed into it so that it became a bird by My permission; how you would heal the blind and the leper by My grace; how you raised those who were dead (spiritually or near death physically) by My grace; and how I protected you from the Children of Israel when you came to them with a clear message. Yet those who persist in denial say: 'This (Jesus and his message) is nothing but a manifest enchantment (deception)!'"

Remember when I[God] inspired the disciples of Jesus: Believe in Me and My Messenger, to which they all replied: "We believe and do take our testimony that we submit to God [as muslims]." (Also remember) when his disciples said: "O Jesus, Son of Mary, is your Sustainer able to send us a repast from Heaven?" Jesus replied: "Be mindful of God if you claim to have faith." They said: "We desire to partake in it so that our soul might find comfort (in our belief), that we come to know that you speak the truth and that we can be a witness to all of these." So Jesus, Son of Mary, prayed: "O God, our Sustainer, send down from Heaven a repast to us—a source of ever-recurring comfort, to the first of us and to the last of us, and a symbol (of grace) from you. Provide for us; You are the Best of those who provide."

God replied: "Surely I am sending (as I always do) such repast as you asked for, but if afterward any of you continue to deny the truth, then I will inflict punishment like the one that has not visited anyone on the earth before." God said: "O Jesus, Son of Mary, did you tell people: 'Take me and my mother as two gods beside God'?" He will reply: "O God, Your Glory is limitless; how can I say something that I have no right (truth) to say? If I had said such a thing, You would have known. I do know what I had in my mind, but I do not know what is in Your mind. You are the Knower of all that is hidden and unseen. I said to them nothing other than what you commanded me to say: 'Serve God, who is my Sustainer and your Sustainer.' I (Jesus) was a witness among them as long as I was with them, but after my death, You were their Keeper, and You are a Witness to all things. So, if you chastise them, then surely they are your servants, and if you forgive them, then you are ever Almighty and Wise."[324]

God will say (on Judgment Day): "On this day truth will benefit those who were truthful—theirs is the garden (of peace and plenty) in which the river flows, and they will reside there forever; God is well pleased with them, and they are well pleased with Him. God's dominion extends all over the heavens, the earth, and all that are in between. His will encompasses everything."[325]

---

[324] The story of Jesus and his mother is related in simple clarity in regard to their relationship with God and the favor that God bestowed on Jesus, his mother, his disciples, and his followers. The extraordinary favors that God endowed Jesus with so that he could do things that ordinary mortals could not do has led many to ascribe divinity to him, though he was never party to such claims and always maintained his servitude to God, as did his mother. This part of the Qur'an lays the foundation through telling the real truth about Jesus and his followers.

[325] The Day of Judgment is the time when truth will reveal itself in its full Glory and those who accepted such truths about God and human purpose in their lives

will be rewarded by being allowed to reside in Paradise—a garden of peace and plenty. This is a result of their earning the pleasure of God and being pleased with God as well in their lives and in the Hereafter.

REFLECTION

The Qur'an is consistent in the way Messengers are introduced and how they comply with God's commands and convey messages as they were empowered to do. Starting with Adam (who was created without parents) and moving on to Abraham, Moses, Jesus (born without a father), and then to Mohammad—all were mortals but endowed by God with the command and wisdom of revelations. The purity of this relationship has to be maintained to be true to the message and our relationship with God. The nature of Jesus is a major point of disagreement among Christians and Muslims and Jews. Muslims and Jews are more affirmative about Jesus being a mortal and a prophet. Muslims accept the birth of Jesus as possible by God but reject any notion that he is God's son, whereas Jews have rejected the birth of Jesus as a pure event and have attacked the honor of Mary for having a son without being married.

ACTION

Despite such differences, we should focus on our common belief in One God—the God of Moses, Jesus, and Mohamad—and strive to work together to serve humanity for our collective betterment, since such belief in God and our demonstrated good deeds will be two things that will save the day, the Day of Judgment, and fulfill our purpose in life on this planet.

Key Concepts in Surah Maidah (The Repast)

1. Dietary rules explained (5:1, 3, 4–5, 87–88, 93)
2. Honoring the signs of God (5:2)
3. Avoiding transgressions and maintaining justice at all times (5:2, 8–10)
4. The perfection of faith and guidance (5:3, 11)
5. Marriage to people of faith (from other religions) (5:5)
6. Ablution for prayer detailed (5:6–7)
7. Lessons to be learned from people of previous revelations (5:12–26, 41–47)
8. Lessons from Abel and Cain (5:27–31)
9. The killing of human beings and corruption on land is forbidden (5:32)
10. Success requires sacrifice and a sense of purpose (5:35)
11. The punishment for disrupting social order (mischief, loss of life, and property) (5:33, 38–40)
12. The Torah, the Bible, and the Qur'an all lead to the same God and goodness (5:44–48, 69)
13. God's warning about failing to remain true to His guidance (5:54–56)
14. Warning against the excesses of clerics (5:59, 62–66, 68)
15. The nature of Jesus explained (5:72–77, 109–118)
16. Christian priests and monks are praised for humility (8:82–85, 66)
17. The importance of keeping oaths and promises (5:89)
18. Injunction against intoxicants, gambling, and fortune-telling (5:90–92)
19. Good and bad are distinct (5:100)
20. The desire for overclarification is discouraged (5:101)
21. God's protection (5:67, 105)
22. The need to draw up a will and protect it with witnesses (5:106–108)

1. Dietary rules explained (5:1, 3, 4–5, 87–88, 93)

Dietary rules in Islam are relatively simple and few in restrictions, in contrast to Jewish and Orthodox Hindu practices, for examples where complicated rules have been in place with a fervent attitude against the food of other people (or even sharing the same pots and utensils), irrespective of their faith. Christianity and Buddhism, on the other hand, have almost no restrictions or concept of dietary rules, though Christians were supposed to follow the Jewish rules regarding pork, for example.

Dietary restrictions in Islam include: (1) carrion or animals that died on their own, (2) blood, (3) pork, (4) any sacrificial animal other than what is sacrificed with God's grace, (5) animals strangled or beaten to death, and (6) animals killed by a fall, wild beasts, or being gored to death. Also, based on prophetic traditions (Hadith), all quadrupeds with split hoofs that are vegetarian (not eating other animals) are allowed. All birds (other than birds of prey) and fish are allowed. In general, anything other than what is explicitly prohibited is allowed, and the food of Christians and Jews is also allowed. With the advent of science and the understanding of the nutritional contents of various animal foods, one should make wise choices, use a variety of food types, and be moderate in food intake. Being moderate in consumption is also spiritually and physically responsible in view of widespread poverty around the world today, even in developed countries.

All plant-based food and fruits are allowed, except what might be toxic or poisonous or might alter the human brain (such as opium and alcohol), or any synthetic chemical or drug that is addictive and adversely and seriously affects the human body and mind functions, such as cocaine, LSD, and other drugs that are proliferating in the world today. The consumption of tobacco and cigarettes, though it poses no immediate danger, is addictive and leads to long-term harm to the body. Based on Qur'anic principles of wholesomeness and purity of diet and potential for long-term harm to individuals and societies, we need to create clearer guidance regarding substance such as tobacco, and so on. I am personally not in favor of tobacco, chewing or smoking, and discourage others from doing so. Smoking is very common in many Muslim societies around the world, mostly among men.

2. Honoring the signs of God (5:1–2)

Honoring and showing respect to the symbols of God is mentioned soon after the very first statement in this surah—every human being has to be respectful and mindful of our covenant with God and with fellow human beings. A covenant (*aqd*) is a natural commitment that exists between the Creator and the created being and among the created beings by virtue of our common relationship with the Creator. Some people also include the natural covenant that exists between our physical self and the spiritual self. This guidance is given in the context of pilgrimage and Kabah, where the sole purpose is to visit the principal house of God's worship on earth for a faithful person and to confirm our relationship with God as His created being. Such a gathering of humanity from all corners of the earth, where race, color, gender, ethnicity, wealth, and so on have no bearing and we are asked to be mindful of God's grace and His symbols of worship and creation.

As stated in volume 1 (page 206), during Hajj there is specific guidance on mutual respect and the absence of any altercation or ill behavior with another human being, as well as prohibitions against hunting, cruelty to animals, profit motives from transactions, and so on. Symbols of God are His creations and those that are specifically made to honor and remember God. Every human being, every creature that walks and moves on earth, every tree that burst forth from the seed and reaches out to the sun, every atom of oxygen and nitrogen that constantly enters our body, every fruit that we long to relish, every grain that we eat to nourish ourselves, the sun that touches every one of us, the moon that defines our calendar and causes tides, and so on and so forth, are all markers for us to think about God and to remind us of our mutual responsibilities, not only to living beings but also to the natural world.

3. Avoiding transgressions and maintaining justice at all times (5:2, 8–10)

Justice and fairness in our dealings with one another, a society based on justice and equality, and an absence of moral or ethical transgressions are fundamental to faith, and without these commitments, faith is not very meaningful. As an analogy, there is a verse in the Qur'an that says your prayer (*Salat*) to God should keep away from evil and shameful acts. In other words, if you perpetrate or participate in evil and shameful things, then your worship of God or your faith has no meaning. Being able to connect our faith to basic moral and ethical tenets and to establish a society based on justice is something missing in many Muslim societies. There are Muslim countries whose rulers or judges, in the name of Sharia Law, want to cut off the hand of someone who, out of poverty, has stolen, whereas these same leaders and judges spread corruption in the land and abuse national wealth for their personal benefit and consumption.

Several basic tenets of a society are provided here:

1. No individual or society should violate these tenets out of hatred of another people or society, no matter how badly they have been treated. The end does not justify the means, no matter what a terrorist might think as he or she murders innocent civilians—or, for that matter, what a leader of the free world might think as he justifies water boarding and torture to prisoners under US custody.
2. One should support others in matters of righteousness, with a sense of duty to others.
3. One should not perpetrate or participate in aggression and sinful acts against others, even if one disagrees with or hates them.
4. Be just and establish justice; do not commit acts of injustice, even to those you may dislike or hate.

All of these are requirements of faith, and being just is a testimony for faith and one's sense of duty to one's Creator and fellow humans.

At the end of all this firm guidance, God reminds us that He is fully aware of all our intentions and our acts so that we do not have any false notion that transgressions and acts of injustice will go unnoticed or unaccounted for by God, even if such acts go unpunished or undeterred for some time due to lack of countering by other human societies. God also promises in these verses that those who have faith and follow the tenets of faith for justice and peace will have His forgiveness and reward even beyond what will be awarded in this world. And as for those who violate such tenets due to lack of faith, or even if they claim to have faith, God will take accountability even beyond being accountable to fellow humans on this planet during one's life.

4. The perfection of faith and guidance (5:3, 11)

Verse 5:3, by all accounts, is the last revelation that came to the Prophet Mohammad during his last pilgrimage, and he lived for another eighty-one or eighty-two days beyond this revelation. This revelation confirms that God had finally completed the guidance in the Qur'an and to this last Prophet, guidance that came to people throughout history (ref 2:213), about which they have differed time and again, separating into different religions. But people of conscience always go back the basic tenets of faith and goodness and question the emphasis on and distortion of rituals. They all want to go back to the universal guidance toward faith and goodness. Faith in God and our natural endowment to connect with God and His guidance is self-evident and further corroborated in verses such as 7:172 and 30:30.

Verse 7:172 states: *"When your Sustainer (God) brings forth from children of Adams their descendants from their wombs, We[God] made them be aware: 'Am I not your Sustainer?' To which they replied: 'Yes, we bear witness.' Lest one say on the Day of Resurrection that s/he was unaware of such truth and reality."* This awareness of God is built into each one of us, and every human being, at one time or another in his or her life, asks such questions. Verse 30:30 further corroborates how that happens: *"Set yourself to the guidance with commitment and purity to truly align with the nature of God into which human nature has also been created. This alignment is the true guidance, but most people are ignorant of it."*

Verse 5:3 not only conveys the completion of guidance but also confirms that God's blessings and favors have also been completed in the sense that the generation that received and accepted this final guidance will prevail in the long run, as well as those who come after them as long as they also continue to be guided by such messages of faith and goodness, and they will continue to receive God's blessings and favor. This verse also confirms that Islam (complete commitment to faith and goodness) is the only acceptable means to God's grace and human salvation, as opposed to any other forms of belief in deities or human beings without regard to One God and any form of society that does not ensure goodness and justice for its members. Such a concept is also reflected in various other parts of the Qur'an, and assurance is given that if we stay true to the faith and goodness, then we cannot fail. *"Whoever commits to guidance from the Book (Book of Revelations such as Qur'an) and commits to serve (God and fellow humans), for such who perform and reform themselves, God will never make their effort go to waste." (7:170)*

One piece of evidence of such grace and support from God is stated in 5:11, when God reminds the faithful that there were people who were determined to stop the spread of guidance and eliminate the prophet and his followers, which the early followers were acutely aware of since they suffered with their lives, their property, and their well-being to remain steadfast in the cause. Such a situation has been equally true of other followers such the Christians and the Jews—Jesus was dishonored and crucified, and Moses suffered from the Pharaoh as well as from his own followers. Human history is full of such struggle and sacrifice. God, by finally declaring the completeness of His guidance and His favor, is confirming that such will remain true for the entire stay of the human race on this planet. If we remain true to the commitment to God, God will reciprocate with His grace and abundance.

5. Marriage to people of faith (from other religions) (5:5)

In this verse, the Qur'an opens up the single most important human relationship outside of blood relationships, which is the marriage relationship. In a society and at a time when marriage within the same tribe or extended family was the norm (some of it is still true in some counties, where the marriage of first cousins is encouraged despite known scientific reasons against such marriages), Islam made the broad proclamation that marriage among people of faith, irrespective of color, social status (including slaves), language, ethnicity, or religious affiliation, is allowed. Opening up marriage with the People of the Book as indicated in this verse implies any people who have faith in One God. Some conservative Muslims takes the literal meaning of the sentence and impose the restriction that such marriage is allowed only for a Muslim male with a female from Judaism or Christianity.

I personally believe that such interpretation is too narrow and should be applicable to both males and females and should include people of faith (in One God and who subscribe to guidance from the books of revelation) from any religious affiliation. Historically, Muslims have spread around the world and adopted local cultures and built relationships with local people in large numbers and with an openness that was indicative of its inclusiveness and its alliance with all that is good in any society, a trend from which contemporary Muslims (especially since the colonial times) have retrenched considerably. Our scholars and social leaders have to take the responsibility to reverse this trend rather than leave it to so-called mullahs and imams to continue to propagate narrower interpretations of our Book of Guidance.

6. Ablution for prayer detailed (5:6–9)

Verse 5:6 is the most detailed verse regarding the instructions for physical cleanliness (ablution) and mental preparedness for formal prayer and worship (*Salat*) to achieve spiritual cleanliness and nearness to God and to justice. We are instructed to use clean water to wash our face, wash our hands up to the elbows, wipe our head and ears, and wash the two feet up to the ankles. This assumes that we are already in a state of general purity—that is, we have taken a shower after engaging in sexual intimacy or washed ourselves after responding to call of nature (using the toilet). If not, we need to do those first before ablution, as instructed here. This is a further measure of cleanliness and getting mentally prepared for the formal act of worship and prayer.

In the event water is not available, the Qur'an has allowed the use of pure dust (soil) by touching it symbolically and then simply wiping the face and the hands to fulfill the need for ablution. In the Prophet's tradition, he also allowed just wiping one's feet, if the person is wearing socks or shoes. In the first instance, God has allowed alternative provisions if the first provision is not easily available, and in the second instance, the prophet of God allowed one not to use water when one's feet (a relevant part of the body) are already covered and clean. In both instances, not imposing undue hardship and using a simple, commonsense approach to achieve cleanliness is stressed and provided for.

Many people have asked me, since most of them work and live in relatively clean environments (white color workers and telecommuters) and most of the time are not engaged in activities between prayers in which they get dirty from soil (such working in the field or in construction, etc.) or other materials that will call for the need to use water to clean themselves, if they have to use water to perform ablution. My recommendation is as follows: be honest with yourself and not use the excuse of being lazy. If you know and feel that you are clean, then just wash your hands (if water is easily available) and then simply wipe (pass over) your face, hands, and feet with your hands and say the intention (*niyat*) for prayer in your mind. There is no need to find a piece of earth, but if you choose to do it that way, it is a choice you can make. But you should not feel that it is a necessity given where you might be at the moment.

In our current world condition, in many places available water or soil will do more harm than good, or where drinkable water is in short supply, doing symbolic ablution (*tayammum*) is adequate and recommended, in my opinion. Each one of us can make his or her own choice. We should not impose or require one way of performing our ablution, and never think less of or judge in a negative way someone who might do it differently than you might do. Be humble, reflective of the purpose of the worship you are preparing to engage in, and conscious that God always know the true state of our mind and our intention in all that we do. We should be critical of ourselves before we even feel that we have the right to be critical of others, especially in matters of the worship of God, Who alone can make those judgments.

7. Lessons to be learned from people of previous revelations (5:12–26, 41–47)

The Qur'an confirms the books of previous revelations, namely the Torah and the Bible, as well as all other guidance that came to people through numerous prophets who came in different generations and different geographic areas. One God means one faith and a singular purpose to do good to others and maintain peaceful coexistence among people. Every generation is given its challenges and is asked to be faithful to the guidance that came to them from God, especially Jews, Christians, and now the Muslims in the books that are still present among us, namely the Torah, the Bible, and the Qur'an. From each group God took covenant by their faith and by their commitment to follow the guidance in their Book of Revelations. In these verses God reminds the Muslims, who now offer allegiance to the last Prophet, that others broke previous covenants with God and with their prophets, and Muslims should not follow the same path.

The Prophet Moses came to the Jewish people and brought with him the Torah, which is called a Light and a Guidance for people. Many of his followers refused to obey him (and by implication God) during his presence, broke the covenant made for Sabath and dietary rules, worshipped idols while worshipping God, refused to fight for their own rights and justice, and ignored the rule of justice and social order laid out in the form of the Ten Commandment and other guidance in Torah. Their priests and rabbis became powerful and oppressed people for their own benefit and ignored the message of the Torah and messages from other prophets who came to them, such as Jesus. The opposition of the Jewish priests to Jesus is well documented in the Bible and historical records. The Torah itself documents the lawlessness and persistent denials of faith and goodness by the followers of Moses in his own time, and subsequent history has plenty of examples to reflect on.

Similarly, Jesus came with the same message as did Moses and brought the Bible, being a Light and a Guidance to the Jewish people and to people at large. His early followers did not have the courage or the commitment to defend him against the wrath of the rabbis or the Romans, who were the rulers of the land at the time. His followers introduced new concepts such as Jesus being the Son of God or being God Himself or being one of the Trinity (Father, Son, and Holy Ghost)—all concepts that are considered false and without intellectual merit or grounded in reality by many, including some Christians. The Qur'an is very emphatic about such false notions, as explained in these verses. The Christians turned into numerous sects and groups based on divergent interpretations of theology and the nature of Jesus, who was a mere mortal, a prophet and a guide for people who wish to believe in one God and to do good to others.

Each sect developed its own churches, introduced its own methods of worship, and embarked on serious theological conflicts among themselves, which led to physical conflicts among various Christian rulers, groups, and nations on a scale that human societies had never witnessed before. The atrocities of the Crusaders, repeated a number of times; the Spanish Inquisition; the horror of slavery on the American continent; the two world wars, which caused millions of lives to be lost; the horror of the Holocaust; the ethnic cleansing in Bosnia; and the effect of the war on terror on innocent civilians in Afghanistan, Iraq, and Syria, and so on are some examples of the excesses of the part of the world dominated by Christianity.

The course of action that is more pertinent at the moment is not to dwell on the past and continue to point fingers at one another but to do the following two critical assessments of our current conditions:

a. First and foremost, for most Muslims the critical question is, as much as the Qur'an wants us to understand the failings of the previous receivers of the revelations so that we can learn from and avoid their mistakes and misdeeds, have we fallen victim to the same sort of corruption, injustice, and ignorance despite God's guidance on faith, social justice, human progress, sectarian differences, violence against one another. It would serve better if Muslims all over the world were to focus on their own condition, be mindful of their responsibilities as people of faith, and focus on doing good rather than blame their condition on other nations or people of other faiths.

b. All people of faith and good consciousness need to come together; celebrate our different religious traditions and modes of worship in synagogues, churches, mosques, and temples; recognize our collective failure over the course of history, no matter what the justifications might be; and renew our focus to have faith in a God Who is our common God and to truly reflect on the collective messages from revelations and our collective wisdom and knowledge to charter a better course for the human race.

It would be very useful to remind ourselves of two verses from the Qur'an that should be very instructive and compel us to act accordingly: *"For every group (of people) We (God) had allowed different rules and different ways of life (as they opted for). If God had willed, He could have made all into a single community, but He wanted to test each group in what they find themselves. Therefore, compete for goodness (no matter who you are, what faith you subscribe to). Since to God all of you will return, He will then inform you in all that you were differing."* (5:48). The other verse is explained in volume 1: *"Surely, those who believe (meaning Muslims), and those who are Jews, and the Christians and the Sabians, whoever believes in God and the Last Day (accountability and Afterlife) and does good work, they have their reward from their Lord; there is no fear for them, and they will have no regret."* (2:62).

8. Lessons from Abel and Cain (5:27–31)

Based on revealed scriptures such as the Torah (Genesis 4:3–12) and the Qur'an, Abel, a farmer, and Cain, a shepherd, two of the sons of Adam and Eve, had a dispute that led to the first unjust murder of a human being by another. Their being brothers made this act of murder even more heinous, and that the thought of killing another could reach the consciousness of Cain is another example of the evil that resides in all of us; it can lead to horrible conduct if we are not driven by our faith and commitment to do only good on this earth.

Their dispute was not substantive by any measure; it was more a case of jealousy and envy. Cain felt that God had accepted the offering from Abel and not from him. This caused him to be angry at his brother and at God also. When the thought of killing his brother came to his mind, according to the Torah, God asked him why he was feeling that way, reminding him that God would accept only offerings that were pure and made with good intentions. In the Qur'an, God reveals further that when Abel realized that his brother was harboring evil intentions against him, he reminded Cain to be conscious of God and that Abel would never do to Cain what Cain was contemplating against Abel. Abel finally succumbed to his evil desire and killed his brother, which eventually brought intense remorse, but the evil was done. The Qur'an further adds to the story by relating that a bird (a crow) came to show Cain how to dig in the ground and bury his brother, increasing his remorse even further because he did not know how to bury his brother while a bird knew better.

The killing of a human being by another has become a daily routine in our world today, and in Hollywood and Bollywood, killing and torture are becoming a form of entertainment. Trivializing human lives for entertainment or killing a person out of envy or jealousy or unjust causes are things we have succumbed to. It appears that no one is immune—from superpowers to tiny terror units, from political operatives to gangsters, from farmers and relatives in land/property disputes to landlords with rent disputes, from husbands accusing their wives of disloyalty to their own secret promiscuity, from rich businessman denying living wages to laborers who want proper wages—the world finds too many reasons to kill other human beings, a crime that is told time and again in all Books of Revelations and by all people of wisdom to be uncharacteristic of a human being who should believe in God and commit to goodness and justice on this planet.

The Prophet Mohammad, in his last sermon during Hajj prior to his death, reminded people that the life and property of another human being is sacred and should not be violated and that no person or race is superior to another person or race except by means of God consciousness and good works. Today we all accept from scriptures and science that all human beings are cousins of one another, and we have come to comprehend and accept equal rights and equal opportunity for every human being. The question remains: How are we going to put into practice what we have come to accept as the truth and as the human norm? That is the test for our generation. God is watching, and so are people who are oppressed and humiliated each day on this planet.

9. The killing of human beings and corruption on land is forbidden (5:32)

Respect for human life, personal property, and social norms is an important part of faith and commitment to goodness that resonates in all revealed texts, and it is found in all religious and human discourse. The Qur'an mandate on safeguarding human lives as stated here is a fundamental human right and a right that should be extended to every creature of God. This verse specifically mentions that the Torah contains similar guidance that says that killing one human being without just cause (manslaughter or containing social order and peace against mischief, violence, corruption, and oppression) is like killing the entire humanity. In a similar vein, saving a human being is like saving all of humanity. Such a declaration of human dignity and human rights is truly the foundation of all faith—certainly that of Judaism, Christianity, and Islam—and to find ourselves killing one another is a testimony to what God says in this same verse: that many of us commit excess in the land.

The level of corruption in many Muslim countries and the lack of civil rights and human rights are indeed alarming. It is precisely such conditions that lead to extremism and terrorism, which exploit vulnerable human beings who are caught between corrupt leaders and a corrupt society that does not give its citizens the kind of dignity and safety that each human being aspires to have. The wholesale glorification of so-called Jihad and the sale of Paradise by clerics and terrorists to innocent, impressionable, and restless youths who are yearning for freedom and dignity are causing havoc in many failed states. This is not a situation that can be solved by more autocratic rules and counterterrorism but by restoring social justice, responsible leadership, freedom to pursue life's dreams, and education for the masses for social consciousness that is deeply rooted in faith and God's guidance.

Even though the dialogue in this book is based on the Qur'an, other people of faith, as already stated in the Qur'an, have fallen victim to and continue to perpetuate similar oppression—if not in their own land, then certainly by supporting autocratic leaders or turning away from oppression in the name of political expediency or material and business-related greed and preoccupation. Each human has the responsibility and accountability to restore such imbalance in our society, irrespective of whichever faith that person belongs to or does not belong to. It is a human issue and an issue that takes prominence in all revealed books and enlightened human discourse. We have no choice but to address this among the nations, in every society, as people of faith and goodness.

10. Success requires sacrifice and a sense of purpose (5:35)

This is important advice given to a person of faith:

1. God consciousness (and by implication social consciousness) should permeate his or her day-to-day life and define the purpose of one's pursuits and efforts.
2. Seeking alignment with God implies alignment with His creation in human societies and in the natural world.
3. One has to strive hard and dedicate one's purpose and efforts to establish the guidance on which God intends to found human society, a peaceful society that respects each human being, creates a level playing field for all human beings, makes education and seeking of knowledge within the reach of every citizen, and staunchly resists any temptation to evil, oppression, and injustice.

These three things are defined as the conditions for achieving success. Time and again history has proven to give credence to such human conditions, human development, and the creation of human civilization. The emergence of the modern world manifests some of these conditions: our collective struggle against colonialism, the French Revolution, the American Civil War, and the fight against the evils of communism on one hand and the advancement of human knowledge and the proliferation of democratic values brought about by the American Revolution and the American Constitution on the other hand, along with a general sense of empowerment by ordinary citizens due to communication technology, the rise of small to medium businesses, and micro financing.

But there have been setbacks as well. Technology has emboldened autocratic rulers and even democratically elected governments to put their citizens under surveillance, large businesses are routinely using monopolistic tactics to thwart competition and pollute our environment and our food supplies with toxic chemicals, weapons of mass destructions have been stockpiled, used in preference to social goods, and special-interest groups are infringing on the democratic foundation of our societies—these are cause for concern, and the above advice from verse 5:35 goes a long way to show us how to reverse the tide of such setbacks in the face of immense human possibilities and potential evident in our world today.

11. The punishment for disrupting social order (mischief, loss of life and property) (5:33, 38–40)

The sanctity of human life, protection of property and environment, the safety of individuals, the preservation of social orders, justice and equality for all citizens, equitable distribution of social wealth, and so on is of fundamental importance, and societal norms should be built upon these things and preserved. The rule of law, civil society, human dignity, human rights, leadership, the representation of such rights, and the corresponding obligations by citizens are incumbent on us as individuals and as a social entity.

The Qur'an encourages us not only to understand and internalize such human and societal norms but also to implement them in a way that can be sustained and nurtured in tune with human progress and our ever-expanding knowledge of the human condition, natural laws, and sense of purpose. It is important in this context to reflect on the verse in chapter 3 (3:7) where God reminds us that as we read, study, and understand Qur'anic guidance and instruction, we have to sort out the fundamentals, such as the Oneness of God, human equality, justice for all, equitable distribution of wealth in a society, and so on, versus rules and examples, such as social laws or inheritance laws that were given in the context of the time and can be and should be, if needed, adjusted with the passage of time and evolving human conditions based on consensus building and vigorous debates and intellectual discussions among citizens. People of scholarship should be forthcoming in providing their sincere, humble, and informed opinion but should avoid the arrogance of knowledge or the presumption of being the superior voice as some of the so-called scholars, imams and political leaders have done and continue to do so in many societies, including Muslim countries, societies, communities, and numerous Islamic centers. A sizable segment of Muslims, especially from Middle Eastern countries, have been conditioned to believe that these imams and so-called scholars (sheikhs) are the only ones who can interpret and pass judgment or rules by so-called fatwas in the name of God—a shameful practice that was shunned by true Islamic scholars such as Imam Hanifa, Imam Malik, Imam Gazzali, and others of high scholarship and wisdom, who understood their position as students of God's guidance, demonstrated genuine humility, were truly concerned about human welfare, and were keenly aware of their human failings.

The verses in question provide guidance for deterrence and punishment, if such deterrence fails in the long run, for those who refuse to accept social norms and laws established by people (not by autocratic rulers, which, by itself, is a tyranny and mischief) and create mischief and disharmony, destroy lives and property, and steal unlawfully. Various forms of punishment have been prescribed with the caveat that time, opportunity, and environment have to be extended first for remorse, repentance, and potential correction of personal and collective deviant behaviors. Counseling and education, family intervention, confinement in prison based on proper judicial processes, and even physical punishment if the individual is guilty of harming others physically are options to consider before irreversible punishment can be rendered, such as death for creating anarchy and mischief (to be duly defined) or cutting off the hands for persistent thievery when the social conditions do not warrant such behaviors.

It is important to note that those who are blind proponents of such punishment at the slightest excuse are also the ones who live under autocratic and corrupt regimes and do not condemn the crimes of the powerful and wealthy but use the excuse of so-called Sharia Law to inflict punishment on the weak and vulnerable, such as women or petty thieves. It is also unfortunately true that some of the most corrupt and autocratic Muslim countries or communities adopt and impose so-called Sharia Law, which the political leaders and their religious counterparts conveniently declare themselves immune from, a practice not much different from what the kings, queens, popes, clergy, and rabbis have done in Christianity and Judaism. This is an unfortunate human condition that tempts every generation and every society unless people are diligent about social consciousness and commit to the true purpose of our existence on this planet. For Muslims in particular, there is a serious responsibility, given the current level of corruption and lawlessness and the rise of extremist groups, to refocus on the core values and principles found in the Qur'an on faith and goodness and reexamine rules and regulations to govern our lives in true harmony with those values and principles. We need to use our collective understanding to harmonize our differences in each community, one at a time.

Human history is full of examples of false religious doctrine being used to thwart those who are true to God and to their fellow human beings or the powerful and wealthy using one means or another, including religion, to exploit people and increase their power and wealth. Burning Galileo for saying that the earth is round, putting Jesus on the cross for asking the Jews to go back to the teachings of Moses, branding our founding fathers and American revolutionaries as mischief makers by the King of England, imprisoning Nelson Mandela for speaking out against apartheid, and abducting innocent girls from their school by Boko Haram are some examples that we all are aware of, and we need to work hard to prevent any repetition.

12. The Torah, the Bible, and the Qur'an all lead to the same God and goodness (5:44–48, 69)

One of the distinct features of the Qur'an is that it proclaims the unity of God's guidance. It confirms time and again that the Torah and the Bible and other books that were revealed to previous generations through prophets and messengers—some of whom are clearly mentioned in the Torah, the Bible, and the Qur'an—contain God's guidance for mankind and that the carriers of these revelations and their followers were expected to follow that guidance, establish their society accordingly, and judge using the standards put forth in those revelations. It refers to each book with its core attributes of guidance (for life) and light (of human knowledge and social consciousness). It adds the further attribute of caution and admonition regarding the Bible, as it came to direct its attention to the excesses of the rabbis and Jewish priests in their faith and social practices, contrary to the teachings of Moses and those contained in the Torah. The Qur'an, while confirming the same guidance and light, is given the further attribute of being the guardian of the books—it will continue to exist in its original form (something that cannot be said of the other Books of Revelations) and will continue to guide human societies, if we choose to follow it and not deviate from the foundational guidance of human relationships with God and with one another in regard to human equality, justice, and freedom.

Despite God's ability to make us all conform to His guidance and light (as is evident in the rest of the creation) and as a consequence of the fact that He has given humans the gift of knowledge and freedom of choice, He allows us to differ in our religious discourse and create different religions and customs and rituals, as is very evident in our current time among the Jews, Christians, Muslims, and other religions. In verse 5:48, God makes the point that He will inform all of us where and how we have created differences about faith and ritual, but at a human level, we all should try to do good and compete with one another in preserving human dignity, equality, justice and freedom for all. We should work equally hard and lead one another in eliminating oppression, poverty, social and income inequality, environmental degradation, and anything else that adversely affects us in our physical, mental, intellectual, and spiritual existence. In each of these books of revelation, there are sound judgments for social justice and human dignity such that, if one were to follow them exclusive to other books, one could establish a just society, as had been evidenced from the long history of Jews, Christians, and Muslims. It is when a group deviates from its teachings that we find turmoil in the world, as we have seen during the Crusades, world wars, apartheid, ethnic cleansing, and modern-day income inequality and environmental degradation.

As if such admonitions and urgings to do good and to avoid evil were not enough, in verse 5:69 God formally declares, as He did in verse 2:62, that He will reward anyone—whether that person calls himself or herself a Muslim, a Jew, a Christian, or a member of any other religion—who believes in God and commits to do good to others. This is the universal truth and assurance that we all can subscribe to without dwelling on our petty religious and ritualistic differences. The Muslims have not done a good job in adhering to these principles in the recent past, and the world has not fully accepted such broad principles at large in their relationships among nations, communities, and people of different ethnicities, races, and religions. Such human conditions will inevitably lead to chasms, violence, injustice, the diminution of democratic values, the loss of human dignity, and a reduction in human potential as a species.

13. God's warning about failing to remain true to His guidance (5:54–56)

The essential characteristics of human beings are that we are made in the same nature as God, and we are made His representatives on this planet to establish peace, justice, equality, and human dignity for all. These are essentially the capabilities that each of us is built with and attuned to as our human nature. This harmony with goodness and truth is innately human, and to deny such predisposition in our character is to deny our own existence and purpose as a human being. In these verses, God wants us to realize that as people of faith and goodness, we have a responsibility to fulfill our purpose to build communities and nations aligned with such guidance and principles that God had programmed us with and endowed in our very nature. If after having such endowment and periodic guidance, we as people of faith are unable to fulfill our human obligations to God and to one another on this planet, then God will bring about new generations and new nations who will exceed others in fulfilling such obligations, and they will be given the mantle of leadership and human progress.

Human history is full of such examples. The Jewish people were removed from the slavery of the Pharaoh and given freedom and prosperity under Moses, David, and other leaders in their long history prior to Christianity. Their failure to maintain justice and moral standards led to the rise of Jesus the prophet, and his followers, who were committed to faith and human dignity despite severe persecution by the Jews and the Romans, continued to prosper and build empires and civilizations that exceeded all that preceded. But in time Christians corrupted their faith and partnership with God and failed to uphold the principles of human equality and social justice as leaders became corrupt and oppressive. Clerics and preachers became more aligned with power and wealth but less with the teachings of Jesus to uphold human dignity and social justice. This gave way to the coming of the Prophet Mohammad and his followers, who came to unite the faith of all faithful and to bring back all people to one God and to one message of human equality, human dignity, social justice, and protection of the most vulnerable in contemporary societies. For over a thousand years, Muslims demonstrated commitment to human values in their different societies, whether in Egypt, Iran, Turkey, India or Spain, and they were able to bring harmony to people of all faiths—Jews, Christians, Muslims, and people of other faiths.

There is a similar turn of events and God's ways of dealing with people when they commit to goodness as opposed to when they fail to preserve the covenant of human beings with God, and this has been played out in constant repetitions in various parts of the world—be it in China, or India or Africa or Europe—from times of antiquity to the present generations that we are witnessing ourselves with our own eyes. The excesses of the Muslim rulers, overreliance on wealth, inability to continue the march of human knowledge, and general failure to uphold human dignity and social justice for its own citizens led to their gradual demise throughout the world. The story of Bolshevik Russia, the rise of Mao in China, the two world wars, the rise of American Revolution, the French Renaissance, the fall of apartheid in South Africa, and so on all point to this constant upheaval and reversal of the human condition in favor of more justice and equality, however flawed those efforts and leadership might be. God's directives and guidance have been to align with faith and goodness in our endeavors, to deter all evils and injustice, to be firmly committed to such guidance, and to be undeterred by any opposition against such goodness. We can look at the world today, irrespective of what faith we practice, and see that societies that follow such norms are progressing at a faster rate than societies that do not value education, social justice, and human freedom, which are the cornerstones of faith and the teachings of all great leaders, including Moses, Jesus, and Mohammad.

Verse 115 is a final reminder that the more favor a nation or a group of people has gotten from God, the worse will be their downfall if they fail to appreciate such favors and fulfill their obligations to be a better society. This is something each one of us as Jews, Christians, and Muslims can attest to and look back at our long histories to draw lessons from.

14. Warning against the excesses of clerics (5:59, 62–66, 68–69)

Islam came to unify the religious discourse among the Jews, Christians, and Muslims—it is a theme that is constant in the Qur'an. Moses came to take people back to the beliefs of Abraham, provide them (the people of Israel) with a way out of Egypt, and establish their own just society. Jesus came when the Jews and the world at large (the Romans) were ignoring the message contained in the Torah and the rabbis, in collaboration with the Romans in power, were oppressing their own people and acting contrary to what the Torah was teaching them to do. Over time the Christian clerics and followers of Jesus corrupted their faith in one God and oppressed people on a large scale, some of which we have witnessed in the rise of Papal Institution, contemporary world wars, during colonialism and in the large-scale slavery practiced on the American continent. The Prophet Mohammad came and brought the Qur'an to confirm the truth that is contained in the Torah and the Bible and reconfirmed our faith in One God and our common purpose to create a peaceful and just world for everyone.

In these verses the Qur'an recounts some of the excesses committed by people of previous faiths, namely Jews and Christians, and perhaps it is time for the Muslims to reflect to see if they have gone down the same path that the Qur'an so strongly condemns. The Qur'an asks the People of the Book (Jews and Christians) what faults they find in the teachings of the Prophet Mohammad when he is asking people to believe in One God and to be true to the teachings of the Torah, the Bible, and the Qur'an—three major sources of revelations that reinforce one another. Despite the clear guidance from their prophets and the books that are present, they ignore these teachings; compete in creating chaos, mischief, and evil in the world; destroy life and property; and devour the property (and profit) of others with means that are not legal or wholesome, thereby destroying the essence of life and social justice. The Qur'an further asks the rabbis and the clerics who claim to be men of God why they support such evil and excess in their conduct while they read the books and claim to know better. The arrival of the Qur'an and the Prophet Mohammad, to some extent, created further divisions and enmity among the people who claimed to faith rather than uniting them. This was due to their own envy, enmity, lack of understanding and devotion to God, and lack of commitment to social consciousness and the human condition. The Qur'an further mentions that the people who lack faith and understanding of human purpose are constantly creating fires of chaos and mischief in the world, and God is constantly putting out such fires to preserve human society by overpowering one group with another and by inspiring people to the truth.

Knowing the conditions that the Qur'an finds unacceptable for the People of the Book, it is time to reflect on the conditions and the conduct of the Muslims after 1,500 years to see if we as people of faith, our so-called clerics and scholars (imams and sheiks), and our leaders are committing the same kind of excess and tyranny in our societies while claiming the guidance of God and the Qur'an. In many parts of the Middle East, North Africa, and East Asia, Islam and so-called Sharia Law are used to oppress citizens, dehumanize women, and punish people for petty crimes while the powerful and the wealthy are scot-free, stealing national wealth, devouring people's property, and building palaces and businesses to enrich themselves to a level that human societies have not seen before. Many Muslim societies have failed to make education a national priority for its citizens. Political and social corruption have destroyed the basic fabric of society, and everyone is for himself or herself. Fringe groups with extreme views have sprung up in a number of nations where the government and people are unwilling or unable to control such aberrant behaviors, injustice, and oppression of average citizens, partly because the government and society have created conditions of despair, injustice, and contradiction, which fuel such extreme behaviors.

Despite such repeated failures, it is important to note the optimism that the Qur'an declares for the human race with God's repeated assurances that (1) if they observe the Torah, the Bible, and the Qur'an and keep a moderate course, God will certainly bless them all with abundance from the earth and the sky (ref 5:66) and (2) irrespective of who you are—a Muslim, a Jew, a Christian, or a Sabian (a representative of any person of faith)—if you believe in God and do good things and have firm faith in the Day of Judgment, there is no reason to fear or have regrets. These are assurances that we all can feed from and nourish our mind and soul with to become better human beings and create a better world for all of us.

15. The nature of Jesus explained (5:72–77, 109–118)

This chapter in the Qur'an, like several other chapters in this volume and volume 1, as well as in Chapter 19 in the Qur'an, titled *"Mary (Mother of Jesus),"* contains various aspects of information about Jesus to confirm his stature as a prophet (second to the last Prophet, Mohammad) to the Jews and the guidance that came to him in the form of revelations known as the Bible or the New Testament. The verses also refute any concept of divinity that many sects of Christianity ascribe to Jesus or the notion of Trinity that is also prevalent among certain, if not most, Christian sects.

Verses 75–77 draw attention to the fact that both Jesus and Mary were human in origin, they lived among people, ate the same food, and died just like any other human. People who claim to follow Jesus are cautioned in verses 72–73 not to exaggerate in matters of faith by ascribing Godhead to Jesus or to create multiple godheads and not to go down the path of people who have corrupted the truth to seek their own narrow and deviant views about God and His teachings that came through prophets such as Jesus and Moses.

In verses 109—118, God comes back to resolve the issue of Christian belief about Jesus by foretelling the events that will unfold on the Day of Judgment. On that day, all the prophets will be gathered around God, and He will ask them about their knowledge of their followers, to which they will respond that they had no knowledge after their death. God will recall the favor that was bestowed on Jesus and his mother, how God strengthened Jesus with the help of the Holy Spirit (Angel Gabriel), how Jesus was given knowledge and wisdom with revelations such as the Gospel and the Bible and the books that came to Moses (the Torah), the various healing powers that God endowed Jesus with, and how God had helped Jesus prevail in argument with Jewish priests and rabbis about faith and the guidance in the Torah and the Bible. The narrative of Jesus with respect to his disciples is then recounted, as is how God sent food requested by the disciples as an extraordinary favor but also with a caution that should they not live up to the guidance that came to them through Jesus, they would also be faced with similarly extraordinary consequences. Throughout Christian history, ordinary Christians have suffered at the hands of oppressive kings and queens; the Crusaders who killed Jews, Christians, and Muslims indiscriminately in the land of Jesus's birth; the excesses of the Pope and the clergy even to this day; the constant battle among themselves, as was evident in the two world wars, which were fought primarily among Christian nations that pulled other nations into the mayhem. The horror of large-scale colonialization of people, apartheid in South Africa, and the slavery of Africans on the American continent provide further evidence of faith gone wrong.

Social justice is a cornerstone of all faiths, especially the faith of Abraham, to which Jews, Christians, and Muslims subscribe. As the Qur'an repeats many times, faith without social justice is no faith at all, and history is full of examples where people of faith failed to uphold social justice. The Muslim world today has many nations and societies that are filled with the lack of social justice, where corrupt practices prevail, sometimes in the name of Islam and perpetrated by leaders who rule not with legitimacy but on the claim of birthright, by forceful autocratic leaders who gain power under the guise of democratic institutions, or by political parties that perpetuate corruption and personal wealth accumulation. This social injustice is also creeping up in developed countries in the form of increasing polarization of political processes, campaign financing that gives rise to disproportionate influence by the wealthy, rising income disparities that leave a large segment of the population uncared for, and unprecedented abuse of the environment with indiscriminate means of production and consumption. When we begin to act like God ourselves without the humility and wisdom that can govern our belief and behavior as created beings, when we falsify the notion of truth and justice with or without affirmation of faith in God, and when personal ambition and accumulation of wealth and power overshadow social justice and concerns for human condition, we violate the teachings and guidance of God and all prophets and ignore our own innate human nature. This is a trend that people of faith and goodwill needs to address with a sense of urgency in our world today.

16. Christian priests and monks are praised for humility (8:82–85, 66)

Islam aspires to create a community of faithful who walk the moderate course, devoid of any extremism. The presence of several extremist groups in different parts of Middle East, North Africa, and Southeast Asia is given more attention in the media than what their numbers would indicate. These groups' use of Islam and so-called Sharia Law are nothing but a way to garner support from groups of people who are subject to corrupt rule in countries that lack basic human rights, the rule of law, and a functioning civil society and have extreme poverty though the countries may have a wealth of natural resources. In other instances, in some of these countries (notably Afghanistan by Russians and Iraq by US forces), outside powers have intervened on false pretexts and disrupted the social order within the country, acerbated the divisions among various ethnic groups, caused death and dislocation on a scale that has seriously damaged people's faith in humanity and social consciousness, and led to rise of extremist groups that provide simplistic solutions on a small scale and express their suppressed anger and anxiety on innocent civilians or corrupt governments and their institutions in their countries.

Unfortunately, these types of extremism are not isolated events in human history, and every religious group has suffered from within and from without and has also practiced such extremism on a larger scale, as was evident in the Holocaust, the Spanish Inquisition, the practice of slavery on the American continent, and the IRA atrocities in Northern Ireland and the response of the British army. Even groups that are devoid of faith, such as the Bolsheviks in Russia, the communists in China, and the Japanese army during Second Word War, committed atrocities and destruction against their own people or their enemies on a scale that human societies had not seen before.

The Qur'an has always taken a strong position against social injustice, human indignity, and oppression and anarchy in societies and in human conditions, which was predicted by the Angels when Adam (i.e., the human race) was being prepared to inhabit the planet. The Qur'an's condemnation of Jews and sometimes of Christians are not against their faith but against the conduct of individuals and societies that exceeds the limit set by God with regard to social justice, human equality, and human freedom. As we look at the world today, such condemnation would also be rendered against many Muslim communities and countries that have corrupted their social order, created corrupt government and leadership, and pay lip service to their faith in God and human goodness. The Qur'an in these verses praises the middle course taken by many followers of the Torah and the Bible and makes special mention of Christian priests and monks for their humility, sincere devotion to God and His message, and genuine desire to lead and establish a peaceful and purposeful life. It is time that people of faith, especially Jews, Christians, and Muslims, renew our vows to our common faith in one God and follow the guidance that Moses, Jesus, and Mohammad provided to the world that corroborate, support, and build on one another, rather than be at odds with one another. As the Qur'an says earlier (5:48), God has allowed different people to create different ways (rituals) to worship God, but they all should vie with one another in doing good in societies where everyone can peacefully coexist.

17. The importance of keeping oaths and promises (5:89)

The keeping of one's promises and mutual trust are critical as a foundation of faith and for any functioning relationship and society. God's guidance in 2:177 makes it very clear in a very assertive manner that turning east or west (in prayer, orientation, or ideology) is not the fundamental thing, but one must have faith in

- God;
- human accountability (during life and in the Afterlife);
- Angels who operate under God's command;
- the Books of Revelations;
- the prophets who guided people to faith and goodness;
- charity without expectation;
- taking care of relatives, orphans, the needy, fellow travelers, and those who seek help or support;
- freeing a human being in bondage;
- worshipping God;
- sharing wealth with fellow beings as a condition of living;
- keeping promises when they are made; and
- exercising patience in times of difficulties, calamities, and conflicts.

This is an expansive list of twelve attributes that define a person of true character and humanity and one who acts responsibly. In this list, keeping promise is a critical element that too often gets overlooked in human societies, which leads to all kinds of conflicts, large and small, in personal life or in international relations. Lack of trust is at the core of the long-standing Palestinian-Israeli conflicts, where neither party trusts the other party and neither party believes that other party is genuine in its intention to make good on the promises that it proposes to make. Isaac Asimov, in his book, demonstrated through game theory and real experiment that when parties in conflict put forth their intentions clearly (without trying to deceive each other) and act in accordance with their commitment (and promises), conflicts get resolved with the least amount of damage or waste, and this can lead to peace in shortest amount of time.

The verse in question and another verse (2:224–225) relate to personal oaths and promises that one makes to oneself in moments of anger and sometimes deliberately (perhaps without adequate reflection) when one denies one's own or others' obligations. In such an instance, if it was done in a moment of emotional disturbance, one should upon reflection not follow through on such a vow, oath, or promise. But if it was done with adequate deliberation and the person realizes that such an oath was inappropriate and a better course of action is more advisable or breaking the oath is appropriate, then the notion of atonement for irrational behavior is upon him or her. The Qur'an suggests several ways to atone for it: feeding ten needy persons in a manner similar to how you would feed your family, clothing them in the same way, or freeing a person from any form of bondage. But if one is unable to do such things due to lack of material possessions, then that person should fast for three days to suffer the pain of hunger and have time to reflect on the irrational decision so that next time he or she can be more deliberate and thoughtful about it. In today's context, doing community service, volunteering in a homeless shelter, helping with other social causes for underprivileged children, visiting nursing homes, and so on can be used to expand the list of ways one can atone for such rash and poor judgments in our day-to-day social interactions.

18. Injunction against intoxicants, gambling, and fortune-telling (5:90–92)

In this one verse (5:90), prohibitions against several substances due to their mind-altering capabilities and several social practices based on games of chance or the use of arbitrary means to define future events or outcomes has been pronounced. Islam came to define social justice in a more holistic way, to remove any form of superstition or arbitrariness in our social conduct and to restrain anything and everything that gets in the way of inhibiting human intelligence, human responsibility, and social justice and destroys or diminishes human lives and compromises our meaningful and purposeful existence on this planet.

The prevalence of drinking or the use of opium or other natural substances that are altered to form drinks or powders that can be inhaled, snorted, eaten, or, in more recent times, injected into our bodies and are habit forming can alter our mind, senses, intelligence, and awareness of our surroundings and mutual conduct in ways that are harmful to us individually and to our families, our communities, and our nations. The ill effects of drinking are well documented and established in terms of slowly and sometimes violently destroying lives—causing highway fatalities, spousal and children abuse, binge drinking and gang rapes on college campuses, the loss of productivity from hangovers, and so on. The list is quite long, and it only gets longer when one considers other substances such as cocaine, LSD, and various forms of manufactured and synthetic drugs that lead to organized crime and violence on our streets and communities, especially poorer communities; sexual abuse of women; and destruction of lives in general. In more recent times and in developed countries, the fatalities from overdoses of prescription drugs, powerful pain killers and mental-health-related treatment leading to increased incidence of addiction, undue impairment in life, mental imbalance, suicide, and accidental death to the extent that abuse of prescription drugs has become the leading cause of death in the population, exceeding highway fatalities due to drunken driving.

Gambling and games of chance persist in societies and in many developed countries such as the United States. Legalized gambling exists and is being voted on, on the pretext that it generates revenue for the state or the community that permits it. We all know that this is an unfair trade, with the odds stacked against the gamblers in favor of the operator/owner, and it is an indirect form of shifting income from the poorer part of society, who form the majority of gamblers, rather than the few rich and attractive gamblers profiled in Hollywood movies, and giving it to another part of the community, mostly touted to benefit senior citizens. Such an equation is very misleading when one considers the well-being of the entire society as opposed to isolated groups within a society, and an end should not justify an unfair and unwholesome means of achieving it. Not to mention that many socials ills such as fraud, abuse and organized crime seem to be become part and parcel of the gambling industry.

Superstitious practices with respect to fortune-telling or predicting the future by occult means and practices of sacrificing to idols or ascribing any form of divinity to something that has no claim to divinity are all considered harmful, unwholesome, and unethical from an Islamic perspective. All such substances, meaningless practices, and religious rituals without foundation are labeled as inspired by the Devil and contrary to godliness and are an affront to human intelligence and human dignity. Every human being should avoid, and every society should discourage, such practices.

These things are clearly stated, but despite clear statements, these substance and practices persist in many parts of the world, including Muslim societies. We all have a role to play not only in avoiding such substance and practices but also in joining hands with others to speak against substance abuse, gambling, and superstitious practices.

On a related note, let me also mention that at some level human beings and human societies can see the impact of this, yet they persist in such abuses in a way that causes substantial harm to individuals and communities. Our inability to abstain and curb such evils is a stark reminder of our own human folly and lack of resolve to rid ourselves of such evils. There are other harmful practices that are equally prevalent. Illiteracy, lack of political and social freedom, political corruption, corporate greed, and wanton disregard of human and environmental health are becoming even greater as destructive forces, and on a wider scale than was ever imagined possible. These things will require even stronger resolve to address and solve.

19. Good and bad are distinct (5:100)

The notion of good and evil or what is moral versus what is immoral or what is just versus what is unjust is already built into our innate senses. This is in fact a reflection of our origin as creatures of God made in God's image or as creatures into which God breathed His essence, as was the case with Adam and Eve and with every child that is born. Each and every human being is endowed with such predisposition and has been wired to distinguish between good and evil. So when the Qur'an says that good and evil are not the same, we fully comprehend such a statement as self-evident, and it requires no further proof. Such statements in the Qur'an also confirm its own truth as a Book of Revelations from the Almighty, and it is with the utmost consistency that the Qur'an brings out the self-evident truths in our universe and in our makeup that define us as human and define our common humanity.

But having such a predisposition, innate understanding, and natural affinity to good does not provide a guarantee that good will prevail or dominate society or our human condition or actions. As a matter of fact, throughout human history, we have had periods or geographically dispersed communities or nations in which evil dominated in a society, by will or by coercion, such as apartheid in South Africa, the persecution of Jews in Nazi Germany, discrimination and racism during the colonial rules in large of parts of the world, autocratic rule in parts of Middle East, communist rule that resulted in loss of life and human dignity in countries such as Russia and China, and widespread corruption in countries such as Pakistan and Nigeria. Other times, there have been societies where good has prevailed but there were systemic evils in isolation, such as slavery on the American continent and hegemony and immoral excesses of the ruling class or ruling family, such as Gaddafi of Libya, to name a few examples.

It is easy for a person to fail to distinguish sometimes the evils of society if it dominates the social norm, or for intelligent and cunning men to exploit such evils deliberately for their personal benefit. The Qur'an warns against such failings of human beings and urges people of knowledge and understanding to be mindful of such guile and deceit and to be true to their moral and ethical bearing, which God has ingrained in all of us so that as a society we can be successful. Each and every Muslim, each and every person of faith, and each and every person of goodwill has a responsibility to seek out good and oppose evil no matter how temping evil might be or how abundant such evil may be in our contemporary life or society.

20. The desire for over-clarification is discouraged (5:101)

In matters of laws, regulations, and social norms, Islam had laid out a set of broad guidelines that resonate with human nature, again reflecting the fact the Qur'an came from the Creator Himself. The Prophet Mohammad and all other prophets such as Jesus, Moses, Abraham, Noah, and so on were human beings who deeply understood the nature and make of the human species, its potential, and its limitations, with the result that their teachings and the revelations that supported their endeavors confirmed human nature, human yearning, and human dislikes, again confirming the fact that human beings are endowed with the essence of God's sublime attributes but with inherent limitations that each one of us is intimately aware of and experiences each day.

There are rules about worshipping God, which comes in the form of worship, personal discipline, and the basic demands of social consciousness, as exemplified in the Five Pillars of Faith in Islam, namely:

- **Declaration of Faith (Shahada).** The Declaration of Faith brings crystal-clear and simple but deepening clarity around our nature and our relationship with God, the Creator—we are His creation, made in His nature and bound by His cosmic, moral, and social laws, and prophets such as Mohammad, Jesus, and Moses came to communicate such understanding and to gain commitments in human terms. Every faith demands such clarity, but most have fallen short, including today's Muslims, which is also inherently human since our failings are as much of us as our accomplishments. Judaism has marginalized its relationship with God and revolted against prophets time and again, whether with Moses or Jesus, as is well known and documented. Some sects of Christianity, in their excess of love and adoration for Jesus and Mary, have positioned God Almighty as one of three rather than the only God and have imposed celibacy, monastery, papal hegemony, and so forth on people who were not in accordance with the teaching of Jesus. Muslims, despite spectacular success during their first millennium (600 AD to 1600 AD) in all spheres of human endeavor—godliness, moral clarity, social consciousness, science and technology, governance—have fallen behind most civilized countries despite adherence to rituals and Qur'anic memorization by one group and marginalization of faith and Qur'anic guidance by another group. Holism of God and Prophet, the spiritual and the material worlds, the human and the natural universes are becoming less of a norm, whereas our Shahada was meant to unite these two aspects of our existence.

- **Worship of God (Salat).** The Worship of God is meant to align us with the spiritual and to continually renew our commitment to expand what is good and diminish what is evil. As the Qur'an says, the Salat should keep you away from evils and shameful acts. Yet I have seen too many worshippers and too much corruption coexist in many religious communities and nations; some Muslim countries and many Muslim communities are no exception.
- **Fasting (Sawm).** Fasting as a way to develop self-discipline—training one's mind and body to deal with deprivation, to deny instant gratification and mindless consumerism, to focus on the spirit, and to temporarily forgo the material aspects of our lives—is an important pillar of human development and spiritual awaking. Yet many of us, as the Prophet warned, only experience hunger but do not gain the spiritual upliftment as it was meant to be, just the way worship (Salat) was meant to develop consciousness and natural affinity to be good and to do good. In many religious communities, ritual prayer and fasting have become a source of showmanship and arrogance, to hide their evil deeds. In a similar vein, many leaders in communities and nations use prayer and fasting to fool citizens as to their godliness and to mask their evils.
- **Obligatory Charity (Zakat):** Islam made charity a form of commitment to acknowledge that all the resources (wealth, businesses, natural resources, source of labor, etc.) we gain or take control of

are a gift and a trust from God, and unless we dedicate a portion of that to better the lives of the less fortunate, we cannot claim to be worthy of God's creation and the beneficiary of His grace. This is distinct from regular charity and requires community and institutional commitments based on collective and purposeful undertaking. I see the leaders in many Muslim countries go on charity shows to distribute clothing and food to the poor, but they fail to institutionalize improving the conditions of the less fortunate citizens through legislative mandates such as social security and entitlement grants, which I have seen in the United States—for example, to take care of the orphans, single mothers, vulnerable children, the old, the handicapped, and so on.

- **Pilgrimage (Hajj):** The once-in-a-lifetime pilgrimage to Makkah, the place where Kabah is situated, is meant to draw people of faith, irrespective of wealth, status, color, race, gender, age, and so forth on an equal and universal footing in our common humanity to come to God with a penitent and purposeful mind to reflect on our past; to seek God's forgiveness and grace in the midst of millions of other faithful; to reenact the footsteps of the great Patriarch, Prophet Abraham, his wife Hagar and his son, Ishmael in rebuilding the first house of worship and dedicating it to the benefit of mankind as a reminder of our perpetual quest to serve God and to serve fellow human beings; and to renew our commitment to lead a socially purposeful life when we go back to our respective communities after Hajj. Yet this great institution of godliness and equality has become a source of corruption when one sees the disparity in the way the poor and the rich are given accommodation for Hajj, how the leaders segregate themselves from the masses when performing Hajj, how one adds the title Al-Hajj to one's name after Hajj, how one becomes arrogant thinking that one is better than those who did not perform Hajj, how rich people perform multiple Hajjes while neglecting what is due to their poor neighbors or their employees, how they commit more sins and corruption and then perform another Hajj to cleanse themselves, and so forth.

I have revisited above the basic and often-repeated Pillars of Faith (also known as Pillars of Islam—see the appendix in this volume for more details) just to make the point that as important as the Pillars are, they themselves can become devoid of life and meaning unless one is consciousness of the essence of faith and its implications in our lives. Similarly, when one looks at the all guidance (legal, moral, and social) that is contained in the Qur'an and the teachings of the Prophet Mohammad, which builds on top of all teachings contained in other Books of Revelations and propagated by other prophets, this guidance is broad, constitutional, and builds a framework for practical implementation. When specifics are given, they are meant as examples to help one understand the meaning and put such guidance into practice. The specifics are never meant to confine the meaning or to deprive continuing generations from applying their God-given intellect and evolving human knowledge to continually reflect on the guidance in the context of time, the situation, and the complexities that will inevitably arise. Hence the reason for this verse: when guidance is given, we should take it in the broadest meaning and not try to confine or unduly specify its meaning and application so that it becomes burdensome, loses its essence, and leads people to question faith and become disengaged, which is contrary to its enunciation in the first place.

So-called Muslim scholars and clerics have contributed much to the multitude of rituals and mundane details while neglecting the essence that drives Islamic faith and its Pillars, its guidance, and its rules and regulations. In addition to this verse, another verse that points to the same thing is 3:7, where it is categorically stated that the guidance given in the Qur'an is foundational in nature, and the specifics are examples to be used for further elucidation by each generation with due scholarship and collective consent. Let me cite an example to make the point.

In the context of setting Hajj as a pillar, the following incident took place with the Prophet and his community: In one of his town-hall meetings (sermons), the Prophet said: *"O my people, God has ordained pilgrimage (hajj) (to the house of Kabah) for you; therefore, fulfill your obligation."* At that point, a person in the audience asked: *"Is it every year, O Prophet of God?"* The Prophet remained silent as the person repeated the question two more times. Finally the Prophet responded: *"Had I said yes, it would become obligatory on you (to perform Hajj every year), and it would have been beyond your ability to do so. Do not ask me about matters that I leave unspoken; for, behold, there were people from previous generations who failed because they put too many questions to their prophets (and leaders) and then disagreed (about those details). Therefore, if I ask you to do anything, do as much as you can, and if I forbid something, then abstain from it."* The implication of this simple exchange and the principle are profound and overarching. The emergence of Shia versus Sunnis and the different alliances with imams such as Hanafi, Maliki, and so on and the consequent sectarian differences or differences about how one performs the rituals are the very essence that the Prophet cautioned against.

21. God's protection (5:67,105)

Belief in God and the fulfillment of our human obligations to God and to fellow humans are the essence of our human existence. The guidance of God that is contained in the Qur'an, the Bible, the Torah and other revealed scriptures is meant to aid in our personal and collective efforts to live up to the intent of God for our creation—a creation that is made in the nature of God and to represent God on this planet.

Our commitment to God and to His guidance also comes with some assurance that if we truly commit to the ideals that are contained in the Qur'an and other Books of Revelations and encourage one another to realize these ideals in our lives and in our communities, then God will aid and facilitate such efforts and afford personal protection and community enlightenment after a period of trial and testing, which is the way for us to demonstrate our commitment to such ideals and guidance. In these verses, on two different circumstances, God makes the following commitments:

- The Prophet should continue his vigorous efforts to educate and guide people, and God would protect him in his struggle against the forces of evil and opposition, which were making attempts to stop his movements and personally harm him. The history of his life and the lives of subsequent generations of Muslims proves the point that as long as we have maintained individual and collective commitment to the ideals of true faith, we have prevailed and made contributions to contemporary human societies on an unprecedented scale. The same has been true for Jews, Christians, and people of other faith communities who have followed the path of truth, justice, and human dignity coupled with God consciousness.
- In verse 5:105, God makes a similar commitment to individuals—that if we take care of our souls, meaning we remain true to our innate nature, the nature of God that our souls are tuned to, and struggle to establish God's guidance as our way of life on this planet as a way to bring peace and prosperity to human societies, then God will make such endeavors and visions successful and render this help to secure such souls from harm, from temptation, from despair, and from laziness. The lives of prophets, great leaders, and ordinary citizens who are driven by God-given ideals and who pursue avenues to build peaceful and just societies have always been successful despite periodic setbacks and times of intense conflict.

We should take lessons from history and rely on the assurance that God provides in His Books of Revelations so that we can strengthen our resolve and seek spiritual and physical nourishment from God's grace that our effort will in the long run be successful and will have staying power as long as our effort and resolve is present. Our resolve and effort have to be uncompromisingly just and based on truth; they have to be executed in the most effective way without violating any of the moral and ethical standards of our relationships with fellow human beings and with God.

22. The need to draw up a will and protect it with witnesses (5:106–108)

The guidance of the Qur'an has been far reaching and over-encompassing in terms of not leaving any part of our human condition out. One of the last rights and obligations is to document a will or testament to bequeath or distribute properties and possession after one's death. With the purpose of minimizing confusion and discontent among the heirs who are entitled to such inheritance, the person approaching death should prepare or instruct others to prepare a will or testament and seek two witnesses from within his kinship—or, if away from home, find suitable and trustworthy individuals to witness the intents of the person as documented in the will. While the person preparing the will has a responsibility to find witnesses, an equal responsibility falls on those who formally witness to provide truthful testimony regarding the will if and when called to. They are forbidden morally and legally to deviate from the truth. Here is first reliance on human dignity and trust that is first order of peace and justice in a society.

Considering our human condition, it is likely that some of these witnesses will fail to uphold the truth and try to benefit in a personal way or benefit their favored ones by changing their testimony in regard to the will. In such event, it is encouraged and allowed that individuals who are being harmed by such falsehood to provide testimony, based on truth that might contradict the testimony of the witnesses, to correct the situations and uphold the truth. This form of checks and balances should be established in every society in matters of legislation and the execution and rendering of justice. Human societies rise and fall based on our adherence to speaking the truth in the first place and then safeguarding it in the event attempts are made to falsify the truth. The behavior and conduct of the Trump administration in USA and the truth telling or lack thereof around the death of Saudi-American Journalist are two living examples of where lies are put in equal footing with truth. If that is not bad enough, attempts are made to let lies overwhelm the truth.

CHAPTER 6

Al-Anam
(The Cattle)

(165 verses in total; revealed in Makkah)

THIS CHAPTER (SURAH) WAS REVEALED in one piece (with the exception of a few verses) on the eve of the Prophet Mohamad's departure from Makkah to Madinah under difficult circumstance and uncertain future. Revealed at a juncture in his life when thirteen years of conveying the message of the Qur'an had produced few followers but enormous enmity and hostility to his person, safety, and dignity and the safety and well-being of his followers, this chapter repeats the unity of faith in One God and reaffirms prophets as agents of reminders from the Creator to the created beings, asking them to be mindful of people of other faiths, especially People of the Book (Jews and Christians), and the relevance of the Torah and the Bible as integral to the message of the Qur'an and condemning evil practices in the name of faith or in the name of superstitions.

The name of this chapter is derived from several mentions of superstitious practices about domesticated cattle where the idol worshippers of the Arabian Peninsula created practices and sacrifices in the name of God where no such injunctions or practices came from God but were of human creation out of ignorance and evil superstitions. Even in today's world, there are faithful who exhibit unquestioned loyalty to clerics and to rituals, dress codes, political corruption, acts of terror, saint worship, and theology that have no basis in the scriptures and are justified in the name of God or scripture. This chapter stands as a constant reminder against such excesses, human folly, and perversion in the name of God or in the name of faithlessness alike.

Following are key concepts from this chapter that are detailed further at the end of the chapter:

1. The Unity of the Godhead in relationship with human destiny (6:1–3, 6,11, 46, 72–73, 94)
2. Faith cannot be arrived at by external means (6:7–9, 111,158)
3. Alignment with God is the real faith and source of success (6:12–17)
4. Denial of God is based on failure to understand reality (6:7, 20, 29, 31–32, 40–41, 46)
5. The Prophet is comforted for people's apathy to his call (6:33–35, 56–58, 104)
6. Unity in the created world (6:38)
7. The mission of the Prophet defined (6:48,50)
8. God has intimate knowledge of the universe He created (6:59–60, 95–99)
9. God will account for all that we do in our lives (6:60–62)
10. God is ever powerful and challenges us to make the right choices (6:65)
11. Choose your discourse properly and with deliberation (6:68, 70)
12. Abraham's search for God and truth (6:74–82)
13. Guidance and prophecy were given to many before Mohammad, a unified guidance to mankind (6:83–90, 92)
14. God has no children (6:100–101)
15. To God all is visible (6:102–103)
16. Respect for other religious practices (6:108)
17. God guides as He pleases (6:124–125)
18. Disbelief will be self-affirmed (6:130, 136)
19. Superstitious rituals and sacrifice are condemned (6:137–140, 143–144)
20. All human output and natural resources deserve sharing (6:141)
21. All assertions need to be verified and proven (6:143–144)
22. Real prohibitions and values that really matter (6:151–153)
23. The challenge of the Torah, the Bible, and the Qur'an (6:154–156)

24. Sectarian divides condemned (6:159)
25. Good works are rewarded disproportionately more than evil works are requited (6:160)
26. The faith of Abraham is what one should strive for (6:161–164)
27. We are constantly being asked to make informed choices and act responsibly (6:164–165)

CHAPTER 6
Verses 1–11

In the name of God, the most Merciful and the Instiller of Mercy [to His creatures]

Let God, Who created the universe and the earth and intertwined light and darkness, be praised. Yet those who deny such reality wish to equate others to God. It is God Who created you all from clay and assigned a term [to each one of you], a term that is only known to Him; still you are in a state of self-doubt. God permeates everywhere in the universe and in the earth, knowing all that is secret or open, and He knows what you strive for.[326]

And there comes to them no message from their Sustainer God except that they turn away from it; thereby, they reject the truth when it comes to them, but soon the news will come to them about what they have mocked previously. Do they not see and reflect how We removed generations before who were established on the earth in ways that were not given to you—an abundance of rain from the sky and waterways flowing in the midst of them. Yet We destroyed them for their deliberate sins (of denial and doing evil) and bring in their place another generation (to see how they behave).

If We had sent down to you a writing on a paper that you can touch [as opposed to revelations], and they could touch it with their own hand, it would still lead those who deny the truth to say: "This is nothing but a manifest illusion."[327] Others say: "Why has not an Angel been sent to him?" If We had sent an Angel, then their term would have ended, and they would find no further opportunity to mend themselves. Moreover, if we had made him [the messenger] an Angel instead, we would have made him appear as *a human, and they would still be confused the same way. Surely messengers before you were made fun of, and those who made such mockery were overwhelmed by that which they mocked. Say: "Travel the earth and see what the consequences of their denials were."*[328]

[326] The origin of the universe, the earth, the alternation of days and nights, the cycle of light and darkness, our humble beginning from earthly matters, the finite span of our lives on this planet, and so on are matters that we need to reflect on. People of intellect, philosophers, and prophets as well as ordinary human beings have all asked the question of why we are here, what our purpose is, and what will happen after we die. The Qur'an and other Books of Revelations are living exposition of those answers from God, Who is the source of real intent behind all creation and the creative power that makes all things possible. It is imperative to us as human beings to reflect, to ask questions, and to seek out meanings in our lives and to do so through various means at our disposal—spiritual discourse, revealed texts, science, anthropology, biology, chemistry, physics, mathematics, and the application of our intellect, feelings, inspirations and things that motivates us and inner consciousness that moves us. The universe around us and the inner core of our beings, our consciousness, and our souls, which bear the semblance of godly qualities (*"God breathed His essence into us"*), are all tools given us freely that we need to use to create certainty in our mind about God and our purpose in life.

[327] Avid readers of human history, historians, and even casual readers see the rise and fall of human civilizations from one group of humans to another group, the transient nature of a society and a nation in a manner similar to our own individual lives. No civilization has permanency but does have ups and downs just we experience in our lives. Each one of us goes through trials and tribulations, and so does a society and a nation. Human history is full of examples of the rise of the weak against the powerful on a large scale, but also in smaller spheres of our existence on a daily basis. As much as we need to reflect on the natural world, we also need to reflect on our human condition and what gives to rise and fall of human civilization to correctly guide us in our personal and collective lives.

³²⁸ People who do not have faith in God have come up with all kinds of excuses and demands. Followers of Moses asked to see God directly and for God to directly intervene in their fights against their adversaries, as is evident from the Old Testament. Jesus was challenged to produce miracles, and he had performed many of them during his lifetime. The Qur'an gives two more examples of the thoughts that go through the minds of those who have doubts in the Qur'an. If the Qur'an was paperbound and were to appear to people in a miraculous way, people who cannot read the essence of God from their own lives and from the natural world would still have doubts. If Angels were to come and guide people, God would have to make them as humans to interact with people in ways natural to human beings. Those who have doubts about God and revelations will continue to have doubts, no matter what miracles and unnatural or supernatural phenomena they are presented with.

REFLECTION

In these verses, as in many different sections in the Qur'an, God brings to our attention the signs of the natural world such as our universe, the planet earth, the cycle of day and night, and the transient nature of our existence. In a similar vein, God draws attention to the human condition, the conditions that lead one nation to excel above another nation, and how one generation gets replaced by the next generation like the tidal waves that flow one after another. There are plenty of signs and clues in the natural world and in our own lives to understand the presence of God and the inner meanings of our existence. In the absence of such awareness, reflection, and sense of accountability, no amount of godly intervention, outside miracle or frivolous demands, will cure the heart and the human condition.

ACTION

We have all the tools and intellect given within us and all the signs of God and His purpose in our lives and in the world around us. Not taking advantage of such displays of God's presence and not leveraging our godly instinct and intuitive understanding will lead to self-doubt and flawed assessment of our lives and our purpose. Our first order of priority is to confirm our faith in God and goodness of purpose.

CHAPTER 6
Verses 12–24

Let them ask: "To whom does all that is in the universe and the earth belong to?" Say: "It is to God, and He willed His grace and mercy to permeate [anything and everything in the natural world]. He will gather everyone on the Day of Judgment—an eventuality about which there is no doubt. Those who neglect their soul will not achieve faith. All that dwell during the night and the day are His—He Knows and He Hears."

Ask them: "Shall I be aligned with others against God Almighty, Who is the Originator of the Universe and the Earth? He [God] feeds others but does not need to be fed." Say: "I am commanded to be first among those who submit to God and not to be a polytheist." Say: "I fear the consequences on a Day of awesome calamity, if I were to rebel against my Sustainer God. Whoever avoids such a calamity on that Day is indeed blessed with God's mercy. This is an achievement to celebrate!"

If God lets a misfortune touch you, there is none who can remove it except He; if He provides you with good fortune, then you should know that God is ever powerful over all that exists. He alone is Supreme above all His creations; He is Wise, and He is Aware! Ask: "What thing is the best as a witness?" Say: "It is God Who is a witness between you and me; this Qur'an has been revealed to me so that I can inform and warn you and those it will eventually touch. Yet do you really bear witness that there are other deities besides God?" Say: "I bear no such witness; God is One, and I am clear of any other divine association [you make with God]."[329]

> *To those who were given books before recognizing this (the Qur'an, the prophet, and the unity of God) just as they recognize their own children; those who neglect their soul will not strive for faith. Who is more unjust than he who invents lies against God and His messages? Surely such unjust will not achieve any measure of success. We will gather them together on a given Day and ask those who associated partners with God: "Where are the deities you asserted?" Their [self-deprecating] excuse on that day would be nothing other than this: "God, You are our Lord; we were not polytheists." See how they will belie themselves and all their false assertions will fail them.*

³²⁹ The presence of fortune and misfortune is a constant reminder of our vulnerability in life, and their numerous alterations throughout our short span of life is another way for God to remind us that we need to be thankful and humble when fortune is gifted to us and to reflect on our own actions and aspirations when misfortune touches us rather than blame others or be disheartened. Both scenarios are there to continuously propel us toward striving for the betterment of ourselves and strengthening our collective responsibility to do good, no matter what the circumstances might be, even in the presence of evils all around us.

REFLECTION

These verses provide a glimpse of our own condition, which might lead us down a path of failing to demonstrate our faith in One God and His messages as contained in the Books of Revelations, be it the Qur'an, the Bible, the Torah, or any other book of such stature. Some of us are comforted by the notion that unlike some other coreligionists, we have not succumbed to elevating some of God's creation to Godhead, which is well and good. But that does not absolve us from failing to act according to what our faith in God and the revealed texts require us to do. We are too quick to blame others for our failures and take credit for our success. We become oblivious to the fact that God permeates all our existence within us and the world we live in, and we are subject to the laws or codes that God has put in place to govern our existence and our accountability.

ACTION

All of us have to strive to be true to our faith in God and our commitment to do good; otherwise true success will always elude us.

CHAPTER 6
Verses 25–32

Among them are those who come to you to listen, but there is a filter over their hearts so that they do not understand, and there is a deafness in their hearing. They will not achieve faith even if all possible signs are shown to them. They only come with an intent to argue with you. Those who deny faith have only this to say: "This [the Qur'an] is nothing but stories of the ancients." They discourage others from it, and they themselves keep away from it; they thus harm their own souls and fail to perceive.

If you could witness when they will be made to stand before the fire, they would say: "Would we be sent back? We would then certainly not deny the message from our Lord and we will be among the believers." The truth that they denied will be made known to them. Even if they were sent back, they would surely go back to what was forbidden before, and they are truly liars. Some of them say: "There is nothing beyond the life of this world, and we will not be raised after our death." Again, if you could only see them when they will stand before their Sustainer God, Who will ask: "Isn't this the truth?" They will say: "Yes, our Sustainer." God will say: "Then face the consequences of your disbelief!"

Lost indeed are those who fail to prepare to meet their Sustainer God. That meeting comes to them suddenly, and they will say: "Too bad for us that we neglected such a meeting!" It is a burden they will have to face [as a consequence], and it is an evil of a burden to carry on one's back. The life of this world is but a play and a sport (unless one makes good use of it), and the life after death will be better for those who act responsibly. What is it that you fail to understand?

REFLECTION

The Qur'an explains the realities of life on this planet and life after death with clarity and purposefulness that is difficult to deny unless one is deaf, dumb, and blinded by one's own greed, ego, and intellectual arrogance. Genuine and sincere discussions and questioning are important and should be encouraged, something that is sorely missing in many religious communities and institutions, including Muslim communities and Islamic centers, which is contrary to Islamic teachings. Without vigorous dialogues and debates, we will not strengthen our faith and be able to find solutions to our social and political issues.

ACTION

As God asks the question, "What is it that you fail to understand?", we need to respond with a sincere desire and a purposeful engagement on our faith and on our social obligations as individuals and as communities serving others.

CHAPTER 6

Verses 33–41

We [God] know what they say pains you [O Prophet], but it is not you that they give the lie to; it is God's message that these unjust people deny. God's Messengers before you were similarly denied, and they faced patiently such denials and persecutions until God's help came to them. God's way of dealing with such situations does not change, as there have come to you the stories of some of these Messengers already.

If their denials are really unbearable for you, then perhaps you should seek an opening into the earth or a ladder to climb to the sky to try to bring them a sign [to accept your teachings], whereas, if God had willed, He would have certainly brought all of them to His guidance. Therefore, do not act in ignorance [of God's ways].[330] *It is only those who pay attention who will accept the message. As for those who are dead, God will raise them so that they will return to Him.*

They ask: "Why has his God not sent him a sign?" Say: "Surely God is able to send a sign." But most of them are oblivious (to such signs)—there are no animals on earth nor birds that fly on two wings but that are creatures and communities like yourself. We have not neglected anything in the Book (the Qur'an). Eventually to your Sustainer all will be gathered.[331] *Those who deny God's message are like those who are deaf and dumb and (live) in darkness. Whom God wills, He leaves in their errant ways, and whom He wills, He puts them on the Straight Path.*

Say: "What would you do if God's displeasure were to affect you or you are faced with the hour of judgment? Would you call upon God or someone else? Let's be truthful!" Yes, it is to Him that you supplicate, and He removes what you prayed for; you forget (in those hours) what other deities you subscribe to.

330 Here is lesson in life for the prophet as well as all of us, especially those of us who are impatient, judgmental, and want to set things to our ways without the due process of the law or social norm or God's will. All prophets have faced persecution, ridicule, and animosity despite the sublime and grand vison they were preaching to mankind. Being the followers of such prophets and being people of faith, we have to exercise similar patience and persistence in the face of obstacles and not compromise our values of justice, ethics, and social norms. Unfortunately, many Muslims—and this applies to Christians, Jews, and others as well—commit acts of terror and unfairly treat people of other faiths and people of our own faith in ways that are unacceptable socially, ethically, and morally. On one hand, we have too many overly jealous religious people who have no patience with those who question their ways, while, on the other hand, there are people who have marginalized the value of faith in their lives, persistently devaluing the lives of those who wish to live their faith.

331 People throughout the ages and even today have demanded of prophets, saints, and their perceived spiritual leaders direct evidence of God through miracles or signs coming from the heavens. We know that the Prophet Jesus performed extraordinary acts of healing, walking on water, getting food from Heaven for his disciples, and so on. The stories of Moses turning his walking stick into a serpent and his people getting manna and salwa from Heaven are well documented and widely believed. The Prophet Mohammad also faced similar demands, but the Qur'an refused to give into such demands, one reason being that these demands were not well intended. Instead God in the Qur'an asks us to look at nature, the positioning of the sun and earth in the solar system, the properties of water as the source of all living beings on earth; the alternation of day and night; the cycle of rain and growth of vegetation; the extraordinary capability of the womb to initiate and sustain life until birth; seeds of all kinds that have memory, sensors, and actuators to germinate and grow; the birds that fly; animals that walk on four legs; milk that comes out of cows' udders; and so on and so forth. Other signs were given in terms of how small groups of faithful were able to overcome

obstacles from larger societies, how God made old enemies into friends, how God helped people mend their tribal ways and build universal human bonds, how events that appeared to be disadvantageous turned out to be of tremendous benefit and so on—all these are lessons from life in which there is an abundance of signs of Providence. These are the real signs and evidence of God's presence and His everlasting love and mercy to mankind.

REFLECTION

Faith is a continuous conversation between God and humanity, and life is a conduit for such enlightening conversation. To know God is to know ourselves; to see God is to see nature below the surface; to taste God is to taste a variety of fruits that we relish but did not make; to see God in action is to look at how a tiny mustard seed retains the encyclopedic know-how of creation, uses its microscopic sensors and actuators to sense water, soil, and sunlight and then germinate into a beautiful plant ready to photosynthesize and construct itself from light and nutrients from air and soil and produce the intense and beautiful flowers that then create the same seed from which it started its life. This tiny seed knows more about physics, chemistry, and how to follow God's command as manifested in natural laws than any of us will ever know or fully appreciate. Who created the first mustard seed? Or, was it the first mustard plant? As the Qur'an says: *"To God is the Beginning, and to God is the Ending."* ("The Night", 92:13)

ACTION

For each one of us, no matter what our profession or passion is, there needs to be intense focus on how we function as individuals, what triggers our social instincts, and why harmony exists in nature to support life on this wonderful planet in the middle of a vast expanse of the universe. To truly appreciate God's bounty and to be thankful, we have to mindful of our presence and our purpose!

CHAPTER 6

Verses 42–50

We [God] did indeed sent messengers to communities before you and let distress and afflictions touch them to see if they would find humility. Why did they not seek humility when misfortune decreed by Us [God] fell on them? Instead, their hearts hardened, and the Devil [their evil inclinations] made their activities as if it were good for them. While they were negligent of what they were told to be mindful about, We opened up the gate of all things—so that joy and abundance seemed permanent to them. Then We seized them suddenly, and they found themselves in utter despair. So, in the end, the stance of those who did evils was removed. Praise be to God, the Sustainer of the Universe![332]

Say: "Have you considered this possibility—If God were to take away your hearing and your sight and harden your heart, who is there besides God that can bring these back to you?" This is how We expound the message in different ways, yet they walk away in arrogance. Say: "If God's displeasure were to descend suddenly or in a perceptible way, would it destroy anyone other than those who do evil?"

We [God] do not send messengers except as the expounders of goodness and to warn; therefore, whoever believes and acts righteously will have no reason to fear or grieve, but for those who reject Our Guidance, evil consequence will envelop them because of their corruptions. Say: "I do not claim [as a prophet] that I own treasures from God or that I know what is hidden by God or that I am an Angel; I strictly follow what has been revealed to me (by God)." Are the blind and the one who has sight the same—how can you not then reflect?[333]

³³² I truly believe that all misfortunes and difficulties that we face are due to our own doing (or to the failure to do what we should do) and that all good fortune comes as a result of our endeavors and God's grace. Sometimes God's grace comes even when we do not deserve it. In all our conditions, we are constantly being tested and evaluated as to how we conduct ourselves and how we serve the purpose of our individual and collective existence. We should never take our good fortune for granted or feel that our good fortune validates our way of life. As God has said in other places in the Qur'an, and as we have seen through our own lives and throughout human history, we use our good fortune to persist in evil and unjust ways without realizing that God uses good fortune and misfortune equally to drive us toward consciousness of human purpose and to propel us toward correcting our way of life, which should be based on truth, human dignity, and acknowledgment of God's grace to us.

³³³ Our physical and intellectual capabilities, such as the abilities to see, hear, comprehend, and so on, are all finite and time bound. Making maximum use of such gifts and abilities in our lives is an obligation and should be directed to enhance our personal well-being, improve human condition on this planet, and establish truth and justice for all as God has endowed us to do. Despite our ever-increasing technical competencies and human knowledge, we are still bound by such limitations and are under the same obligations to be grateful for and thoughtful of our God-given capabilities. Such realization and consciousness are fundamental human attributes and an expectation from God. Only by conscious exercise of such capabilities we can prove our true faith in God and our alignment with His guidance.

REFLECTION
Life and living is a constant reminder of our wonderful capabilities and endowment from God, the Creator. Our intellectual and physical capabilities and our human conditions—whether it is good fortune or

misfortune—all coalesce in a holistic way to help us develop ourselves further each day and to get closer to the vision of that God has for us.

ACTION

The key challenge for each one of us and for the human race is to what extent we desire and endeavor to fulfill our common goal of a peaceful coexistence and continually improve human potential by submitting us to the Will of God and to His Guidance!

CHAPTER 6

Verses 51–60

Remind them with this revelation, those who recognize that they will be gathered in front of their Sustainer—where they will have no protector and no one to intercede on their behalf—perhaps this will make them mindful of their responsibility. And do not drive away from you those who call upon God daily in the morning and in the evening seeking God's blessings. You are in no way accountable for them, nor are they accountable for you. Should you ignore them [in favor of others], then you will become one of those who are unjust. It is this way that God tries some of them against others when they say: "Are these the people whom God had favored over us?" Do they not know that God is the best in knowing who truly is grateful?[334]

When those who accept Our [God's] messages come to you, say: "Peace. Your Sustainer has willed upon Himself Mercy; therefore, if any among you does evil in ignorance and then turns away from it and lives righteously, he will find God full of Mercy and Forgiveness."[335]

Say: "I am forbidden to worship anyone you call upon besides God Almighty. I cannot follow your conjectures; otherwise I will lose the way and will not be among those who are guided." Say: "I am firmly rooted on evidence [of truth] from my Sustainer, and you call it a lie. It is not in my power to fulfill what you ask for in haste. Judgment and decision belong to God alone. He expounds the truth, and He is the best to decide (between truth and falsehood)." Say: "If I were empowered to fulfill your demands, the matter would be settled already between you and me. But it is God Who knows who does evil (and will settle the matter on His own terms). With Him is the knowledge of what is unknown—none knows but He. He knows what is in the land and what is in the sea. Not a leaf falls but He knows, nor is there a grain in the deep darkness of the earth or a thing green or dry; all are clearly defined and documented. He is the One Who takes your soul away as you sleep at night, and He knows what you accomplish during the day. He lets you rise each day so that your appointed term for life can be completed. Eventually all of you will gather back to God, and He will inform you of the end results of your lifelong pursuits."[336]

[334] Those who are politically or financially more prominent in society and can demand more attention are contrasted with those who are socially conscious, are driven by faith in God, and wish to do good. The Prophet Mohammad was a magnet for people of all classes—socially prominent, intellectually driven, courageous, poor but noble in their aspirations; the seekers of truth and justice, those who are slaves but dignified human beings, women of stature, women subject to social injustice and so on and so forth. Certain individuals such as tribal leaders, moneyed individuals, and people with a false sense of pride and privileges were annoyed by the presence of people whom they considered not their equal when they were with the Prophet. Such demand and arrogance were noted by God, and He clearly instructed the prophet not to lend ear to such demands and to treat everyone equally. He is even cautioned that should he listen to such demands and shift his attention away from a certain group of people, he would be guilty of injustice to his fellow human beings and fail in this role as the Messenger from God. Such an attitude from certain individuals is also considered a trial from God when they fail to understand how God values human positions and human conditions.

[335] This is a fundamental posit from God—that all human beings, irrespective of their past conditions, should feel comfortable to approach God for mercy and forgiveness. In this way God is also reminding the prophet to do the same—that is, his door remains open for everyone who wishes to seek the truth and be just even though in the past he or she may have been anything but. The general proposition is that anyone who has done evil or opposed the truth out of ignorance (not deliberately and repeatedly), mends his or her ways, and demonstrates

righteous inclinations and behaviors should receive forgiveness and mercy from God. Similarly, the Prophet should give attention to such individuals. This is a lesson and an instruction that should not be lost in our social interactions and the way we treat one another.

336 Faith in God calls for not only a deeper awareness of ourselves and our human condition but also for a fuller acknowledgment of the God's infinite capacity to know our own condition better than we do and to know the details of His created world. Giving examples of things as mundane as the falling of a leaf, a small grain lost in the soil, who is alive and who is dead, or the whereabouts of everyone's soul are powerful reminders of how God cares for His creations. The current advancements in technology whereby we have developed unprecedented and widespread ability to deploy sensors and use mobile devices and massive computing powers to capture and track data, information, movement, identity, weather, temperature, and so on provide us with a glimpse of what God has enabled us to do to date and what He has kept for Himself. All our capabilities and enhanced abilities should result in the betterment of the human condition and achieving our human purpose within the span of our lifetime on this planet; failure to do so will prove our negligence and dereliction of duty to one another and to God, the Creator. Such failures have serious causal and moral consequences in this life and in the Afterlife (see also 39:42).

REFLECTION

Personal accountability is paramount in the Islamic concept of God consciousness and social consciousness and should be the norm for all people of faith and goodness. Accountability toward others—that is, commitment to serving the larger community is as important as accountability to oneself. By the same token, we also are accountable for what we do and not what others do.

ACTION

We should solidify our faith and our commitment to do good and not get overly consumed or distraught when larger society or others fail to do the same. This is to preserve our sense of sanity, patience, and moral clarity so that in our haste or impatience or ignorance, we do not commit acts of excess that are counterproductive and wrong.

CHAPTER 6
Verses 61–70

God has dominion over His creation, and He deploys preservers [Guardian Angels; see also 13:11] over you; when death comes to one of you, Our Messengers [Angels] cause his death, and they never fail. Then those who have died are brought back to God, their true Master. To Him belong all matters of judgment, and He is ever prompt in taking accountability.[337]

Say: "Who removes the calamities of the land and the sea? You call upon God in humility and in secret: God, if You deliver us from this, we will commit to be grateful." Say: "It is God Who saves you from this and every other distress; yet you ascribe divinity to others." Say: "God has the power to send a torment from above or from under your feet or to confuse you with your mutual distrust and disagreements so much so that you suffer the violence of others." See how We expound the realities and the messages so that you might understand. Your people call it [the message] a lie, whereas it is the truth. Say: "I am not responsible for you [my job is to convey the message]; for every prophecy there is a term set, and in time you will come to know."[338]

When you come across those who indulge in vain talk regarding Our message, do not engage until they move into some other discourse. Should you forget, then do not continue with such evil folks after you have realized your lapse. Those who are conscious of their responsibility [to God and to themselves] are not responsible for such evil folks except that they should continue to remind such folks so that they might attain consciousness as well. Such people who take guidance for mockery and sports and who are beguiled by the life of this world should continue to be reminded, lest an individual life come to nothing for its actions; such individual will have no friend nor an aid to intercede with God nor an offer of compensation, which will be accepted. It is these people who reduce life to nothing by what they do and by what earn; they will face extreme and unpleasant consequences and a chastisement from God that will be severe—all because of their persistent denial of truth.[339]

[337] These verses refer to matters that are hidden from our human sensory perceptions but are within the realm of our mental, intellectual, and spiritual experience and comprehension. We cannot see God, but He permeates all aspects of the created world, some of which we see and understand and others we do not understand but can make intelligent guess about to try to understand. Those are guesses or conjectures only and may not be the reality of what exists or how it functions. We have not seen Angels, but according to the Qur'an, they are with each and every one of us, assigned to aid us, record our deeds, and cause our death at the appropriate time, among many other functions that we are aware of or know about. In the realm of science and technology, we continue to uncover the physics, chemistry, and biology of things, living or otherwise, as if there is no end to the ever-unfolding mysteries of this universe and our own planet, which sustains life with the aid of the distant sun and has stockpiled and seasonally replenishes all that we need to exist. The existence of the Afterlife is also hidden from us, but our transient life on this planet will come to end, which we know for sure. In our Afterlife, we return to the Creator, we face the consequences of the choices we made during our life on earth, and we are judged by God, who is the most fair and generous Judge and a Master for mankind. Such beliefs are essential elements of faith (see also 2:3).

[338] In our current world, natural calamities seem to be happening each year with increasing frequency—whether it is tornadoes or violent storms that come from above or earthquakes or volcanic eruptions that come from below (under our feet). The ever-increasing level of global warming, environmental pollution, and depletion of natural resources are threatening the very survival of our species. If that is not enough, mutual distrust; racial, ethnic, and religious discord; mental

health epidemics; widespread lack of respect for human lives; and relentless development and use of weapons of mass destruction are causing more lives to be lost—a tragedy that is neither hidden from humanity nor from God. Unless we truly reengage with the purpose of life and our relationship with God, which also defines our relationships with one another—other humans and the natural world—we are on an ever-increasing path of violence and discord in this world. With God's aid and genuine faith in humanity, nothing is impossible, whereas without God's aid or our humility as human societies, we are making calamities for ourselves with ever-increasing dimensions that affect every aspect of our lives, including the balances in the natural world in which we live, breathe, drink, reproduce, walk, and pursue happiness.

[339] In our age of instant communication, proliferation of social media, and fluidity of capital market, there is unfounded euphoria about our human condition. Yet the fundamental law of changes to human condition is what is inside the human mind and human spirit and not what is external to it. The tools and technology may affect the rate of change, but in no way will these define the direction of such change. That is the realm of our inner devotion to truth, justice, equal opportunity, relative value of human resources to capital resources, and our harmony with the Creator and the created world (see 13:11).

REFLECTION

The true reality of our existence on this planet, our relationship with the Creator, our eventual return to God, the personal accountability that comes with this relationship, the acute awareness of our dependency on God for benefits that He provides and protection from calamities, the presence and role that Angels play in preserving our lives, documenting our activities and causing our death, and so on, are all matters of truth that cannot be directly seen but are within the realm of human cognition, perception, and spiritual awareness. Those who want to rely on physical science to prove such matters will be frustrated, since matters relating to the spirit cannot be defined and experienced in physical terms but can be hypothesized and deduced from our human experiences, inspirations, and aspirations.

ACTION

Proper discourse on such matters is an important element of our upbringing and human education that every individual and every society should undertake and continue to enhance. Despite a thousand years of spectacular rise and demonstration of such thirst for knowledge and wisdom by Muslims around the known world, which also inspired Europe and people of other faiths, Muslims over the last several centuries have regressed, a trend that needs to be reversed for their own benefit and for the benefit of the world.

CHAPTER 6

Verses 71–83

Say: "Shall we call upon or rely on anyone or anything, other than God, which can neither benefit us nor harm us—only to prove our turning away from God after guidance has come to us? This is how the Devil [and his evil companions] entice and beguile ones who are prone to earthly (low-value) desires—by saying: 'Come to Our guidance.'" Say: "True guidance comes from God, Who has inspired us to submit to the Sustainer of the Universe— to maintain constancy in prayer and to be mindful of our responsibilities; it is to Him that we will all be gathered."[340]

He is the One Who has created the universe and the earth in truth [in the same principles that He governs Himself]. Whenever He says: "Be," it comes into existence [according to the same principles]. His words define the truth, and His Dominion will be evident when such manifestation will be announced [Trumpet is blown]. He knows what is manifest and what is hidden; He is Wise and Aware![341]

[Remember] when Abraham said to his father, Azar: "How is it that you consider idols to be gods? I see this as you and your community straying from reality." We helped Abraham to comprehend the essence of the universe and the earth in a way that he might be of those who have full conviction. He reflected on a star that became visible during the night. He thought: "This is my Sustainer God." But when the star went down, he said: "I cannot worship that which is not permanent." Then he reflected on the moon rising and said: "Could this be my Sustainer?" But when the moon disappeared, he said: "If my true Sustainer does not guide me, I will also become one of those

who stray from reality." Then he reflected on the sun rising and said: "Could this be my Sustainer God? Is this greater than anything else?" So, when the sun too set and disappeared, he said: "O my people, I am clear of all that you worship besides God. Indeed, I have accepted and oriented myself wholly to the Originator of the Universe and the Earth, being truthful, and I do not associate anything or anyone with the divine God." (note: this last statement is also used to initiate Islamic Prayer as one stands and gets ready to pray – a fitting homage to Abraham)

His people did argue with him, and he responded: "Do you dispute with me regarding God and the fact that He has guided me to Him? I am not afraid of those whom you have set up with God, unless my Sustainer wills as such. My Sustainer encompasses all things in His knowledge. Why would not you reflect on these? How could you want me to accept partners that you have set up with God while you are not afraid to set up partners with God for which you have no confirmation from God? Which party, then—you or me—should feel more secure, if you really want to know?" Those who believe in God and do not taint their faith with evils of inequity will have security and are properly guided. He is how We inspired Abraham with Our arguments against his people. We honor by increment whom We please; God is Ever Wise and All Knowing.

340 The concept of monotheism is central to Islam and Judaism. Such monotheism is also the foundational teaching of Jesus Christ, even though some groups of Christians have encumbered their religious theology with irreconcilable concepts of Trinity or assigning divinity to the Pope; saints; Holy Ghost, Mary, mother of Jesus; and to Jesus himself. Abraham being the founding father of monotheism, this concept is introduced as a prelude to the discussion of Abraham and his life story in the section that follows. Just as our grandparents—Adam and Eve—were driven away from Heaven due to the evils of Satan, who made false promises and was jealous of humankind, the same evils continue today, and they come from the Devil himself and ignorant people who subscribe to such evils and wish to create divisions among human beings by causing them to depart from their natural disposition to One God to multiple godheads or conceiving divinity

in created beings. Human beings have been endowed with divine attributes (*"I [God] breathed into Adam My spirit"* [15:29]), but we are not divine, and we do not have partnership with divinity. But we do seek alignment with divinity through acknowledging God and shaping our lives and our society in the way God had guided us and in the way God has already programmed those guidance, values, and morals into our souls.

³⁴¹ As a further prelude to the story of Abraham, who searched for God within himself, looked at nature to assess how one should define and understand God's presence, and debated with his community about their religious beliefs and practices, in these verses it is clearly established that God is the source of all creation—this universe that we are part of and this planet Earth that is able to support us with light and warmth from the distant sun. God's creative power is expressed as His will to create something, and it becomes. The universe operates, and so do our lives, accordingly to certain truths that God has established and to which He binds himself. These truths are manifested in natural laws, the nature of our inner core, the ways our human communities and communities of all living beings operate and behave. The original endowment of knowledge to Adam and Eve and the constant pursuit of knowledge and wisdom by humankind is itself a manifestation of the natural laws that God put in place in His creation. Some aspects of these laws are kept hidden, and others are being revealed to us each and every day through science, technology, thoughts, inspiration, and revelations. The nature of the Afterlife is something kept hidden but explained through revelations of certain aspects of it and will be made known when God so wills, when the world as we know it comes to an end. Each human being will then find itself alive after its death in this earthly life and facing God to account for her or his life.

REFLECTION

The story of the life of the Prophet Abraham, central to three of the major religious traditions in the world—Judaism, Christianity, and

Islam—is kept at the core of the narrative of Islamic teachings and traditions. Not only from the perspective of lineage, where the prophets Moses, Jesus, and Mohammad are the great-grandsons of the Prophet Abraham, but also in terms of teachings of monotheism and an uncompromising attachment and devotion to truth, social justice, and human dignity, all of which stem from the teachings of the Prophet Abraham, found in the Torah, the Bible, and various parts of the Qur'an.

ACTION

To take lessons from the life of a prophet and magnificent human being such as Abraham is to reaffirm our commitment to our common heritage as human beings and as followers of the same guidance that Moses, Jesus, and Mohammad brought to mankind.

Key Arabic Terms

100. *Sur* (Trumpet, or event that exposes reality of Afterlife)

CHAPTER 6
Verses 84–93

We [God] blessed him [Abraham] with Isaac and Jacob; We guided each as We did guide Noah before and from his descendants—David, Solomon, Job, Joseph, Moses, and Aaron. This is how We recognize those who do good to others. So was Zacharias, John, Jesus, and Elias—all of them righteous. We also made Ishmael, Elisha, Jonah, and Lot to excel among people. We did select and guide from among their forefathers, their descendants, and contemporaries to the Straight Path.

This is God's guidance with which He guides whom He wills among His servants; so, if any of them has associated partners with God, then all their activities will have been in vain. These are the [chosen] people whom We gifted with the book, sound judgment, and prophethood. Now if there are some who deny [the truth], [know that] We have entrusted such truth to a group of people who will remain faithful—these are the people whom God has guided; it behooves you to follow their guidance. Say: "I seek no reward from you; this guidance is just a reminder to all people."[342]

They fail to understand and acknowledge God the way He should be acknowledged, when they say: "God has revealed nothing to a mortal." Ask: "Who revealed to Moses the book, which is a Light and a Guide for men; yet you consider it a bundle of paper to claim it but ignore and conceal much of it; it teaches you things that neither you nor your previous generations knew." Say: "It is God [who sent the book to Moses]. Let them be consumed in their meaningless conversations [if they so choose]!"

This [Qur'an] is a blessed book that We have revealed; it confirms all that came before it, and with it you may inform and inspire people of this Mother of Towns (Makkah) and all around it. Those who have firm conviction in the Hereafter do believe in this book, and they are ever vigilant over their services to God. [On the other hand], who is more perverse than the one who constructs lies against God or says: "I have been given revelations while no such revelations have been granted, or I can reveal the likes of which God has revealed." If you could only comprehend the consequences of such a perverse stance when such persons will face agonies of death and the Angel of Death will approach them (and say): "Separate yourself from your soul; This day you will suffer the consequences—disgrace and humiliation—for speaking against God without any truth and for arrogantly denying His messages."[343]

[342] The unity of God's message and guidance is evidenced by the fact that all known prophets as mentioned in the Qur'an, the Bible, the Torah, and in these verses were on the same Straight Path that Abraham, Noah, and Adam had walked. We also understand from other verses and from the sayings of the Prophet Mohammad that God sent prophets to all known communities over the course of human history, starting with Adam himself and ending with the Prophet Mohammad, with 124,000-plus messengers in between. The presence of other religious books in Buddhism, Hinduism, Confucianism, and so on, and the convergence of their message around the unity of Godhead and social consciousness further testifies this central truth about God and about the pluralism that God has allowed to emerge among people of faith.

[343] Throughout human history we see people who accept the centrality of God's presence and the spiritual and social consciousness that emanates from such faith. In parallel we also see people who not only reject such truths but also go to extreme lengths to oppose such truth. The widespread oppression of the Pharaoh against Israelites, putting Jesus Christ on the cross, and the atrocities of Crusades and the Spanish Inquisition are further examples of not only denials of this pluralism of faith expression but of wanton disregard for social consciousness and

respect for God's message. It is sufficient for God to say that we need to reflect on the eventuality where each one of us will face death and come back to the same God Who created us in the first place. While some people may have transient opportunities to deny and disregard God's message and even oppress those who disagree with them, they should reflect on the certainty that God will bring them back to Him and make them accountable for such actions. Sometimes such a face-to-face meeting with reality will take place even on this earth before their death. People such as Saddam Hussein and Adolf Hitler have witnessed such outcomes in our contemporary history, as we all know.

REFLECTION
Belief in the unity of faith, the criticality of social consciousness, and the conviction in life after death should be sufficient to keep us away from denial of God's message and to engage in activism to create a better world for every generation.

ACTION
Apart from those who have no such faith or conviction, the key question for those of us who claim to have faith, irrespective of our religious affiliations, is how to enable this faith to enrich our lives with deep social consciousness and generate a constant drive to better the lives of all human beings on this planet of ours.

CHAPTER 6

Verses 94–99

[On Resurrection Day, God will say]: "You have come back to Us (God) one by one, just as We created you in the first instance, and you have left behind all that We gave you [in your earthly life]. We also do not see your intermediaries with you now whom you had asserted to be partners with God for your sake. Now the bond that you imagined with your intermediaries has been lost, and such relationships have failed you."[344]

It is God Who enables grains and seed kernels to germinate. He brings back life from the dead, and He causes death to those who are living. This is your God; how is it that you turn away from such truth? He is the One Who makes the dawn to appear, the night for rest, the sun and the moon to follow prescribed courses. These are the determinations [taqdiru] from God—the Mighty, the Knowing. He it is Who placed the stars so that you may find ways in the darkness on land and sea. We have thus detailed the messages and signs for people who wish to seek knowledge. He it is Who brought you forth from a single soul and defined for you a term limit and a place to rest. This is how, again, We have detailed the messages and signs for those who wish to know the truth.

It is He Who rains down water from the clouds and causes such water to bring out new growth in all living plants (and vegetation), turn those into lush green foliage, and then produce flowers and grains in clusters, dates from the spathe of date-palm in dense clusters hanging low, and gardens full of grapes, olives, and pomegranates—all alike, yet different. Look at the fruits—how they come forth and ripen. This is how We detail the message for those who wish to believe![345]

³⁴⁴ Throughout the Qur'an, God helps us to visualize and comprehend the notion of creation, accountability, and Afterlife. Such narrative is also aimed at debunking the notion of intermediaries that some religious groups or sects within larger religious groups have come to establish and practice—such intermediary and practices negates the notion of the Oneness of God and the absence of any other entity that has any share in divinity. Each of us comes to this earth alone and one at a time, as we all know and can see. God gifts us with parents; communal support; water to drink; air to breathe; fruits and grains coming from the earth; resources embedded in the earth's crust; light from the distant sun; an atmospheric shield to protect us; and, above all, His own spirit, the capacity to think, acquire knowledge, and make informed and wise decisions to lead our lives. We have a defined life span and a place and an endowment to grow, mature, and eventually die. Such realities should make any person who wishes to reflect seek to understand and be inclined to accept the truth to become a believer in God and develop consciousness that leads to a constant drive and endeavor to better himself or herself and our way of life on this planet for everyone.

³⁴⁵ God is the source of all creation, and we see it every day with our own eyes, yet we fail to reflect, appreciate, and acknowledge it—the cycle of cloud and rain; the seasonal changes with plants and vegetation bursting forth with foliage, flowers, and fruits; the placement of the sun and the moon to give us light and measure our days; the cycle of day and night so we can rest and rejuvenate; the placement of distant stars so that we can find our way not only on earth but also reference our cosmic presence in the vast universe. The incredible diversity of life, flora, and fauna on this planet is awe inspiring and humbling for any human being who takes the time to reflect and explore deep within himself or herself to find meaning and purpose. (see also 21:30).

The ultimate cycle of life and death that each one of us experiences is a further reminder that each one of us has a time-bound gift and an opportunity to explore and accept the truth about God, His creation, and the life that defines our existence and purpose. Not taking on that spiritual journey in our lifetime, not being able to find that purpose that defines our existence, and not shaping our activities and conduct in alignment with such realities are the sources of ultimate failure for a human being, given that we have been gifted with all that is needed to fulfill that purpose within ourselves and the universe in which we have been placed.

REFLECTION

Our lives, the planet earth with its life-supporting construct, the solar system creating the balance and light, and the expanding universe—all are sources of deeper reflections that have inspired human beings in all ages and will continue to do so as long as we continue to exist.

ACTION

A vision for our existence, a mission for our life, and persistent activism to align ourselves with the realities of creation, our existence, and the betterment of the human condition are things we all need to be deeply attached to as favored creations of God. We need to do this with knowledge, with heart, with humility, and with genuine openness to each and every human being who walks on this earth along with each one of us.

Key Arabic Terms
101: *takdir* (determinations, measurement, outcome)
102: *qawme yalamuna, qawme yafqahuna, qawme yu'minuna* (people of knowledge, people of insight, people of faith)
103: *mustaquarrun* (term limit) and *mustawda'un* (resting place)

CHAPTER 6

Verses 100–111

They consider the Jinn to be God's partner, whereas God created them. They also falsely ascribe sons and daughters to God out of ignorance. God is glorious and above anything that one might ascribe to Him. He is the Originator of the Universe and the Earth! How can He have a son while He has no consort? He created all that exists, and He encompasses everything in His knowledge. Such is God, your Sustainer—there is no god but He—Creator of all things! Therefore, serve Him—in His care is all that exists. Human vision cannot behold Him, whereas He envisions all vision. He is truly Subtle and Aware!

Insightful evidence has already arrived from your Sustainer; therefore, whoever can envision it, it is for his own good, and who remains blind to it will have its consequence. [Tell them]: "I am not responsible for your conduct!" This is how We reinforce the messages lest they say: "You have indeed studied it well." Thus We enable the people of knowledge to understand (Our message). Follow the truth that your Sustainer has revealed—there is no god but He, and remain undeterred by those who subscribe to polytheism. If God had willed, they would not practice polytheism. (Also), We did not assign you as a protector for them, nor are you in charge of them. Be mindful, and do not criticize those whom they invoke besides God, perchance they then revile God out of ignorance. We have made every community to see their conduct as fair in their views, but they will be informed about their activities once they return to their Sustainer.

They swear by God with a strong declaration that if a miracle were to come, they would certainly take faith in it. Say: "Miracles are at God's disposal." Do you not realize that even if such miracles were to happen, they would not believe? We keep their hearts and sights turned off, as they did not believe the first time around; We leave them alone in their arrogance, blindly stumbling around. Even if We have Angels descend on them, let the dead speak to them, and assemble all things (evidence) in front of them, they would not believe unless God wills (according to their merit); most of them are steeped in ignorance.[347]

[347] Attributing divine attributes to others besides God has been around throughout human history. Lack of knowledge and understanding, superstition, lack of humility, evil design, greed, ego, and so on to control the human mind and secure the loyalty of the ignorant and the innocent have led human beings to claim divinity, such as the Pharaoh (and other kings and queens in various parts of the world) or to ascribe divinity to objects (e.g., stones and mountains), animals (e.g., snakes by the Aztecs, elephants in certain Hindu beliefs, cows by followers of Moses), saints (to dervishes and pirs by Muslims or living saints by Christians), to Angels (e.g., the Holy Ghost in the Trinity), and even to prophets (e.g., Jesus in certain sects of Christianity). Conscious human minds and human beings have always questioned such fallacies and felt disturbed by such human conditions. Prophets and people of divine inspiration, philosophers, social leaders, scientists, and ordinary human beings have questioned such polytheism and guided human beings and societies away from such beliefs and practices, which lead to all kinds of social evils, including the loss of human dignity and divine grace.

REFLECTION

Faith in God and understanding the purpose of our creation come from deeper reflection of our existence and the world around us, a sense of accountability for our actions, conduct, and a genuine appreciation for one another as human beings. Reason will play a definite role in this, but we have to have hearts and minds to comprehend and accept reality and commit to the truth. As Pascal said, heart has its reasons that reason does not know. No amount of direct evidence will be sufficient unless one is inclined to reflect, feel, and use his or her intuitive sense and is willing to go beyond mere reasoning.

ACTION

We need to stay away from any form of polytheism that compromises our reasoning, stifles our intellect, and makes us subservient to anyone other than God Himself.

Key Arabic Terms
104. *basaayiru* (proof, enlightenment, insight)
105. *aaridh* (turning away, being unaffected)

CHAPTER 6

Verses 112–121

God allowed enemies against every prophet—the devils among men and Jinn, some of them inspiring others with gilded speeches and arguments, only to deceive. If your Sustainer had willed, they would not have done that. Therefore, remain aloof from them and from their falsehoods. (This is how God) inclines the hearts of those who doubt the Hereafter toward such gilded enticements so that they may earn what is due (from such evil inclinations). (Say:) How can I seek a judge other than God when He is the One Who has revealed this book, explaining and differentiating? Those who received the Book (such as the Bible and the Torah before) know that this book is revealed from your Sustainer with Truth; therefore, be not of those who doubt.

The Word of God has been fulfilled with truth and as promised. There is none who can change what God intends. He is the Hearer, the Knower. If you were to follow many of those who inhabit the earth, they would lead you away from Guidance coming from God. They follow nothing but their own conjectures and manufactured lies. Your Sustainer God surely knows who moves away from His Guidance and who stays on it.[348]

Eat of the meat on which God's grace has been acknowledged as a means to demonstrate your belief in His message. What reason you may have not to eat of which God's grace has been acknowledged? He has already made it known to you what is forbidden and its exceptions if you are compelled to it. Certainly, many people deviate from guidance by their ignorance and errant views. Your Sustainer God knows those who transgress as such. Stay away from any sin—in public or in secret. Those who commit sins will face the consequences. Do not eat of which God's grace has not been acknowledged— this a practice of transgression. Certainly, the Devil within people instigates them to contend on these matters with you. If you incline to them, they will bring you to the practices of polytheism.[349]

[348] History is full of examples of human conditions where a prophet or a leader of the community who wishes to do good and lead people toward a higher plateau of human existence faces stiff challenges from those who are threatened by human aspirations to establish higher morals, justice, and equality and to remove injustice and financial tyranny. In our recent memory we have seen the struggle of our founding fathers against the British king to establish democratic rule in America, the struggle of Nelson Mandela in South Africa against apartheid, the atrocities against African Americans, and the movement to establish civil rights by Martin Luther King. Each of them faced resistance and enemies not only from the ruling class but also from citizens who were opposed to such movements of human empowerment. The resistance and oppression faced by Moses and his followers; the followers of Jesus, including Jesus himself; and the followers of the Prophet Mohammad are all well-known and well document in history. The hegemony of communism, colonialism, and monarchies against average people and human suffering provides many examples of human conditions that God allowed to evolve as a result of our own lack of commitment to human dignity and the universal equality of each and every human being. This is also how God finds the truly committed souls to His causes while at the same time identifying and establishing those who are opposed to such causes.

[349] The devil (evil inclinations) in each one of us and the Devil himself are the source of so much contention among people of different faiths, different races, and different ethnicities on issues of peaceful coexistence, gender equality, wealth distribution, and so on. The Qur'an provides foundational guidance, in consonance with our inner core consciousness, on such matters. As people of faith, we need to be grounded in such basic tenets of human life and human society, without which we will sway toward charisma, false ideologies, and the transient understanding of our society and human nature, all of which lead to human

discord, gender inequality, income disparities, and lack of true governance by people as God's representatives on this earth.

REFLECTION

Evil and human discord are ever present throughout history. Such a condition forces us to make choices, choices that will define us or ruin us individually or collectively as the human race. Our ability to discern that which is good and that which is evil; our ability to guide our lives that resonates with our human values and inner consciousness, which are also detailed in the revelations from God such as the Qur'an; and our ability to act accordingly even in the face of stiff opposition and enormous difficulties are the real hallmarks of a true human being. This is what God wishes to uncover in each one of us no matter where we are and what context defines our lives at the moment.

ACTION

Having a good understanding of our purpose and our calling and shaping our lives accordingly is an age-old challenge that each generation has to face and prove again and again before we go before God and justify the gift of life that He had given us.

Key Arabic Terms
107: *kitaba mufassalan* (book full of explanation, details to make distinct)

CHAPTER 6
Verses 122–135

Think of someone who was dead, and then We (God) brought him to life and gave him a light by which he is able to walk among people; is he the same as the one who is in darkness and has no light to come out? For those who deny the truth, their doings are made to appear good to them. Thus, We allow the leaders in every land to be its evildoers so that they plan in it; but their plan is against themselves, which they do not perceive. When a message (from God) comes to them, they say: "We will not believe until we are given the same message that God had given to His messengers." But God knows best where to place His message. Humiliation and serious chastisement will come to these evildoers for what they scheme (against people and God).

Whomever God wills to guide, He opens up his heart to Islam (faith and goodness), and whomever He wills to leave in their errant ways, He constrains and restricts their breast as if he is rising up in sky. This is how God does not guide those who deny the truth. This guidance is the true guidance from your Sustainer—a straight path. God makes His message clear to those who mind. For such is the residence of peace with their Sustainer who is their Friend for what they do.[350]

On the Day when We will gather them all and ask: "O assembly of Jinn (leaders of evildoers), you have diverted a great many among people," their erstwhile friends among men will say: "Some of us have benefited from others (in our lives), and now we have come to the end of our terms, terms that you have fixed for us." God will say: "Fire is where you will reside, except whom God wills; Your Sustainer is Wise and Knowing. This is how We make the evildoers befriend one another on the basis of what they do." (God will address): "O community of Jinn and Men, did not My Messengers come to you giving you the Guidance and making you aware of this Day of Our meeting?" They will reply: "We bear witness against ourselves"; indeed, the life on earth deceived them and they will testify against themselves that they denied the truth. This is a norm from your Sustainer, Who does not destroy a town where its inhabitants are unaware. Each town is treated according to a measure of what they do. Your Sustainer God is not unaware of what they do.[351]

Your Sustainer is Self-Sufficient, Full of Mercy. If He wills, He may remove you and make whom He wills to succeed you in a manner that He made you to succeed your predecessors. Whatever you have been promised [death, Day of Judgment, etc.] will surely take place; you cannot escape such an outcome. Say: "O my community, act as you are able, and I will do the same. You will soon come to know who will inherit the future, because the unjust will not succeed."

[350] God's guidance is like a light that shows the way, whereas lack of guidance is like darkness that prevents us from making any movement, or, at worst, makes us do evil things without knowledge. Then there are corrupt and evil leaders who not only ignore such guidance but are driven by their inner evils (ego, lust, greed, love of this world, etc.), and their manufactured lies (claiming divinity; misguiding people to acts of injustice and oppression such as racism, ethnic cleansing, religious superiority, gender bias, terrorism, fake news, alternative facts, etc.) induce others to not only commit acts of evil and shamefulness but also entice and compel others to follow their path. It is our deliberate choices that we make to have faith and to do good, combined with God's will, that help us stay the course—on the Straight Path—and give us true honor and dignity in this life and in the Afterlife.

[351] God's address to the assembly of Jinn and Men on the Day of Judgment is a reminder and a way to help visualize and be mindful that the results awaiting us come from what we do on this planet and in this life. Corrupt leaders in the

community, business enterprises, and political systems will lead us down a path of disempowerment, economic disparity, political upheaval, and environmental degradation that we can witness already in our current human condition. While God will question those and take their accountability on the Day of Judgment, we as people of faith have to prove our worth by resisting such leaders and establishing alternative ways of creating and sustaining a better world.

REFLECTION

Blaming others for our misfortunes or remaining aloof to the undesirable conditions of the world is no way to justify our presence in this world or the purpose of our lives as God intends. Deeper reflection, creating a vision for our community, our country, and our world that is steeped in faith and goodness for all, and striving to establish such a vison is the responsibility of every individual, every community and people of faith no matter where we are.

ACTION

We need to work within the system where it makes sense and in other cases build a consensus to envision and implement alternatives that offer the best that human beings can conceive and put into practice in all aspects of our community, financial, and political lives—to better the lives of each and every human being on this planet.

CHAPTER 6

Verses 136–144

They assign from which God has created for them of produce and cattle a portion to God—at least that is what they assert, and a portion to other deities (whom they associate with God). The portion assigned to other deities never comes to God but what is assigned to God somehow reaches the other deities. (See how) their judgment is corrupted with evil practices! Their belief in these deities justifies them to kill their children; such belief may cause their destruction [as a society] and confuse them regarding their faith. If God had willed, they would not have behaved as such; therefore, stay away from what they falsely assert.

They say: "Specific cattle and produce from the field are forbidden; none shall eat from these except as we please"—this they assert and more— "certain cattle you cannot ride, and on certain cattle you cannot grace by God's name." All of these are falsely ascribed as if injunctions from God; all such false assertions will have consequences as defined by God. They say: "What is in the womb of such and such cattle is reserved for males only and forbidden to females, but if it turns out to be stillborn, then all can partake in it." God will make them face the consequences of such false assertions (to God); God is Ever Wise, All Knowing.

Failure is bound to come to those who kill their children perversely and out of ignorance and who forbid people from what God has provided for—all to forge a lie against God; these are deviations from truth, and they are certainly not guided.[352]

God is the One Who produces in fields cultivated or growing wild—date palms, fruits and grains of various sorts, olives and pomegranates, similar and in varieties. Consume of the fruits as they ripen and share their due to others when you harvest. Don't be wasteful; God does not love the prodigal. Among the cattle, there are some that carry your burden and others for you to consume. Eat from what God had gifted you with, and do not create evil practices by following the Devil, whose evil is openly declared (against humans).[353]

Regarding the eight in pairs—two of sheep and two of goats—ask them: "Has God forbidden the two males or two females or what the wombs of these female may contain? Inform me with knowledge, if you are truthful." Now as regards the two of camels and two of cattle, ask them: "Has God forbidden the two males or two females or what the wombs of these female may contain? Were you a witness to God's prescribing any of these?" Who is more perverse than the one who falsifies in the name of God and leads people to devious ways without the benefit of any real knowledge? God certainly will not guide such corrupt people.

[352] Many societies over the long stretch of human history have developed superstitious practices in the name of religion and in the name of God. Practices of human sacrifices, using divination to predict the future, creating evil practices that defy logic or are devoid of human knowledge, devil worshiping, worship of animals such as elephants or monkeys or snakes, offering food and drinks to deities that are nothing more than mere sculptures or stones or tree trunks, allocating harvests or animal offspring to deities or even people based on gender, the killing of children, specially female children, and so on are all based on superstitions, false beliefs and attempts by corrupt leaders, religious personalities, and opportunists to deprive human beings of their dignity, human equality, God-given knowledge, and instinct to worship the true God. Some remnants of these types of practices continue even to this day—saint or pir worshiping, expecting Santa Claus to deliver gifts on Christmas day, aborting female fetuses in greater proportion than male fetuses in countries such as India and China, clergy and clerics as intermediaries between God and His people, and the list goes on.

Even mainstream social, financial, and political practices prevalent in the world today that lead to alarming income disparities; extreme profiteering by businesses, especially players in the financial market (e.g., Wall Street); the prevalence of monopolies and oligopolies in the name of free market; the favoring of political-party ideology over human dignity and social justice; the wanton disregard for the natural balance that is needed in human existence on this planet; excessive consumerism and adoration of celebrities; excessive preoccupation with physical existence and creature comforts; and negligence of the spiritual dimension of our being—all of these practices are in urgent need of rethinking and revamping to restore human dignity, social justice, and God consciousness.

353 The notion of sharing with others what God gives us as a result of our direct effort and what becomes available to us as part of the existing social, physical, and market constructs (analogy: a field cultivated and wild growth from above verses) is a fundamental expectation from God and a social imperative for human societies. Too many businesses, political leaders, societies, and nations are exploiting natural resources in the ground, fish in the ocean, and social media–based technology; encouraging consumerism and excessive consumption; using monopolistic practices to set high prices, and so on to their exclusive benefit, with serious consequences to human poverty, the global environmental mess, human health, and the lack of quality of life to a majority of the world population, irrespective of the developed counties or underdeveloped countries in the word today.

REFLECTION

Every generation has to look at the current religious, social, political, and financial practices in its communities, in its societies, within its national boundaries, and across the globe to make sure these practices are based on knowledge and sound judgment, reflect social consciousness and human dignity, ensure a minimum living standard for each and every human being on this planet, leave our planet in a better shape than we found it, and be mindful of God's gift to mankind and the corresponding human obligations to one another and to God.

ACTION

Each and every one of us comes from God, and to God we will return; this reality and the covenant that binds us to God and to one another as a result should make it abundantly clear that we have an urgent need to reflect on our lives and our world as we witness and experience it today and do something, within our own sphere of influence and resources, to make the world a better place for ourselves, our children, and for humanity at large!

CHAPTER 6
Verses 145–153

Say: "Based on what has been revealed to me, I find nothing forbidden to eat for anyone desiring to eat except what died of itself, blood poured forth, or flesh of swine—these being filthy [undesirable]—or where a transgression has occurred by blessing a slaughter with a name other than God's. But if someone is driven by necessity—neither desiring it nor consuming more than his immediate needs, then he will find his Sustainer Forgiving and Merciful." As for the followers of the Jewish faith, We [God] prohibited animals with claws, oxen and sheep (Leviticus 7:23), and all their fats except what is on their backs or in the intestines or internal organs or what is inside the bones—these restrictions are a form of punishment for their continued rebellion; indeed We [God] speak the truth. Therefore, if they deny you, say: "Your Sustainer is expansive in His mercy, but for those who persist in sinful acts, their negative consequences, as prescribed by God, cannot be avoided."

Those who are Polytheists say: "If God had willed, we would not have set up partners to God, nor our forefathers, nor we would have prohibited things that are allowed (by God)." Similar was the behavior of those before them until the evil consequences, as prescribed by God, touched them. Say: "Do you have any documented sources that you can produce before us? (Perhaps) you follow conjectures and are telling lies." Say: "With God rests the final evidence to truth. If He willed, we all would have been guided (to the truth)." Ask them: "Bring your witness regarding such prohibition." Even if they bear witness, you should stay away from such witnesses and *never follow the unworthy desires of those who reject God's messages, have no conviction in the Afterlife, and regard others as equal with God, their Sustainer.*[354]

Say: "Come and let me convey what God has forbidden: Assign no partner to God, and be good to your parents; do not kill your children for fear of poverty—God provides for you and for them; do not get close to anything shameful—openly or in secret; do not take a human life that God has made sacred, except for reason of justice. These He directs you to so that you will have a better understanding." Do not touch the property of orphans except with the best of intentions; wait until they attain maturity, and then give what is due and be equitable; We (God) never impose a burden on anyone except what s/he can bear. When you speak, speak the truth and be just, even if it goes against those with whom you have relationships with. Fulfill your covenant with God. These, again He directs you to so that you will become conscious and mindful.

These are the directives to the Straight Path (to God)—stay on this path, and do not follow other ways that might lead you away (from God). Such are God's directives so that you become responsible and fulfill your obligations.[355]

---

[354] Dietary prohibitions are relatively few in Islam—primarily against pork, alcohol/drugs, carrion, blood, and any slaughter on which a name other than God's has been pronounced. On another level, the Qur'an declares that anything and everything that is wholesome, other than these explicit prohibitions, is allowed. It also allows the food of the People of the Book (Jews, Christians, and others who follow Books of Revelations) to be acceptable to Muslims, since they also believe in the same God and use God's name in their slaughter of animals. For all our consumption needs, which consist of drinks, fruits, vegetables, grains, and meat, these limited restrictions are minor and should impose no undue burden on anyone. We should rejoice and be thankful for all the variety and tasty food options God has created without our asking for it. We need to preserve the quality and purity of these food ingredients, especially in our commercial food production, where we use pesticides and other chemical-based fertilizers; on store shelf, fast

food and other ready-made food, which has other chemical preservatives, additives, and excesses of sugar and salt; not to mention the risk of genetic manipulation without adequate testing, evaluation, and monitoring against greedy commercial and business interests.

355 On a spiritual, moral, and ethical level, the restrictions are also few, but overarching that are the requirements of careful understanding, conscious awareness, and a full commitment to follow through even if it means going against oneself or one's relations. Prohibitions included here are

- any partnership to God or assigning divinity to any creation of God,
- the killing of children for fear of poverty or gender bias,
- the killing of any innocent human being of any faith or no faith, except for just cause as permitted by God, and
- any shameful acts or conduct (adultery or fornication, bestiality, pornography, torture, oppression, racism, gender bias, insult, altercation, aggression, oppression, violence, religious persecution, ethnic cleansing, hoarding, excessive profiteering, mischief, corruption, lying, cheating, bullying, stealing, robbery, etc.) done in secret or openly.

In the same vein, God warns us against any unlawful way of confiscating and consuming others' properties, especially those who are vulnerable, such as orphans and widows. There is also the strong injunction to always speak the truth, since lying is the source of all major sins and shameful acts. For every action that we take, we need to ask three core questions:

- What is my intention for this act?
- What are the spiritual, moral, ethical and legal boundaries applicable for this act?
- What is the consequence of this act in this world and in the Afterlife?

REFLECTION

Attention is drawn for each one of us to think; be consciously aware; commit to doing good; and stay away from all evils, injustices, shameful acts, and limited prohibitions for animal-based food. Undue preoccupation with dietary restrictions and imposing unnecessary restrictions by some religious clerics and scholars is unwarranted, and their total negligence and ignorance on issues around food quality, genetic manipulation, chemical toxins that are causing havoc with human health and environmental pollution, and social injustices and corruptions are disappointing, to say the least.

ACTION

We all have a human responsibility and a commitment to our covenant with God to follow the guidance given in these verses. Honest adherence to these basic guidelines is more than adequate to create peace and empowerment for human societies.

CHAPTER 6
Verses 154–160

We (God) gave Moses the book, to complete (Our blessings) on those who would do what is good and beautiful, proving clear exposition of all things, a guidance and a mercy so that they might develop faith in meeting their Sustainer God. This is a book [the Qur'an] that We have revealed as blessings; therefore, follow its teachings and be mindful of your responsibility [as a human and person of faith] so that you might receive His blessings; lest you say that books were revealed to two parties before us and we were not informed of what they read. Or, you say: "If the Book was revealed to us, we would have guided ourselves better than they did." Now then, the evident truth from your Sustainer has come—a source of guidance and blessings; whoever now denies such messages from God and walks away from them will be the one doing evil indeed. We will return such negligence and opposition to our Messages with negative consequences that befit such conduct.[356]

Is it that they are waiting for anything other than Angels to come to them, or that your Sustainer God should come, or some other evidence appears from your Sustainer? The day when such evidence will arrive, their faith in it will benefit no souls that did not believe before or did not use their prior faith to do good. Say: "Wait then, and we will wait with you as well." (Beyond belief) those who create division in their faith and turn into sectarian divides, you have no relationship with them. Their affairs will be in the hands of God, Who will inform them [in due time and on the Day of Judgment] with respect to their conduct. Whoever earns a good and beautiful deed, God will multiply its rewards ten times, and whoever brings about an evil deed will face its consequences accordingly; no wrong will be done to them.[357]

[356] The constancy of messages from God Almighty in the form of Books of Guidance that have come throughout human history is a central message of the Qur'an. The book given to Moses (the Torah) and the book given to Jesus (the Bible) and this Qur'an (given to Mohammad) are but chapters in the larger Book of Guidance that God has revealed in portions over time with the evolution of human societies and their diverse lifestyles and experiences as part of the human experience. The unity of the Godhead and the unity of God's guidance is a fundamental aspect of the teachings contained in all Books of Revelations, and the receivers of such revelations must remain true to their teachings to be guided and blessed by God. The challenge has been not only to develop faith in God and faith in our meeting with our Creator but also to maintain the purity and the unity of such faith and thoughts. The fact that we have created different religions (Judaism, Christianity, and Islam, to name the major ones in our world) out of the same guidance and then, within each religion, created divisions and sects, is further indication of our failure in remaining true to the oneness of message from God.

[357] Attention is drawn here that developing faith in the fullness of life and acting accordingly will benefit us as individuals and as societies; this is the challenge for all of us during our transient existence on this earth. To wait until death comes to us or to have faith on the Day of Resurrection will confer no benefits, as we will have, by then, lost the lifelong opportunity that God had gifted us with to use our souls and minds to find the truth about our life and our purpose.

In their jealousy to outdo their fellow faithful, some groups have turned prophets into Godhead and people into saints and Angels. Other groups have created theological differences, religious hierarchies to compete for worldly gains, and deviant doctrines to control the masses, in direct opposition to God's call for human equality, religious tolerance, and coexistence and to refrain from any divine partnership with the Creator and His creation. God, in his infinite mercy and to encourage goodness in all of us, also assures us that he will amply reward all good works but will make evil suffer its evil consequence in due measure of its transgression.

REFLECTION

The Torah, revealed to Moses; the Bible, revealed to Jesus; and the Qur'an, revealed to Mohammed, are sequels to the same guidance that God promised to Adam and Eve (and by implication to mankind) and if we follow such guidance together, we will have a peaceful world that will enable human beings to reach their highest potential of knowing God, understanding the natural world, and fulling our mutual commitments and obligations.

ACTION

People of all faiths who believe in God and the true guidance in their respective Books of Revelations should uphold that guidance of mutual interactions and freedom to practice their faith in their own way and strive for peaceful coexistence among all people. This is certainly the message contained in the Qur'an.

CHAPTER 6

Verses 161–165

Say: "As for me, my Sustainer God has directed me to the Straight Path—a path that is steeped in righteousness, in the tradition of Abraham, the bearer of truth and faith, who was not a polytheist." Say: "My prayer and my worship, my sacrifices and perseverance, my life's pursuits, and my ever-approaching death—all are directed to God's will, the Sustainer of the Universe! He has no partners [in creation or its sustenance]. I am commanded to this, and I am the first to accept and act accordingly (be a Muslim in its true sense, not for label only)."[358]

Say: "How can I seek out a Sustainer other than God Himself, since He is the Cherisher of all things?" No soul bears but what it earns (see also 53:33–41), and no soul will be made to face the consequence of what someone else has done. At the end of your life, you return to you Cherisher God so that He can inform you on matters that you differed on (while alive). He is the One Who made you [the current generation] the successor on earth and made some of you excel over others (in matters of intelligence, leadership, wealth, spirituality, morals, ethics, kindness, freedom) so that He may ascertain your worth with respect to His gift He has given you. God is prompt in requiting (your actions as He deems appropriate), and He is ever the Forgiver, the Merciful![359]

[358] The notion of a *"Straight Path"* (the shortest distance to truth and peace)—ascribed to Abraham, as the chief architect of that guidance inspired by God and the subsequent messengers from his lineage, including Moses, Jesus, and

Mohammad, who continued to perfect and elaborate this guidance through succeeding generations—is itself something to take note of. It is a theme that permeates the entire Qur'an, which very strongly confirms the truth contained in the Torah and the Bible and continuously reaffirms the unity of faith in One God and the unity of guidance to serve humanity to attain the highest human potential as creatures of God endowed with knowledge, wisdom, and freedom of choice. A better understanding of God's will and developing a keen awareness of how we define purposefulness in our existence on this planet is critically important for us individually and as a society, the lack of which is evident in our current time, when human suffering and oppression, income inequality and extreme poverty, racial tension in developed societies, corrupt government in less-developed countries, the polarization of social discourse along political lines, environmental degradation, monopolistic business practices, and so on are on the rise.

³⁵⁹ Central to our purpose in life on this planet is a sense of accountability to fellow human beings and a covenant with God, the Creator. God has indeed gifted us with all that we need to lead a life full of human potential. On one hand, He breathed His essence into each one of us so that we have the capacity and affinity for knowledge and wisdom and an innate desire to feel connected with and serve fellow human beings. On the other hand, God has equipped this planet earth with all that we need to survive and support our growth on two levels: (1) on a physical level, it has all the amenities and resources, such as air and water, the capacity to produce sustenance for us, vast oceans, mineral deposits, sources of energy from sun, air, water, and fuel in the ground, and so on to sustain life and its physical needs, and (2) on a spiritual level, the cycle of life and death, day and night, light and darkness, good and evil that coexist, the emergence of intelligent life in the vast universe, the diversity of life—plants, birds, flowers—provide a rich spiritual environment to sustain our souls and spirits and to connect with God, the Creator. As every generation succeeds the previous generation and excels in new ways, we need to demonstrate individually and collectively how we are using gifts from God for the betterment of humanity or be accountable for its misuse and abuse.

REFLECTION

Commitment to truth and justice that is inspired by faith and a covenant with God, the Creator, is something each one of us in every generation has to reflect on and find our call to duty to reflect our current condition and social and global context. If each one of us is driven such that he or she has found his or her unique passion that that person finds fulfilling, then collectively we will have addressed all the needs of humanity.

ACTION

We need to create the social conditions and the human drive that comes from leadership, honest and sustained dialogues among people, respect for freedom of choice, and an unwavering commitment to peaceful coexistence among people of all faiths and races.

Key Concepts in Surah Al-Anam (The Cattle)

1. The unity of the Godhead in relationship with human destiny (6:1–3, 6,11, 46, 72–73, 94)
2. Faith cannot be arrived at by external means (6:7–9, 111,158)
3. Alignment with God is the real faith and source of success (6:12–19)
4. Denial of God is based on failure to understand reality (6:7, 20, 29, 31–32, 40–41, 46)
5. The Prophet is comforted for people's apathy to his call (6:33–35, 56–58, 104)
6. Unity in the created world (6:38)
7. The mission of the Prophet defined (6:48–50)
8. God has intimate knowledge of the universe He created (6:59–60, 95–99)
9. God will account for all that we do in our lives (6:60–62)
10. God is ever powerful and challenges us to make the right choices (6:65)
11. Choose your discourse properly and with deliberation (6:68–70)
12. Abraham's search for God and truth (6:74–82)
13. Guidance and prophecy were given to many before Mohammad, a unified guidance to mankind (6:83–90, 92)
14. God has no children (6:100–101)
15. To God all is visible (6:102–103)
16. Respect for other religious practices (6:108)
17. God guides as He pleases (6:124–125)
18. Disbelief will be self-affirmed (6:130, 136)
19. Superstitious rituals and sacrifice are condemned (6:136–140, 143–144)
20. All human output and natural resources deserve sharing (6:141)
21. All assertions need to be verified and proven (6:143–144)
22. Prohibitions and values that really matter (6:151–153)
23. The challenge of the Torah, the Bible, and the Qur'an (6:154–156)
24. Sectarian divides condemned (6:159)
25. Good works are rewarded disproportionately more than evil works are required (6:160)

26. The faith of Abraham is what one should strive for (6:161–164)
27. We are constantly being asked to make informed choices and act responsibly (6:164–165)

1. **The unity of the Godhead in relationship with human destiny** (6:1–3, 6,11, 46, 72–73, 94)

In these verses, one gets a glimpse of God—his Oneness as it manifests itself in the creation and the purposefulness of creation, especially of human beings. God is the Creator of the universe, a vast enterprise of billions of stars and planets constantly forming and norming in billions of clusters and constellations of stars, galaxies, nebulae, and other constructs that we attempt to organize the vast universe as we uncover more and more. Our own Milky Way galaxy, for example, is home to 400 billion stars, including our own sun and solar system, nearly 120,000 light-years across, an example of one galaxy.

Recent discoveries and scientific investigations will perhaps lead to earthlike planets where life like us is plausible and perhaps already exists. Our planet, Earth, is home to 6 billion human beings who undergo the constant cycle of birth and death while the earth goes through a cycle of day (light) and night (darkness) and seasonal variations, a cycle that also plays out in our lives in the form of joys and sorrows, success and failure, fear and hope, despair and aspirations. Every human being is given a term by God—a term to define a life span with a set of possibilities informed by knowledge we seek and shaped by choices we make. God is intimately aware of our conditions, individually and collectively.

We are bound at a physical level by His physical laws, which govern the universe, and by our covenant as conscious beings at a moral and spiritual level. God, using the earth as a vehicle, provides resources for our sustenance, gifts knowledge we seek, and provides inspiration to elevate our human existence. His ultimate gift is our innate alignment with Him, as we are created in His image, as described in the Bible and our human nature being the nature of God Himself, as described in the Qur'an. Our senses and our spiritual awareness and compass are gifts from God with accountability to use them properly and to suffer consequences for their misuse and negligence. The Day of Judgment that happens every day and every moment that we exist will also manifest in its full exposition when we all come back to God individually and collectively to account for our lifelong pursuits and bear responsibility for the consequential impact on our continued existence beyond our earthly life. As God advised the prophet: *"Remind (people) with it (the Qur'an), lest a soul suffers from what it earns (or fails to earn)."* (6:70)

Verse 94 is awe inspiring if you can imagine standing in front of God on the Day of Resurrection and remember what God told us already: *"You have come back to Us (God) one by one, just as We created you in the first instance, and you have left behind all that We gave you [in your earthly life]. We also do not see your intermediaries with you now whom you had asserted to be partners with God for your sake. Now the bond that you imagined with your intermediaries has been lost, and such relationships have failed you."* (6:94)

2. Faith cannot be arrived at by external means (6:7–9, 111, 158)

Throughout history some people who are not inclined to believe in God—or, for that matter, in any factual matter (a poignant example is global warming for our generation)—will find all kinds of excuse and false narratives to stay affixed to their positions. In these verses God refers to several such demands that people asked their prophet regarding God—perhaps God should send a piece of paper from Heaven that people can touch with their hands, or an Angel should come down, or dead people should come alive and tell their stories, or some other sign should come directly from God—or worse, God Himself should come down to them on this earth.

In some sense, all of these things have already happened if we only seek knowledge, have humility, and genuinely aspire to know who we are and where we come from. The books (pages) of divine guidance are already in everyone's hands in the form of the Torah, the Bible, the Qur'an, and other sources of divine knowledge and guidance that came to other generations and communities around the globe. Angels have appeared to Mohammad, to Abraham, to Moses's mother, and to Mary, among other human beings, to convey directly, for example, God's inspiration to receive the guidance of the Qur'an (Mohammad), to face the trial of causing death to his own son (Abraham), to follow God's directive to protect Moses (mother of Moses), to face the societal challenge of giving birth to Jesus (Mary, mother of Jesus). As we travel around the earth and explore the universe, the past (the dead, old relics, stones, fossils, retreating stars) is in constant communication with us, eager to tell us our origin and open up a window to reflect on our existence and purpose. God is ever present in our lives as the sun rises each day, bright days come after the lonely nights, a child is conceived in the mother's womb, a person goes through the cycle of life just like another animal or plant, and a persistent agitation is in our consciousness to seek God and find meaning in our common humanity.

But such evidence is not sufficient to make someone accept God and the realities of life unless that person genuinely aspires to know God and himself and seek knowledge and deeply reflects on human nature and the human condition and the natural world we live in. As the Prophet of Islam once said, *to know God, you need to know yourself.* Also, some of our human demands go contrary to established norms. As God says, if He were to send an Angel as a prophet, He would make him in the form of a human, and then we would not know the difference. And if God were to appear as He will on the Day of Judgment, when all human beings will gather to find the results of their lifelong pursuits, there would be no going back. Belief on that day in God and in our humanity will have no benefit to those who misused their lifelong opportunities and did harm to the world, be it to other humans or to the natural world.

3. Alignment with God is the real faith and source of success (6:12–19)

God makes known certain realities of this universe in various scriptures, through prophets and the continuous evolution of human consciousness as manifested in human knowledge and the sciences. God is the Creator of this universe and the planet Earth that we inhabit. He Himself placed mercy at the core of creation—a concept that permeates all our human experiences, be it the extraordinary love and care a mother (a human mother or an animal mother) exhibits toward her child; how the earth takes care of and preserves all its creatures and natural resources in an awe-inspiring way—a small mustard seed that germinates in its soil and then comes out as a seedling to be nurtured by air, rain, and the sun; the river that starts as vapor over ocean and land, is carried by wind, drops on top of mountains into gushing streams that collect to form rivers, and then travels back to the ocean while serving human habitation and nature along the way on a scale that only God can create.

God makes known that we all will be gathered back to him on Resurrection Day, about which there should be no doubt, and nobody can escape from it. God confines and guides us through covenants and natural laws like nobody can, and He distributes knowledge and choices to human beings like to no other creatures.

God feeds everyone, and He does not need to be fed, thereby establishing our total dependence on him. All that dwells either during the day or during the night is known to him. Given this simple framework, it behooves each one of us to acknowledge God and to align ourselves with Him as He guides us through the Qur'an and other books of scriptures and evolving human understanding of our own existence and the world around us, such knowledge itself being a gift from God, sometimes given freely as He wills and at other times as a direct reward to human aspirations and endeavors.

It is up to us to acknowledge God and be true to our human nature, which is a reflection of God's nature and the natural world. To be misaligned with God is to deny such reality and to disturb nature of humanity and the balance in the natural world. Polytheism is also considered a form of gross misalignment as well as atheism, since these negate the very foundation on which creation is established—a singular source of creation and human purpose, without which our society will continue to disintegrate into chaos and marginalization of human spirit. Simple belief in God is not enough, as many religious leaders and religious rituals would lead us to accept; a deliberate commitment to align with our human nature is essential, knowing full well that such natural alignment brings us to God in this life and on Resurrection Day.

4. Denial of God is based on failure to understand reality (6:7, 20, 29, 31–32, 40–41, 46)

Every generation must reflect on its current condition, priorities, and lessons learned from previous generations and make God's guidance relevant to their generation and the generations to come. Material abundance does not guarantee success, and negligence of the human spirit as it aspires to connect to its Creator and to one another will lead to the eventual demise of civilizations and ideologies, no matter how vigorous it might seem at any given time.

Many human beings are prone to considering this life to be the end-all and find no meaningful purpose other than to maximize personal creature comfort and amass materials gains, whereas God reminds us that this life is an opportunity to demonstrate our human potential and establish our natural connection to God and His grace. Such purpose is achieved not through a *"savior,"* as some of my Christian friends might feel, or through an alliance to a tribal code of ethics, as some of my Jewish friends might claim. I believe that the teachings of Jesus are fundamentally more important than who Jesus was and that Moses was visited by God to honor him and humanity as opposed one human tribe, even though it was a great honor for the descendants of Jacob and Joseph to have such close proximity to God through Moses, as it validates God's deep connection to people in need and in despair. Mohammad has been declared as a *"mercy"* to humanity, though he appeared among the pagan Arabs, and he continued to build on the teachings of Moses and Jesus and did not claim to bring a new faith but provided a narrative that brings all prophetic teachings together into a "way of life" labeled as striving for peace (Islam) and a human condition aligned with God and goodness (muslim), independent of where one lives, what tribe or race one belongs to, and what gender one was born into.

In the face of a life-threating accident or overwhelming turmoil in our lives, we all instinctively turn to God, but on normal days prior to or after such events, some of us tend to gravitate to conditions that assume self-sufficiency and marginalize God's role in our lives. We consider life as sport and enjoyment as long as it lasts while ignoring its present and eventual purpose to be responsive to our human instinct and innate nature of goodness and purposefulness, always striving to be on the side of God and not pulling God to our side. As God challenges us in this last verse (46), if He were to take away our sight, our hearing, and our heart (our ability to comprehend and connect), how could we ever get them back and be human again? Despite our endowment to be the best of God's creation, we run the risk of becoming the worst as current world events, unfortunately, bring us to the edge of a cliff. Let's be reminded of God warning: *"We have created human beings with the best of attributes and capabilities, but then [We let] some of them render themselves to the lowest of the low, except those who believe [in God and in their humanity] and do good."* ("The Fig," 95:4–6).

5. The Prophet is comforted for people's apathy to his call (6:33–35, 56–58, 104)

As we know from stories of Jesus, Moses, and other prophets, the tenure of a prophet is not an easy one. Not only did they have to deal with the awesomeness of God's directives and communication and encounter Him directly or through the Angels or through inspirations that they were unfamiliar with, they had to go through internal debates and reconciliation to comprehend and convince themselves of the message, and finally, they had to persuade their contemporary communities to believe in the message while the responses from their communities were not the most kind in most cases. As God says in the Qur'an, there is never a prophet to whom God does not assign adversaries.

The Qur'an is full of such stories of previous prophets to acquaint the Prophet Mohammad with what to expect and to adequately prepare him for the tasks ahead. Mohammad was in pain to see the denials from his society, and God comforted him by saying that their denial was not about him but about the message of God and reminded him that prophets before him were similarly denied and insulted. God even challenged the Prophet that if he was overly grieved by his lack of success and wanted to speed up the process, perhaps he should go on his own and look for signs that he felt could possibly make his tasks easier and reminded him that if God had willed, all would have come to His guidance. But he was leaving it up to the people to convince themselves though knowledge and conscious deliberation. Therefore, he should not be in personal turmoil for other's ignorance.

God decreed certain terms and covenants with his creation that would be carried out, and no one can advance or delay those, just as one cannot delay or advance one's death, for example. God implies in the Qur'an that such terms are not only set for each individual human being, but also for communities and nations, all other creations on this planet, and for the planet Earth itself as part of the larger universe. Therefore, the prophet should not feel any responsibility or need to speed up results but should focus on carrying out his mission the best he can and leave the results to God.

It is not up to the prophet to make us believe; rather, each of us has to come to that conclusion himself or herself by paying attention to God's message and our internal reflections on the realities of this world. The Prophet advises that one has a choice and will be responsible for the choices that one makes, and his job is to convey and explain as further corroborated in the following verse: *"Insightful evidence has already arrived from your Sustainer; therefore, whoever can envision it, it is for his own good, and who remains blind to it will have its consequence. [Tell them]: I [Mohammad] am not responsible for your conduct!"* (6:104)

6. Unity in the created world (6:38)

We understand from our own experience as human beings that we are created as social beings and that our happiness, our sense of purpose, our progress as a human society, and our understanding of the world around us depend on our ability to bring to bear a collective purpose and shared sense of responsibility. Human beings are uniquely equipped, through the gifts of godly attributes such as seeking knowledge and exercising free will, to create a world that can either fulfill the promise of peace and goodness as God intended and delegated to us, or we can create a world of chaos, mutual destruction, and self-service, as Angels feared, and we can see this being played out in our own generation around the world. Such self-evident truths are a constant reminder for us to reflect on the sense of unity in our own society that we can create or shatter and to seek further corroboration from the world around us.

In this verse, God makes us aware of the creative truth that by itself is not necessarily obvious, but through science and observation, we are beginning to appreciate this truth and benefit from such understanding by being better prepared to preserve the world and bring technological innovation and scientific discoveries that could accelerate positive human development, assuming we are genuinely inclined and feel responsible to do so. This verse also seem to imply that all creatures will go back to God on resurrection, not just humans but God will call to account for human conduct and behavior since we were gifted with informed choices and freedom to act while the rest of the creation is subject to natural laws and instinctive (programmatic) behaviors without free will.

Even our solar system exists and can sustain life as a unit and not by individual planets or moons. The emergence and sustenance of life on earth is a function of the sun's and earth's relative positions, the earth's rotations around the sun and around its own axis, and the unique coupling between the moon and the earth. We are yet to fully comprehend the benefits and the needs of the other planets in our solar system—perhaps to show us what the earth might eventually become as its term, set by God, comes to fruition and perhaps how they these planets could provide additional resources and accommodations to prolong our human existence. It is only by recognizing our own predisposition to community building and finding common purposes, as exhibited in nature as well as in the natural world, as the handiwork of God and as proof to his purpose and plan, that we can reinvigorate our commitment to collective well-being and reaching our common destiny of peaceful coexistence and alignment with the Creator.

7. The mission of the Prophet defined (6:48–50)

God made a promise to Adam and Eve and hence to humanity that He would send guidance on earth to continue to reinforce what had already been built into our souls, which have all the attributes of God and goodness. This was a commitment made to reassure Adam and Eve in the face of an open declaration by the Devil that he will do all he can to derail humanity from alignment with God and peaceful coexistence among themselves.

But God is also committed to allowing human beings to make free choices as He Himself has, and He has made provisions for such freedom in our lives on this planet. In exchange, He will also hold us accountable for choices that we make. This causal relationship is no different from what we see in physics—for example, for every action (e.g., force applied), there is an equal and opposite reaction. In the human civic and spiritual domains, an act of goodness tends to create one or more act of goodness, as we are driven by inspirations, natural alignment to goodness, and, yes, also herd mentality, being creatures of a social environment. Similarly, an evil act driven by greed, power, lust, impatience, and disregard for human nature and aided by the Devil can produce widespread evils if not checked by our countervailing goodness aided God's guidance.

Prophets who are human themselves and are inspired by God indirectly or directly through the presence of Angels and God's word are commissioned to advise and caution—advise to seek alignment with God and a peaceful coexistence with fellow humans and the natural world, and caution against the consequences that naturally follow if such advice is not given credence and adhered to. The prophets' mission is to be the earthly guide for God among humans while respecting the divine freedom bestowed on each one of us to make his or her life choices.

While they are privileged beings with an endowment from God of superior intellect, insight, inspiration, personal charisma, and communication from God, they are still humans with limited resources and ability to anticipate future events and outcomes, and, as the prophet says, I am not an Angel and only follow what God reveals to me. Such a construct demands that each one of us be faithful to what we see and what we learn and not to be blinded by other transient priorities and carnal impulses over our physical purity and spiritual growth. God ends the verse (6:50) with a rhetorical question: How come you do not reflect on such matters for your own good?

8. God has intimate knowledge of the universe He created (6:59–60, 95–99)

The Qur'an, unlike any other earlier scripture, provides descriptions and accounts of an intimate relationship of God with the created world in a way that is awesomely inspiring and at the same time makes us aware of our own accountability and responsibility as human beings. God talks about the treasure of natural resources that is unknown and unseen in the universe and on this earth, and all that is on the land and in the sea is known to Him, and He makes it known to mankind and to the created world as He wills. The notion that even a leaf that falls from a tree and all organic materials, dry or green, are recorded with precision and care is a testimony of God's awareness and involvement in the world that we live in. The evolution of human knowledge, science, and technology continues to open our own capabilities to get a window of God's creation and the creative power that this generation has been blessed with.

On a spiritual level, God talks about our human souls departing us during our night's sleep, and He returns them at the beginning of the day so that we can rise and continue another day to earn a living and fulfill our terms of life. At the end of our term, we go back to God so that He can inform us about our lives and our performance as human beings.

He draws attention to our creation from a single being, Adam, and provides us safety and security on the planet Earth in a pattern similar to how a seed brings out life to a plant or a tree. He makes us ponder the role that the sun and the moon play to bring day and night and measures our sense of time and passage in life and how the distant stars provide guidance to our travel on this earth as well as in space. He draws attention to how vegetation becomes dense from small seedlings and how buds turn into flowers and then fruits with gradual ripening of an immense variety in size, taste, color, and fragrance, all to benefit and delight the world that we are part of and depend on for our survival and physical and spiritual growth.

He points out these facts about us and our natural world to make us think about ourselves and our world, so that we will be thoughtful and thankful, inspired to seek knowledge and understanding, and gain confidence in our being and our innate connection to the Creator and the created world. He then wonders why some of us turn away from such inspiration, guidance, and responsibilities. The natural world and our own lives comprise another scripture just like the Qur'an to observe, learn from, and emulate in our lives. Those of us who do not see, hear, and smell the world and do not reflect on its construction, inner workings, and mutual dependencies in addition to God's guidance are the real unfortunate ones who may pass a life of creature comfort and enjoyment but have no real purposefulness and connection with the divine. On top of that, when we consider all the evils that we have perpetrated in this beautiful world with total disregard for safety, dignity, and the basic needs of all human beings, it is a shocking illustration of our lack of thoughtfulness and purposefulness in the face of constant reminders from God and our own conscience.

9. God will account for all that we do in our lives (6:60–62)

From the moment we are born to the moment we die, God is aware of what we do, how we do it, and what intent or motivation drives us to do what we do or become what we become. God makes us aware in these verses that our soul, which is the permanent part of our existence and which is built in the nature of God (see 30:30), is always under God's care whether we are awake or asleep, as guardian Angels (*hafazatan*—keepers) are assigned to each one of us. Prophetic traditions tell us that there are also record-keeper Angels (*kiraman katibin*—honorable writers, see 82:10-11) who sit on our two shoulders and record all that we do—good as well as bad.

Accountability is fundamental to human existence. Societal orders and our personal and communal well-being are intimately aligned with our sense of accountability whether we are taking care of own family, working at our workplace, interacting with people in the public square or in our neighborhood, or fighting on the battleground. Some form of accountability is instinctive and natural, such as parents taking care of children—all creatures are drawn to such activities as an innate part of our creation and without exception. Serving others; earning a living by providing products and services; taking care of those who are less fortunate; striving for justice and human dignity; creating civil society; ensuring democratic means to manage our societies, our politics, and our economic means; pursing knowledge and truth, and so on require intentionality and a deliberate preparation and continuity of motivation that varies from people to people, from society to society, and from generation to generation.

As these verses imply, the cycle of life and death is as certain as the alteration of day and night, and God agents—Angels—are unfailing in carrying out their duty to serve humans and bring our death so that we can then go back to God, Who is the best of judges and most effective in taking account of our lives. As the Qur'an speaks in chapter 99: *"On that day [Day of Judgment], people will come forth [out of their graves] alone so that the results of their lifelong pursuits can be shown to them. Then he will see even an atom's weight of good work [he has done], and he will see even an atom's weight of evil work [he has done]."* (99:6–8). Similarly, in chapter 36: *"Surely, We [God] bring life back to those who are dead; We record what they do and their whereabouts [footprints]; all matters are meticulously documented [nothing is left out]."* (36:12)

Throughout the Qur'an, God repeats the message of accountability that we must have toward God and toward ourselves, and only with a sense of responsibility (*taqwa*) can we discharge such obligations and commitments. This is another reason why the Qur'an says in 2:2 that it can serve as a guide only for those faithful who are, first and foremost, responsible (have taqwa – Muttaquin) human beings.

10. God is ever powerful and challenges us to make the right choices (6:65)

This verse relates to events and outcomes that we have all witnessed, yet perhaps we do not reflect on their implications. Natural disasters and man-made disasters have accelerated to an unprecedented level in the twenty-first century. Frequent flooding and tornadoes; severe lightning and storms;

tsunamis; earthquakes; contamination of water; soil, and air; and gigantic sinkholes that swallow up houses and street blocks have become daily occurrences all over the world that were noticed only periodically even a generation ago. God's ability to force us to face the consequences of our own actions through natural disasters and man-made disasters is something any person who reflects on the natural order of things can attest to. Scientific discoveries and analysis force us to confront the causes of some of these calamities so that we can reflect on how we are responsible for some of them with our negligence and misplaced priorities in the way we power our industrial complex, manage our transportation, and influence our consumption of resources.

On another front, there is an even more difficult situation that is emerging, and that is the overall mental and spiritual health of human societies. According to a study by the World Health Organization (WHO), mental health will be the number-one health issue in the coming decades. Large-scale man-made refugee problems due to injustice and oppression by regimes, the proliferation of weapons of mass destruction by the leading members of UN Security Council, serious addiction in prescription drugs perpetuated by pharmaceutical companies and modern medical establishments, the rise of self-serving party politics that give precedence to the hunger for power and disregard human and societal interests, the rise of far-right political establishments that marginalize and demonize minorities and people of other faiths and races, and large-scale apathy to faith in God in favor of secular thinking have been causing havoc on human mental and spiritual well-being, leading to an overall degradation of quality of life, physically, mentally, and spiritually, all over the world and in all races, ethnicities, and faith groups. No group is immune from the man-made onslaught of analysis paralysis, serious disrespect of human beings and human consciousness, uncontrolled exploitation of natural resources, and misplaced priorities in energy production and consumption, to give few examples.

God in this single verse draws attention to conditions where we are thrown into confusion about ourselves and how our mutual enmity leads to violence and disharmony among human beings, a species that has been endowed with the highest moral and ethical standard by God Himself. He also reminds us that despite such failure, we need to continue to reflect, correct, and persevere—a human obligation for each generation in every society.

11. Choose your discourse properly and with deliberation (6:68–70)

The Prophet, and by implication all of us, is reminds us that we all need to pay attention to our discourse among ourselves. Such discourse should be meaningful, purposeful, and relevant to our lives, our living, our well-being, and our spiritual growth. It cannot be only about rituals on one hand, which many conservatives and fundamentalists want to have, and on the other hand, it cannot be only about superficial enjoyment of life without any regard to values, principles, and accountability. Many of us are thoughtful and professional people who aspire to take our faith seriously but are unwilling to engage in deliberate and purposeful dialogue among ourselves and to engage the larger community within our own faith and across all faiths to develop shared views, common purpose, and support of one another for greater human dignity and progress.

As we can see from such verses, guidance in the Qur'an is much more holistic and touches on varied aspects of life—even how to conduct our discussions and discourse than the previous scriptures. We need to take the guidance of the Qur'an not only to perfect faith elements and rituals which are part of a well-crafted training regimen to build self-awareness, develop better discipline and establish personal relationship with God but also to engage our time, energy and knowledge in the most intelligent, productive and efficient way to push us on a path of higher human potential, not only for us as individuals but for all of us as communities and a societies.

12. Abraham's search for God and truth (6:74–82)

Abraham, being a central figure among Jews, Christians, and Muslims, takes a prominent position in many of the narratives of the Qur'an. These narratives give us a glimpse of his aspiration for faith and confidence in God, the Creator of the universe; his attempt to sacrifice his son (Isaac or Ishmael, depending on whether you're reading the Bible or the Qur'an) to demonstrate his obedience to God; his discourse with his own tribe, including his father and the priests of the time, questioning their idolatry and superstition; his quest to find God by observing the natural world and his own consciousness regarding what rings true versus false regarding deities; and his building of the Kabah, the ancient place of worship that not only survives till today but has become the central part of the Islamic faith and ritual where millions of faithful visit each year and commemorate the memories of him, his son Ishmael, and his wife, Hagar. Hajj (annual pilgrimage), one of the five pillars of faith in Islam brings people from all corners of the earth in a unique assembly of humanity, breaking the barriers of race, sect, gender, wealth, and worldly position.

These verses narrate his inquisitive and conscious mind, which not only questioned the existing faith and practices of his generation but went out on a hunt to find the truth about God and the human condition. It is the same hunt that drove Moses, Jesus, and Mohammad to question their generations, to reinterpret the social order in Pharaonic times, reinvigorate the laws of Moses, remove lawless and injustice in Arabian tribes and reignite the passion and truth that Abraham felt when he understood Who God is and what it means to align oneself with God.

Over time, all faith groups, including Muslims, become overly attached to rituals and practices and faith elements and begin to deviate from the real teachings that are in the Torah, the Bible, and the Qur'an. They begin to subscribe to a self-fulfilling and comforting notion that being aligned with one's ethnic group and being God's chosen people or claiming Jesus as the savior (as opposed to God and Jesus's teachings), prioritizing on five Islamic rituals rather than establishing truth and justice will uplift the human race or improve the human condition. Unless we can really understand the drives, motivations, and mandates of Abraham, Moses, Jesus, and Mohammad, those of us who claim to be their followers will fall short, and our world will continue to suffer from human indignity, extreme poverty, and political and social oppression, which have become commonplace in many parts of the world, including the developed world. Let's be reminded: *"Those who believe in God and do not taint their faith with evils of inequity will have security and are properly guided." (6:82)*

13. Guidance and prophecy were given to many before Mohammad, a unified guidance to mankind (6:83–90, 92)

These verses summarize, with specific names of prophets who are also mentioned in the Bible and the Torah, that they all belonged to God, received guidance from the same God, and were committed to believe in the same God. It first mentions Abraham, whom God inspired with consciousness and thoughtful reasoning to refute his community's idolatry and practices that were contrary to reality and human dignity. Abraham is followed by Isaac, Jacob, and Noah (who came before Abraham), and some of their descendants who were given guidance by God. It then mentions that David, Solomon, Job, Joseph, Moses, and Aaron were rewarded for their good work. The list then moves on to Zacharias, John, Jesus, and Elias—each was righteous in the eyes of God. Finally, the list moves on to Ishmael (the firstborn of Abraham), Elisha, Jonah, and Lot (contemporary of Abraham)—they were privileged to excel in their communities.

The Qur'an further corroborates that even the parents of these prophets and some of their descendants and their peers (brethren) were also chosen and guided to the right way. These are some examples of people who were given books containing guidance, authority from God to propagate such guidance among people, and prophecy to predict and caution against the consequences of failure to follow the guidance and to apply it in their contemporary society in the best possible manners. In exchange, these prophets asked nothing of people that might benefit them except that people continue to serve these reminders to successive generations. Yet in their name, the imams, the clerics, and the so-called religious scholars demand payment for such services and became subservient to others by accepting salaries in exchange for calling people to God—a construct that is contrary to prophetic teachings and traditions.

This sequence of verses culminates with the idea that the Qur'an is a blessed Book that confirms all other books that came before it (e.g. the Bible and the Torah, among others) with the sole purpose of reminding and cautioning people in the town it was revealed (Makkah) and to all towns and nations on this globe.

14. God has no children (6:100–101)

In these two verses (among many others in the Qur'an), God simply refutes any notion that God could have children in the way that human beings have children. And for anyone to assign to himself or to others a special relationship to God by ascribing some parent-child relationship with God, God reminds people that He has no mates and has no children. On the contrary, as the Creator of all things, all belongs to Him in a deeper and more intimate way than even a mate or an offspring could, and He oversees everything without the need for assistance or advocacy from any partners or relations in His divine purview.

But the notion of agency, where human beings in general and prophets in particular are given the representative authority to guide and rule themselves in accordance with God's guidance and human intellect and free will, is very different from the false assumption that someone (a false deity) or some creation of God (Jinns or spirits, as claimed by some) have a son or daughter relationship to God and as such call for human allegiance to them in preference to or in addition to God. Surah Al-Ikhlas (Chapter 112), which is one of the earliest revelations, affirms very early on that God was neither born from anyone nor has given birth to anyone and that there is nothing in our universe comparable to Him.

15. To God all is visible (6:102–103)

The first verse confirms and reiterates the constant truth about God being the only deity in this universe Who is worthy of worship and devotion. Not only He is the Creator, He is also in constant charge of His creations, meaning that their survival and prosperity and the working of this world require His grace and attention, and He is able to do so without any fatigue or need for respite (see 2:255). Our physical bodies, efforts to earning a living, nurturing a seed to germinate, keeping our rivers clean, and so on require our constant attention and deliberation with knowledge and practice. At another level, none of this is possible without the natural laws that God laid out, evolutionary forces He put into motion, and a constant tendency in the natural world, including humans, to maintain its pristine state. My wife and I are thrilled to be getting a granddaughter in a few months as I write this book, and I am sure our daughter-in-law is doing all she can to stay healthy, eat right, and stay safe to give the baby a safe haven in her womb. Yet the growth and well-being of the baby is very much in the hands of God, who creates, nurtures, and matures each and every one of us as He wills and according to measures and terms that His infinite capacity and wisdom has laid out for each one of us till death and beyond.

Understanding who we are and what this world is all about is very much a physical act as well as a spiritual act. Our senses, in the form of sight, hearing, smell, touch, space, and time are physical, while our feeling, consciousness, cognition, and aspirations beyond space and time are spiritual. Both of these acts are subject to practice and intense training to harness greater efficacy and dimensions and more so subject to God's will as He informs and manifests Himself and the world to us (see again 2:255). We are subject to tools and technologies that can only see and perhaps comprehend us and part of world that we live in. And what we create as our vision (a proxy for all of our senses and capabilities) is limited, while God's vision encompasses all of His creation, and He has declared Himself as fully Aware (*Al-A'leem, Al-Khabeer, Al-Raqeeb, Al- Shaheed*). And such awareness involves a subtle understanding of the universe that is known only to Him and to his creations that He wishes to endow with it. In the Qur'an, God's attribute of being Aware is accompanied by this additional attribute of being the Knower of Subtlety (Al-Lateef).

For example, in 22:63, He brings our attention to the formation of clouds, rain, and how the world around us turns green with vegetation as an example of that subtle knowledge and awareness that He possesses and over time conveys to humanity. In 31:16, He provides the story of Luqman, who advises his children that God's awareness encompasses even a tiny particle (i.e., a mustard seed, as mentioned) in any part of the universe, while in 33:34, God advises the family of the Prophet Mohammad that guidance that comes to them through the Prophet has to be dissected and internalized with all if its nuances and subtleties. And finally, in 67:13–14, God declares that He knows the condition of the human heart, whether we express it and keep it a secret, as a show of His being aware of the condition of his creation. And how could it be otherwise that the Creator would be unaware of and unconcerned about His own creation?

16. Respect for other religious practices (6:108)

Mutual respect for one another's faiths and the notion of religious plurality as a way to serve God and humanity is something that the Qur'an emphasizes time and again throughout its unfolding messages over twenty-three years, which resonates well with our human condition and aspiration. Verse 2:62 (explained in detail in volume 1) is very eloquent and definitive on religious diversity. So is verse 5:48 (explained in volume 2), which not only allows religious plurality but goes further to say that it was out of respect for human free will, as established and privileged by God, that God allows people to differ and have different sets of beliefs in God and different rituals as they see fit for themselves. Such differences should not be the cause for division and conflicts but an incentive to do good and prove one another's worth to God, in the way our human institutions (e.g. business, social enterprises) allow us to compete while being true to the policies and visions of the institutions that we belong to and advance human conditions.

This verse (6:108) draws our attention to the fact that our human psyche is always attuned to our loved ones and our deities that we worship and that any slight to them affects us as a slight to ourselves. The Qur'an reminds us that we should be deferential to other deities of other faiths, even if we do not subscribe to such faith or accept such theology in light of our own faith, so that we do not incite disrespect to God, who is the only deity that created this universe and governs our lives. I see that fundamentalists from all religious faiths and the extreme elements from various faith groups exhibit disrespect to one another's faiths as a routine part of their discourse, which needs to be strongly discouraged. Especially Muslims, who read the Qur'an and believe that it is the living guidance of God, should actively discourage any disrespect to other deities and to the people who subscribe to such faiths. Only by respecting others we can garner respect for ourselves and have a meaningful discourse about God, faith and life.

17. God guides as He pleases (6:124–125)

The guidance of God is given freely to each and every human being through our own human construct where we are created in the image of God, as the Bible says and as the Qur'an says (30:30) that our human nature is crafted in the nature of God Himself. As a result, we have a natural yearning to be with God and to be aligned with God. God mentions in the Qur'an that he brought together all the souls of the descendants of Adam and Eve (ref. 7:172) and asked them who their Creator was, and they all confirmed that God is the Creator and Sustainer of them. God then posits that this was done so that no children of Adam and Eve could ever come back and say to God that they were unaware of their origin.

Perhaps none of us has recollection of that event when God says: *"Am I not your Creator Lord?"* One way to understand that recollection is the fact that inside each one of us, without any exception, is a sense that there is a God Who is the cause of our existence and our universe, and this has been a constant reminder and desire of humanity as long as we can trace back our human history. Ideas of faith and religion may have been corrupted due to ignorance, superstition, self-indulgence, greed, and other human failings, but central to each faith is a constant desire to know who we are, what we are about, and who created us.

God advised Adam and Eve, on the occasion of their being assigned the agency of God (*Khalifa*) on this planet, to be mindful of God and to teach their children the guidance of God, which would come to each generation by direct communication and the inspiration of prophets and messengers, scriptures that would be given to provide continuity and permanence of such guidance, and inspired human beings who would continue to bear the torch of God's guidance under a variety of human and social conditions, however difficult it might be.

One source of conflict between different faith groups is this sense of entitlement to guidance for them alone and to denigrate or deny that such guidance could come to other groups and societies as well and that these all come from the same God. When Abraham spoke of God and perfected his devotion to God, it was the same God that Moses spoke with, it was the same God Who made Jesus, a special creation without a father to further the laws of Moses and reshape the conversation on faith and humility, and it was the same God that Mohammad was inspired by with a universal message of mercy and human dignity for all of mankind. The emergence of clerics and religious scholars who have a vested interest in maintaining their hold on the masses have throughout the centuries continued to propagate the idea that theirs is the true faith and there is no other religion or expression of one's faith in God. Yet the Qur'an says to the contrary in multiple contexts and occasions, as explained in the previous volume (2:62) and in this volume (5:48), that all the scriptures point to the same God, and our alignment should be based on sincere devotion, well-directed consciousness, understanding, and the shared goal of uplifting all of humanity as a community that aspires to be with God and of God.

Our conflicts, self-serving interests, and narrow interpretations of scriptures are products of our own ignorance, lack of humility, and misplaced priorities, which are unfaithful to our human origin, our sense of equality and human dignity, and our eventual return to God to give accountability for our lives and pursuits.

18. Disbelief will be self-affirmed (6:130, 136)

Denial and disbelief in God manifests in different ways—one is outright denial that God exists (atheists), and another is through polytheistic beliefs and customs (polytheism), where a creature or an object of creation of God is considered an equal, a partner, or a carrier of God's divinity to an extent that these associate godheads are given devotion equal to God and sometimes even exceeding God, and where capabilities and powers are attributed to these entities that truly belong to God alone. Another form is present where God is marginalized and another entity (e.g., the Devil) or custom (e.g., cult) or tribal alliance or nationalism takes precedence over their lives, priorities, and belief systems.

The Qur'an refutes some of these forms of disbelief and denials in the context of the seventh-century Arabian society where the Qur'an was gradually revealed over twenty-three years to the Prophet Mohammad and his faithful followers. Some of these disbeliefs and denials are prevalent in various forms in our contemporary societies as well, either in the mainstream or on the fringes of society. The Qur'an asserts that all these beliefs or reliance on other deities, entities, and belief systems will eventually fail during the lifetimes of their followers, and, on the day of final judgment, when God will question such beliefs, these followers will recognize the fallacy of their faith, and these so-called entities, who or which were presumed to possess divine powers and attributes, will fail to respond or present themselves as such.

Human beings are given every opportunity in life to recognize these realities and to abandon such beliefs and reliance in favor of God, who is the ultimate reality. Through scriptures and our human endowment of knowledge and free choices, we have to ascertain such realities and prove our commitment to enable justice, human dignity, and truth in our social norms and establishments.

19. Superstitious rituals and sacrifice are condemned (6:136–140, 143–144)

Throughout human history, people of various religious affiliations and people of no faith have constructed various acts, rituals, and superstitious supposition to control the human mind, restrict human freedom and dignity, falsify reality, and do things in the name of God when no such allowances have been made. In these few verses, God cites some examples prevalent in the

Arabian society where the Prophet Mohammad was sent to start his mission and work as a prophet of God, in the same tradition that other prophets such as Moses and Jesus had done. Specific mentions are made to the following:

- Setting aside certain produce, fruits, animals, and sacrifices for God and for other deities, a practice common among the Hindus even today. This practice is also a reflection that divine powers are considered to be shared among God and the other deities.
- Superstitions and the falsification of God with other deities confuses people, leading them to make faith and religious practices devoid of meaning, in extreme cases causing undue harm and atrocities against other human beings (the ancient practice of human sacrifices) and animals (burning or sacrificing them to gods) and creating false rituals and practices in the name of God. A justification commonly used in the current counterterrorism measure of collateral damage, where innocent human beings are being killed, maimed, and harmed in large numbers, borders on false belief and false pretext, confusing judgment, and making things appear acceptable where no such moral basis exist.
- Arbitrary prohibition of what crop or animal is consumable and by whom to satisfy greed and self-interest and then justifying this in the name of God is another example of such abuse, superstition, and evil practices. In many of the shrines in the Indian subcontinent, for example, people are encouraged and sometimes forced to pay money, food, and other goods in the name of the dead or in the name of God, only for it to be consumed by the caretaker and the owners of such institutions. Whatever good is done is masked by the evils that they create, but too many people are willing to oblige in the name of faith and God.

As we study some of these aberrant behaviors in the name of God and other deities of ancient people, every generation has to look at its own conduct and remain vigilant against the justification of evils and false norms, some of which are staring at our face in the form of extreme poverty, immoral greed, income inequality, large-scale pollution, and the destruction of our environment and natural habitat for other creatures who inhabit this planet with us, widespread political corruption and atrocities against ordinary human beings, and the glorification of faithlessness in God directly in many communist countries and sometimes overtly in secular countries.

20. All human output and natural resources deserve sharing (6:141)

This verse lays out a foundational principle that the world has forgotten, and it is more relevant to counter the ever-widening income inequality in the world today. Things that we earn and secure for our own benefit, whether they come because of our own direct effort or indirectly through other means, whether personal, natural, business, or institutional, all being directed from God, is to be shared not just out of personal goodness and generosity but as a moral obligation as well as a natural construct of our world.

God is named here as the One Who produces orchards and gardens, whether they come about because of human effort or naturally in the wild, untended by any human. So is the case with fruit trees and plants, seeding that grows into giant trees bearing all kinds of fruits, and other amenities for human consumption and use. God's guidance is that we partake of such gifts from God as these fruits ripen and become ready for consumption and also pay its due on the day of reaping and harvesting. They key concept here is to pay its due as soon as we have these in our possession.

One should be able to think through this simple but encompassing example and demonstration of what should be our mental state and moral stature when we earn and accept such gifts of God. In the world today, earning comes in all forms and from all sorts of endeavors—be it from farming that produces grain, fruits, vegetables, or fish, or from seeking bounties from nature such as a wide variety of edibles grown in forests, mineral resources from earth's crust, fish and other resources from oceans and rivers, consumables manufactured in our industries and by businesses, or technology that improves the quality of life and communication, just to name a few.

In our world today, there is an unprecedented amount of greed and a sense of selfish personal entitlement that have sapped our conscience and moral well-being, the result being that we have created a vast ocean of poverty and impoverished societies with islands of extreme riches that have reached unsustainable proportions in a manner that is no different from our abuse of the natural world through pollution, carbon emissions, and reckless exploitation of minerals that subjects large groups of people to inhuman working conditions, pollutes the environment without any regard to our obligation to the natural world, and allows profiteering to the maximum without any regard to fair-market playbook.

We need to understand the implications of such a simple and elegant verse from the Qur'an and apply it diligently to all our human endeavors in any field that produces output that generates income (fruits) for each one of us, whether a laborer or the owner of an institution or a business, and pay its due when we reap the benefit, be it a paycheck, a harvest, an inventory that has built up, a transaction that has taken place, or a mouse click that earns an advertising dollar, when profit is realized at the end of the day, end of the month, or end of the year.

The key questions are, how should this due be defined and delivered, and for whose benefits, and to what obligation? A couple of thoughts come to mind for us to consider, deliberate, and use in the creation of ground rules, some of which could become the law of the land, if the majority opinion supports such a framework, inspired by our faith in God and our common aspiration to create a world where everyone has the opportunity and social support network to be what he or she wants to be:

- Taxation on such reaping is already a common practice all over the world, where society demands that every income earner pay a certain amount to a common treasury for the running of the country. This is based on income statements rather than balance sheets and applies to individuals as well as for-profit institutions, but with shortcomings that are becoming more apparent as we gain experience, such as the following:
    - The income tax rate is a hotly debated issue, and in many advanced countries, governments rise or fall depending on how they enact policies to tax their citizens and businesses.

In many countries, both developed and underdeveloped, the wealthy find too many ways to evade taxes, either through legal means by influencing tax policies, diligently taking advantage of many tax loopholes in ever increasingly complex tax laws, influencing lawmakers to keep those loopholes untouched, creating tax havens in various jurisdictions, and shifting or hiding income in nontransparent banking systems in different part of the world, or through outright disregard and bribery to avoid paying taxes.

- People of Islamic faith have the institution of *zakat* (asset-based social giving with annual dues of ~2.5% on net assets [as opposed to income]) for those who are wealthy; it is based on accumulated assets to date as opposed to the current year—in other words, it is based on balance sheets and not on income statements. Zakat has been historically applied to individuals; perhaps it is time to apply it to profit-making institutions as well and apply this collective resource strategically to improve the income potential and living conditions of the poor (education, empowerment, health, and infrastructure) as opposed to only consumables such as food and clothing. Here also, zakat as an institution has not given adequate attention and analysis to create a pool of resources across national boundaries for the benefit of poor people all over the world.

But the reaping analogy in the Qur'an seems to imply that this due (whatever we wish to call it) becomes payable at the time of harvest (an analogy would be a paycheck, or the monthly income statement for business) and to be taken from the top line rather than the bottom line—gross income rather than the net income. Perhaps we all do not agree on this interpretation, but it needs to be debated. How does this due relate to the above two items—tax and zakat? Is it already included in these items, or do we need to augment our current thoughts? Many Christian Catholics and Mormon Churches levy such reaping from their congregations to support their missions and activities—10 percent of income is the typical amount that I hear about. We can learn something from their experience to better understand what such due means in biblical and Qur'anic senses and contexts.

21. All assertions need to be verified and proven (6:143–144)

These verses challenge existing social customs or superstitious practices in the strongest terms: *"Inform me (God and His prophet) with knowledge if you are truthful"* and *"Were you a witness when God instructed such practices?"* It ends with this broad denunciation: *"Who is more at fault than who forges lies in the name of God to lead people in error without proper knowledge and deliberation?"*

Over time Muslims have developed additional social customs and practices as well as reverting back to old customs, a phenomenon that is part of our human psyche, unless we remain diligent, seek adequate knowledge and discussion, and continually question our lives, their purpose, and the social norm in which we live and operate.

Here are some examples of what continues to plague Muslim lives, especially in our recent history. I will put them in three broad categories—social, political, and religious, with two examples in each category:

- Several **social customs** are devaluing our human lives in Muslim societies, and they have no basis in the Qur'an or prophetic traditions; for example:
  - **Hijab for women:** The notion of modesty and proper attire—which is common for both men and women—to cover our shame and not to present ourselves as sex objects, has been taken to the extreme, especially for women in some Muslim countries, while a trend has emerged in Western societies where women are expected to expose greater portions of their bodies as a social norm. With respect to women's dress among the Muslims, it is an established fact that the majority of Muslim women do not subscribe to hijab except in Middle Eastern countries, and many Muslim women who wear hijab in the West are from that part of the world or are being influenced by them in their conservative Muslim social circles. This is very much contrary to what the Qur'an teaches, and it is being imposed by authoritarian regimes or ignorant and

arrogant imams and sheikhs in the name of Islam while Islam clearly declares: *"There is no compulsion in the matter of faith and religion"* (2:256).

- **Lack of Education:** While the very first revelation of the Qur'an makes reference to pen and knowledge: *"Read in the name of your Creator, Who is generous, Who taught the use of pen and taught humanity what they did not know"* (96:3–5), and while seeking knowledge has been the pioneering spirit of Muslim scholars, educators, and the ruling class for many centuries, there has been a dramatic decline in making education a priority for Muslim masses in most of the Muslim countries. Too many Muslim nations have come to regard their citizens as mouths to feed as opposed to brains and intellects to nurture and empower.

- On the **political front**, practices and policies that grossly violate the teachings of the Qur'an are on display in many Muslim countries, and two major examples will suffice, as follows:
  - **Authoritarian Regimes:** A regime that is not a choice of the people and that does not operate in consultation with its citizens is contrary to Islamic traditions and principles. There are too many kings, sheikhs, and power-hungry leaders who steal elections and impose their undemocratic rule on people, and many times they use religion, nationalism, socialism, and other defunct ideas to justify their rule and continued exploitation of people. Most recently, two Muslim countries that were showing promise of sustained democracy and economic development, Turkey and Malaysia, overreached the abusive patterns of behaviors by their leaders and their supporters, even if some of their concerns might be legitimate. Here is a verse that all Muslims should understand and commit to: *"God commands you to put trust [governance] on those who are worthy of it, and when you judge among people, judge with justice"* ("Women," 4:58).
  - **Political Corruption:** This has become the major source of evil in too many Muslim countries, societies, and institutions where the rule of law is no longer the norm, national wealth is consumed by

a few in power, corrupt businesses collude with politicians to usurp power and financial resources to the exclusion of average citizens, political freedom and human dignity are curtailed on all fronts of the citizens' lives, and businesses are given freedom to pollute and usurp natural resources such as water, air, and soil for greed and profit for the few. Some of these leaders then pretend that they are doing good and deploy deceptive public relations campaigns to hide their evil doings. Let's listen to what the Qur'an says about these people: *"When they are told: Don't make mischief in the land, they reply: We are doing good and maintain peace"* (2:11).

- On the **religious front**, there has been a general decline of rigorous religious teaching around faith and goodness (as opposed to rituals) and an overreliance on so-called imams and sheikhs, contrary to the need and call for individual and collective responsibility (*taqwa*) and empowerment. Again, two examples will suffice:
  - **Madrassa education:** Though it started out as a genuine attempt to educate the masses on faith and religion in the face of colonial onslaughts during the eighteenth and nineteenth centuries, over time it morphed into a rigid curriculum of rote memorization of the Qur'an and a rigid form of indoctrination by authoritarian regimes and compliant and ill-educated clerics to create a parallel system of education that deprives its students of any meaningful skills to earn a living and instead turns them into ritual practitioners of faith and, at worst, enforcers of such rituals and eventually turning some of them into outright proponents of authoritarianism and corruption of faith along the lines of ISIS, Al-Qaeda, the Taliban, and other fringe groups that are preying on innocent human beings and destabilizing societies in the name of Islam. It is also important to note that some of these fringe groups are also products of failed states, social and political oppression, and sustained exploitation of human beings by their domestic political forces and/or foreign intervention, and we can look at countries such as Afghanistan, Iraq, Syria, Somalia, Yemen, and Nigeria, where such evils have taken roots.

- **Religious clerics:** In Islamic thinking and tradition, the notion of laymen versus clergy is nonexistent, and the idea that one makes teaching faith and religion a form of income generation was foreign to the Prophet, his early companions, great statesmen, and all the great scholars of Islam, all of whom possessed skills and expertise far more comprehensive than simple rituals and pure religious learnings. For them, faith, social laws and norms, and scientific understanding of the world existed together as a harmonious source of knowledge from God, and they committed themselves to serving their community and improving human conditions, but they never made the preaching of religion a source of income for themselves. The corruption of faith by clerics is evident in the Muslim world and even in the Muslim communities in the West, where the community members, instead of stepping up to learn and educate themselves about their faith and combining it with their learning of social and physical sciences, submitted themselves to Madrassa-trained imams to take ownership of their religious practices. This needs to change, and too many young Muslim are walking away from mosques, Islamic centers, and Sunday Schools all over the world because of disillusionment over the teachings and behavior of such clerics.

22. Prohibitions and values that really matter (6:151–153)

These two verses are foundational in terms of real demarcations that one should not cross from faith, moral, ethical, and justice points of view. These verses are preceded by verses 145–146 and 150, in which the dietary restrictions are enumerated and we are asked to faithfully corroborate God's injunction and not create our own without justification and proper deliberation. One could, conceivably, argue that the current verses are meant to elevate the conversation from the physical plane to the moral and spiritual planes. It is important to enumerate these below to organize in our mind the depth and comprehensive of these two verses.

Verse 151 starts with an invitation to come together with a desire to learn and understand and then to impress upon ourselves that with personal honesty and intellectual integrity we can understand and appreciate what God wants us to prioritize and fulfil in regard to prohibitions and guidance that really matter:

1. God should be worshipped and served alone, as He ought to be served without any divine associate—this statement of unity of Godhead goes after, for example, the Christian concept of Trinity, Jesus being elevated to a Godhead or son of God and, by the same token, after any form of polytheism, while negating atheism as a nonstarter.
2. The second injunction is about every human being's obligation to be good to his or her parents and to take care of his or her children, while strongly condemning any belief or practice about infanticide, definitely pointing to the Arab custom of burying female children at the time when such revelations came or the ancient custom of sacrificing children to the Godhead or for fear of poverty, something that is ever present in all times, even in our current generation, where orphans or children are being abandoned by parents or abused in orphanages or institutions.
3. Any form of indecency or shamelessness, either physical or moral, is strongly prohibited, whether done in the open or in secret. This is a broad statement that includes nakedness, illicit sex, stealing, bribery, lying, corruption, humiliation, undue pride, hypocrisy, racism, injustice, misogyny, xenophobia, and other things that the human mind inherently and instinctively considers indecent, shameful, and unjust.
4. Any form of killing or murder is unjustifiable, be it homicide, terrorism, counterterrorism, suicide bombing, wartime excesses, collateral killing, ideological killing, political killing, female infanticide, ethnic cleansing, so-called honor killing, hostage taking and killing, lynching…and the list goes on. We human beings find reasons and means to kill one another like no other species on this planet, in gross violation of God's commandment, in this verse as well as the prohibition articulated in the Ten Commandment by Moses, the unjustified killing condemned

by Jesus, and the declarations made by the UN and other international, national, regional, community, and social institutions in every generation and certainly our current generation, where the killing of human beings is ever present and an ever-widening crisis as exemplified in Syria, Yemen, the Rakhine state of Myanmar, and by ISIS in Middle East and the persecution of minorities and political opponents in countries such as China, Russia and India, Philippine, to name a few.

5. The unlawful possession of another's property, the worst cases being those who are vulnerable, such as orphans (as stated in this verse), children, minorities, women, the poor, or the less empowered. It is incumbent on us as individuals and as a society to protect, preserve, and make use of this property in the best possible way and in the best interest of such vulnerable owners and then hand it over to them once they are mature and able to assume control and proper usage. We need to have legal frameworks and just enforcement in place to help them manage their properties and ownership.

6. Next comes the requirement that in our dealings with others, in all matters such as social interaction, trade and commerce, leadership and citizenship, employees and business owners, we treat one another, at personal, societal, and institutional levels, in a fair and equitable manner, and every generation has to debate, discuss, and continuously build on previous generations.

7. Next comes our own discourse—in all matters of conversation, speeches, and policies, we must speak for truth and justice, even though it might go against us or our relatives, friends, or associates.

8. Last but not the least, God finally reminds us that we have a covenant with Him, our Creator and Cherisher, that we should fulfill, individually and collectively.

God reminds us that all this guidance and these injunctions are for our own benefit. He constantly reminds us of this through the scriptures and through our consciousness so that we not only understand their purpose but also become mindful. God further assures us in verse 152 that no individual is ever asked to do anything by God except that God also endows that person with the capability. There is no better reassurance one can get than this. I am also reminded of what Nelson Mandela once said: Everything is impossible until it is done.

23. The challenge of the Torah, the Bible, and the Qur'an (6:154–156)

The Qur'an is full of references to previous Books of Revelations, especially the most recent books claimed by Jews (the Torah) and Christians (the Bible) prior to the revelations of the Qur'an. In the Qur'an, one is reminded that the Qur'an is for all of humanity and in particular for those who take their lives and mission seriously and feel a strong responsibility (*taqwa*) besides faith in One God. In all its calls, it addresses people of faith, including Muslims, to continually make the point that faith and good works matter and labels do not.

Here is the first (verse 154) confirmation that the Torah was given to Moses to fulfill and deliver [God's favor and blessings] on him [Moses, his followers, and generations to come] who wish to do good; in it things have been explained and made known to serve as a guidance and a source of God's grace; and to further one's belief that we all are destined to meet our Creator eventually.

Then reference is made to the current book [the Qur'an], which is revealed with full blessings from God so that people can follow it and become responsible human beings such that God's mercy will follow. Muslims are made aware that the Qur'an was added to complete the sequel of God' revelations in response to two key outcomes since the revelations of the Torah and the Bible:

- Since the Torah and the Bible were not widely available to the people outside the Jewish and Christian faith for reasons well documented, the Torah was claimed by followers of Moses as an exclusive blessing to the Children of Israel, and they claimed that they were the only ones who could explain and retain the right of who could be guided to God, while the Bible was repurposed to create the concepts of the Trinity and Jesus as the Savior, and it was put forth as the only acceptable faith to the exclusion of any other faith groups and faith elements. It took the papal institute almost two thousand years (1965) before issuing the notion, articulated in Nostra Aetate of religious plurality, a concept that God had articulated in the Qur'an in the seventh century to all of humanity who wish to believe in God and do good, irrespective of religious label (2:62)

- As a consequence, to the first reality on the ground among Jews and Christians, people outside these two communities, especially the Arabs who were very familiar with Jews and Christians, felt left out. They also were aware of their own lineage to Abraham and acted as the custodians of Kabah, a place of worship that dates back to Abraham and Ishmael, the firstborn of Abraham. In the contemporary world in India, with Hinduism and Buddhism and Chinese Confucius and Zen cultures, people were creating islands of religion and religion-based communities to the exclusion of other religions and sometimes exhibited open hostilities, and there was constant strife and theological discord, something that was clearly visible and propagated as a religious doctrine by the papal institute against the Jews and later on against the Muslims. There was yeaning among human hearts outside the prevailing religious norms and communities that God bring another revelation that would unite all and guide them better against the narrowness of religious doctrines perpetuated to date.

It is in this backdrop that the Qur'an came to confirm the truths in all revelations before it (2:4) and to affirm human freedom to choose one's own religious affiliation (5:48) and to simplify and codify the universal notion of faith in God and in goodness as the true expression of faith, giving it a name, Islam (peace), a pungent, pure, and spiritual name that resonates with the human heart; labeling its followers simply as Muslims (those who are aligned with God and goodness); and removing any connotation of tribal (e.g., Judaism), personal (Christ, Buddha), geographic (Hinduism), or any other affiliation that would negate the universal nature of faith and our common humanity. It is in this vein that the Qur'an declares Abraham a Muslim (3:67, 2:128); the disciples of Jesus as Muslims (3:52, 5:111); Jacob, Joseph, and Moses as Muslims (2:133,10:84, 12:101); as well as all prophets and their followers as Muslims (3:84, 29:46).

We have much more work to do in this regard, and our American experiment, in which faith in God is codified in the Declaration of Independence and religious freedom and plurality are established as a norm in our constitution, gives hope to the world that even unity of faith and our common humanity is possible and is worth fighting for.

24. Sectarian divides condemned (6:159)

Apparent divisions among people is ever present, some of which are the natural order of things, such as race, ethnicity, language, and so on, as evolution and creative forces in nature move and shape our onward journey as a species as God intended and constructed the natural world. All creations, other than human beings, use such diversity as an instinctive response to create affinity and collaboration and to improve their survival and reproductive capacities. Human beings, on the other hand, endowed with increasing knowledge of the natural world and the freedom to make choices (sometimes freely but other times from coercion or bias or evil desires), are led to accentuate such diversity to create divisions among people all over the world.

Such divisions happen along the lines of race, national origin, ethnicity, religion, gender, wealth, social class, professional affiliation, and so on, limited only by the imagination of human beings and our propensity to accentuate such divisions for self-interest, greed, lust, and evil. Even though this verse speaks specifically about sectarian divides in the context of religious belief, one could argue that it pertains to all forms of human divisions that go against the notion of truth, human equality and dignity, and sense of justice.

What are some of these sectarian divides? Among the Muslims, the major divides are Shia and Sunni, even though there is no mention of the Shia or Sunni in the Qur'an or in any traditions of the prophet—it is an invention of the latter-day Muslims, but it happened very early in the emergence of Muslims as a new faith group along the lines of Jews and Christians. Among the Sunnis there are minor divides along the lines of schools of thought such as Hanafi, Maliki, and so on, whereas among the Shias there are innumerable permutations of practices, beliefs, and sectarian alliances such as Ishmaeli, Bori, Iranian brand, and many other shades that have not been fully cataloged or explored by academics.

Among the Christians, some of the major sectarian divides are the Catholics, Protestants, Methodists, Lutherans, Eastern Orthodox, Greek Orthodox, and Quakers, to name a few. Among the Jews, we have the Orthodox, Conservative, Reformed, European Jews, African Jews, and so on. Among the Hindus, there are defined caste systems that not only codify such divides but also perpetuate such caste-based divisions by birth as opposed to one's belief or affinity.

The singular advice from God is to deny and refrain from such divisions and divisiveness and not to perpetuate or accentuate such divisions. Other advice from God is to maintain a middle-of-the-road understanding of faith and our actions and to avoid any form of extremism in any manner of belief, action, law, or practice. God encourages such a position, giving further incentive by saying in verse 160 that any good deed and position will be rewarded ten times, whereas an evil will be requited only to the extent that such evil deserves, thereby implying that we ought to demonstrate a propensity to unity ten times greater than to division.

One could also argue that Muslims, Christians, and Jews are themselves major sects of a common faith, a faith that the Qur'an codifies as the *"faith of Abraham"* and a faith to which both Jews and Christians lay claim. The majority of Muslims on the middle road like to think that Islam came to unify such division and continue to believe in a world where such unity is possible even though some of the fundamentalists, extremists, evangelical Christians and orthodox Jews would think and aspire otherwise.

25. Good works are rewarded disproportionately more than evil works are requited (6:160)

In this single verse, which has been repeated with similar examples in a number of other places in the Qur'an, God establishes a simple and pragmatic concept of reward and punishment and makes the commitment that no human being will be wronged by God even by a small margin. This is also a reminder for human beings and human societies of how to treat our citizens when good works dominate evil works and the sheer abundance of good works is brought about because we go out of our way to encourage, facilitate, and reward what is good while enacting a measured and commensurate deterrent and punishment against evil to minimize the presence of evil while not being judgmental or wrongful to those who engage in such evils.

The Qur'an declares that when someone brings about a good work, God (hence, by implication, society) will reward such a work tenfold. We need to be creative as to what tenfold means, recognizing that while God in His infinite capacity and resources will find ways to provide rewards in multiple ways, we in society should also seek and best leverage our resources to encourage, sustain, and multiply such good work. In the same vein, God declares that if someone brings about an evil work, his or her requital will be of similar measure, not any harsher than such evil work deserves when the overriding desire and intent is to stop the evil and not to be unjust to the individual.

In the United States, for example, too many people are put in jail for minor crimes such as shoplifting, while very little effort is being made to help them reform their behavior or find the underlying social dynamics that lead to such behavior. It is also the case that African Americans are disproportionately put in jail for such crimes, which points to biases and injustices that need to be corrected.

A tradition of the Prophet Mohammad corroborates this principle with a story that tells of interactions between God, the Angels, and humans. To bring accountability to human beings and to document their activities in this life, it has been mentioned a number of times (see, for example, 36:12) that God assigns Angels to watch over each human being and records all that he or she does. A pair of Angels is assigned to record keeping and follows a set of instructions that originated in this conversation between angel and God:

Angel to write good deeds: God, how would you like me to record the good works of a human being?

God: When a human being intends to do good, record it and assign one reward for such a good thought. When he or she follows through with the good intentions and accomplishes a good deed, record it and assign ten rewards.

Angel to write evil deeds: God, how would you like me to record the evil deeds of a human being?

God: If a person intends to do evil things or has an evil thought, do not write anything; perhaps he or she will not follow through. But if he or she does commit an evil deed, record it and assign one unit of punishment commensurate with the particular evil act committed.

One of God's names is Knower of Subtlety (*Al-Lateef*), Who has a deep and nuanced understanding of His creation. The challenge of human civilization over the years has always been to accumulate such details; nuanced understanding; and appreciation of our own existence, purpose in life, and how we operate as individuals and as communities to improve our human condition and alignment with God.

26. The faith of Abraham is what one should strive for (6:161–164)

A lot has been written about Abraham in the Torah, the Bible, and the Qur'an, and there have been many references to Abraham in Islamic traditions and Jewish oral traditions, tying the three predominantly Abrahamic faith communities—Jews, Christians, and Muslims—in a tight spiritual bond. This bond has not always been a healthy one, though, since each of these faith groups would rather believe that Abraham belongs to them to the exclusion of others, while some of the secular people are bewildered by some of the epic stories around Abraham, such as attempting to sacrifice his son at the command of God. There is also discord as to which of Abraham's sons was part of the story—Isaac or Ishmael—since the Jewish and Christian faiths draw their lineage back to Abraham through Isaac, and the Islamic faith draws it lineage to Abraham through Ishmael. This is further conflicted by the mention of Ishmael in the Qur'an as the son who was to be sacrificed, while the Bible mentions Isaac as the son to be sacrificed.

In any event, the Qur'an is very emphatic about the unity of faith in One God and upholds Abraham as the sublime symbol of a person's of faith in God and as one who demonstrated a lifelong pursuit of goodness and fervently wished that future generations would continue his path of enlightenment and not fall back to his father's generation's idol worship and ignorance.

In these verses and several other places in the Qur'an (for example, 98:5), the right path and the right religion is defined in its core elements of devotion to God, being just and upright, and serving the people, and these core attributes are then intimately tied to the life and practices of Abraham and subsequent prophets such as Moses, Jesus, and Mohammad. These powerful sets of verses call for our inner consciousness to rise to the truth about God, about faith, and about our pursuits in life with a strong reminder that each soul will be burdened by its evils or enlightened by its goodness, and no soul will be made to account for others but for itself.

27. We are constantly being asked to make informed choices and act responsibly (6:164–165)

I have titled this volume *Social Consciousness* precisely because of an abundance of verses in the Qur'an that point to our individual and collective responsibility to be informed and make informed choices at every stage of life and at every fork in the road that life leads us to. It is not where we are but how we behave is more critical. Circumstances that we find ourselves in are not always in our control, but how we behave is in our control—if not at a physical level, then certainly at a conscious level. Hence the guidance from the Prophet Mohammad is very revealing. He said that if you face or witness an act of injustice, you should actively engage to stop such injustice. If you can't do that, then you should speak up against such injustice. Even if you can't do that, then at least you should despise such injustice, and that is the lowest manifestation of faith and goodness.

Each of us is endowed with specific core capabilities, knowledge, aspirations, resources, and experiences that make us unique, just like fingerprints or brain scans, and each day shapes and reshapes those core attributes in every generation as a natural construct from God. Some individuals have been gifted more than others, some nations excel over others, some positions in our businesses and institutions have more authority than others, but in each case, there is a corresponding obligation, responsibility, and choice ability that ultimately defines who we are and what our accomplishments will be. The Qur'an makes it explicit by stating that *"God will try you with what He has blessed you with,"* and He will take *"prompt requital"* as He pleases. God also provides an assurance that we all can take a note of and emulate in our lives, and that is that He is Ever Forgiving and Merciful to His creation.

In this instance, a conversation of Moses with his people is very instructional as related in the Qur'an (7:129). In one of the darkest days in the life of the Israelites, when Moses was present and they were still in the clutches of the Pharaoh, the people gathered around Moses and expressed their despair—Moses, we were oppressed before you, and we see no abatement in sight even when you are with us. One can only imagine the gathering and the raw sentiments that were expressed, which could mean one of two things: they were calming themselves to endure such conditions with faith in God and confidence in Moses, or they were bitterly complaining that Moses had done nothing to change their condition.

Moses on the other hand, while being fully aware of the current and extreme difficulties faced by his people, was more focused on the future of his people and human beings in general. He did not know how things would turn out and certainly had self-doubt at that moment, but he always had faith that God would deliver him and his people from the Pharaoh eventually. He made the following profound statement that would serve every generation of faithful - Jews, Christians, and Muslims alike. He said: Perhaps God will deliver you from your current difficulties, but then He will see how you behave in turn. This is the quintessential human challenge, and our current generation is failing in so many different dimensions, whether it is poverty, pollution, income inequality, partisan politics and political corruption, ethnic cleansing, or wide-scale dismantling of civil liberties in the name of counterterrorism or one-party rule, just to name a few of the problems of our generation that need to be reversed with a sense of urgency and dedication.

CHAPTER 7

Surah Al-Araf (The Elevation)

(206 verses in total; Revealed in Makkah)

THIS CHAPTER (*SURAH*) GETS ITS name from its mention of people who will be at an elevated place on the Day of Judgment, when they will be able to see people in Heaven and in Hell and fully recognize their own predicament, as they are not sure which way they will land as Judgment Day continues. These people will engage in conversation with those who are in Heaven to wish them peace and congratulate them on their success and to aspire their own future with them. They will also engage with people who are in Hell to question them on their claims during their lifetime that made them arrogant, overconfident in their future, and unwilling to accept the concept of faith and goodness as being the core set of values that defines ultimate success of a human being.

The notion of elevation also implies a higher level of intellectual and spiritual capability to discern and discriminate between good and evil and a resultant aspiration and strive to align oneself with what is good and wholesome. This surah in a way is a manifestation of this constant yearning of a human soul for alignment with its true nature, the nature of God, and the natural world that we are part of. Starting with the opening statement to embrace God's guidance by reflecting on our ancestors—Adam and Eve and their experience with Devil—brings in a sense of devotion to God and a sense of responsibility in our personal and collective consciousness and interactions, avoiding all forms of indecencies and injustice, establishing rule of law and personal tranquility, striving for truth and justice, and so on.

This surah provides stories of a number of biblical prophets in a sequential manner, in a way that would assure the Prophet Mohammad and his followers that they are being given the same universal message of Oneness of God and goodness of humanity that they needed to establish, preserve, and propagate among the people of the world. The story of Moses takes a special place and receives emphasis in this surah with the recognition of the followers of Moses as people who were the recipients of special attention from God and were made an example of how caring God is for His creation, despite our repeated failures and unwillingness to conform to God's vision. Below is a list of key concepts that show the breadth and depth of guidance, encouragement, cautions, and discernments God wishes us to consider during our life on this planet and our journey back to Him. These key concepts are then elaborated at the end of the chapter.

List of key concepts:

1. Embracing guidance with open arms (1–3)
2. All will be questioned, even the prophets (6–9)
3. Earth is a source of provision and a proving ground (10, 24–25, 27, 34)
4. The Devil's plan against human beings is all inclusive (11–27)
5. Adam and Eve's first repentance (23)
6. Sense of responsibility for life *(Taqwa)* as protection against evil (26, 35)
7. Genuine worship and devotion to God (29, 31–32, 204–206)
8. All forms of indecency are forbidden (33, 28)
9. Salvation is through faith in God and humility (40–44, 55–56)
10. The final sequel to the Qur'an (52–53)
11. God, the Creator Supreme and Provider (54–58)
12. The rule of law and tranquility (56)
13. Nature as a constant reminder (57–58)
14. The prophets as guides—Noah, Hud, Salih, Lot, and Shu'aib (59–93)
15. God's challenge and warning to people (94–99)
16. Human failure to maintain God's covenant (100–102)

17. Lessons from Moses (103–129, 148–156)
18. The Prophet Mohammad as a guide (157–158)
19. Moses's followers recognized (159)
20. Human failings and successes (168–170)
21. God reveals to us all (172–174)
22. The inability to use God-given endowments (179–180)
23. Seeking truth and doing justice (181, 159)
24. Our tendency to associate others with God (189–191)
25. Simple guidance of forgiveness, goodness, and knowledge (199)

CHAPTER 7

Verses 1–18

In the name of God, the most Merciful and the Instiller of Mercy [to His creatures].

Alif Lam Mim Swad. (This is) A Book that has been inspired to you. Let there be no doubt about it in your heart so that you may caution people with it, and it may serve as a conscious reminder for those who have attained faith. Follow what has been revealed to you from your Sustainer God and take no others besides Him as Guardians; little it is that you reflect to develop consciousness.

How many communities (that were unmindful) have We brought to their consequences [ruins] while they rested at night or slept at noon? When they suddenly faced their consequences due, their only response was: "Indeed, we have done wrong (to ourselves)!" We [God] will question everyone who received the message, and We will question the message bearers as well so that We can confer to them realities (of life and their doings); We are never absent (from their lives). On that day judgment will be rendered with truth and fairness—for those whose good deeds outweigh their evil deeds will be successful, whereas those whose evils outweigh their goodness will have destroyed themselves because of their rejection of God's messages. You should know that We have given you firm footings on this planet Earth and provided all means to sustain your lives; yet you hardly ever give thanks (to God).[360]

We (God) created you and shaped you (physically and with human intellect and choices) and said to the Angels: "Submit to Adam." They all submitted except Iblis (the Devil), who did not follow through (see also 2:34, 15:28, 20:116). He (God) said (to the Devil): "What got in the way when I commanded you to submit (to Adam)?" He (the Devil) said: "I am better than him (Adam); You created me from fire, whereas you created him from dust (see also 3:59)." God said: "You are removed from your current state; you cannot behave arrogantly (in this state); go forth, and you will be among those who are humiliated." The Devil pleaded: "Respite me till the day people will be resurrected." God replied: "Yes, you are those who have been given such respite." The Devil asserted: "Since You caused my downfall (on their account), I will lie in wait for them along Your Straight Path; I will approach them from their front, from behind them, from their right and from their left. You will find most of them not thankful to You." God replied: "Be gone as despised and disowned. Whoever among the people follow you, I will certainly bring its consequences [Hellfire] to you all."[361]

[360] These few verses provide spiritual nourishment and encouragement to the Prophet to have firm conviction in the revelations and inspirations he had received from God. He is expected to demonstrate and effectively communicate to mankind that God alone is the source of every creation, our lives, and our purpose. We need to develop consciousness regarding our origin and bring purpose to our existence. God not only created us but also made the planet Earth suitable for human habitation and provided all that is necessary to sustain and uplift our lives. Being thankful to God is something we should all strive for. Lack of such thankfulness and ignoring the guidance from God will cause our fall from His grace. Such failures can manifest suddenly or gradually over our lifetime so that when we become aware of such an outcome, we have very little opportunity to correct it; we can only regret the wrongful turns in our lives.

[361] The fall of the Devil (Iblis) from God's grace is another example that reinforces the consequences of arrogance and misplaced pride that destroy our existence and our individual souls in the eyes of God and in the eyes of mankind. The story of Adam and Eve and the Devil is repeated several times in the Qur'an (chapters 2, 7, and 20) over many years to be a constant reminder of our humble

origin with divine grace; the fall of the Devil for not honoring Adam as God commanded, due to his pride and arrogance; our fall from grace as Adam and Eve listened to the misinformation from the Devil and wished for something that only God could grant (the desire for permanency); and the Devil's securing permission from God to tempt and lead people away from goodness toward evil, only to be a party to his misfortune.

REFLECTION

The stories of Adam and Eve and the Devil; the nature of our creation and the natural world to sustain us; and our godly endowment of knowledge, wisdom, and choice—these are collective sources of guidance that comes from the Creator Himself so that we can become conscious and purpose-filled human beings and human communities.

ACTION

Pride and arrogance have no place in our human discourse, and exercising our knowledge and wisdom through proper understanding of our creation and existence on this planet is something that each and every one of us is capable of doing and should strive for to attain God's grace and to create a peaceful world.

Key Arabic terms
107: *khalaqnakum summa sawwarnakum* (created and shaped you)
108: *aghwaitani* (the fall from grace, life made evil, or to be disappointed)

CHAPTER 7

Verses 19–31

(God said): "O Adam, enjoy life in Heaven with your wife and partake of anything it has to offer, but do not approach this tree lest you commit an act of injustice (against yourselves)." But the Devil whispered to them otherwise to expose to them their sense of shame and evil that was hitherto unknown to them and said: "Your Cherisher God forbade this tree lest you become Angels and be of the immortals." He then swore to them: "I am an honest adviser to you (both)."

This is how he (the Devil) caused them to fall from grace by his deceit. So once they had tasted from the tree, they became aware of their nakedness, and they began to cover themselves with leaves from the garden. (God) called out to them: "Did I not forbid you about this tree and also say to you that the Devil is an enemy always ready (to act against your interest)?" They both replied: "O, Our Sustainer God, we have wronged ourselves; unless you forgive us and show mercy on us, we both will be among those who have lost their way."[362]

God said: "Go forth (to the earth), some of you adversaries of others. On the earth you will have your living quarters and your livelihood for a time. It is here that you will live, it is here that you will die, and from here you will be raised (on the Day of Resurrection)."

O Children of Adam (and Eve): We (God) have enabled you to fabricate clothing with which to cover your shame (unlike other animals) and to beautify yourself, but the best of clothing is consciousness and a sense of duty [taqwa]. Such is the message from God so that you become mindful. O

Children of Adam (and Eve): Do not let the Devil deceive you as he caused your parents (Adam and Eve) to be expelled from Heaven [Jannah: garden of peace] and removed their garments (physical and spiritual) to expose their shamefulness (nakedness). The Devil and his hosts can see you, whereas you are (at times) unable to see or perceive them. We (God) have made the Devil (and all your evil thoughts and acts) aligned with those who deny faith in God (and in goodness).

When such people commit an indecent (and unjust) act, they say: "We found our forefathers doing the same, and God has prescribed us to do it (as well)." Say (to them): "God never prescribes indecency (and unjust acts)! Do you ascribe to God something that you have no basis for (no knowledge of)?" Say (to them): "My Cherisher God only commands what is just and what is right. Devote yourself wholeheartedly in every act of worship of God, and seek his blessing with sincerity, and be true to His guidance. (Remember that) He is the One Who brought you into existence, and to Him you will return."

A group He (God) has guided but another group strayed from guidance as a consequence of what they did—they preferred the Devil, instead of God, as their guardian in life, and they think they are on the right track. O Children of Adam (and Eve): Conduct yourself most beautifully in every act of worship, partake freely in every nourishment (God had provided), and be measured in your consumptions. God does not like those who are wasteful.[363]

---

[362] The story of Adam and Eve is repeated several times in the Qur'an, along with the story of their destined life on this planet. They were endowed with knowledge and understanding that even the Angels were not privy to or endowed with. With that knowledge came the obligation to be actively conscious of their responsibility toward each other, toward God, and to the world around them and to make informed and sound choices with their God-given freedom. The tree represents a token of what was to come and how to exercise our free will, and the Devil represents all the evil inclinations within us and the source of evil temptations and counsel from outside. The failure of Adam and Eve to follow God's guidance, to doubt His instruction, to fall prey to the Devil's deception and their subsequent forgiveness by God due to their genuine and timely remorse are all things that will be played out in each of our lives on this planet.

³⁶³ The presence on this planet is transient, as we all know. *"We are from God, and to Him we all return"* (2:156) is the central truth of our existence on this planet, as is also confirmed in these verses when God told Adam and Eve to descend to earth, where they would find provisions for life and a fixed term to fulfill. Along with that destination came instructions and guidance on how to navigate and fulfill the commitment that God took from us to use our knowledge and consciousness. Clothing that we wear to protect and beautify ourselves is a physical gift from God, but more important is the gift of knowledge and consciousness (*taqwa*), which is a spiritual gift to sustain our moral, ethical, and human imperatives in our individual lives and collective society. This inner gift gets exposed and becomes evident only through education, reflection and retrospection, devotion to truth and the realities of this universe, and a sustained effort to connect with God and fellow humans. A proper balance in our physical existence and consumption with our spiritual commitment to God and human dignity is the real intent as well as a test that we will need to fulfil and pass as individuals and as communities all over the world.

REFLECTION

Storytelling is a central element in all Books of Revelations. We as human beings are deeply connected to the common human stories and human conditions that we can innately experience within us, especially the story of Adam and Eve, who represent the beginning as well as the essence of our human existence. Being conscious of our story, our origin, our purpose in life, and our covenant with the Creator God is essential to a successful life journey.

ACTION

In one of his famous prayers, the Prophet Mohammad implored God to increase his knowledge. But at the same time, he also asked God to keep him away from knowledge that did not benefit anyone. By this he was not saying that he wanted to shy away from knowledge but, rather, he wanted to understand the implications and responsibilities that come with knowledge—that is, every gift of knowledge should be directed to benefit human beings and uplift human conditions on this planet.

Key Arabic terms
109: *sawatihima* (of their shame or nakedness)
110: *khasirin* (loser, or to be lost)
111: *rishan* (bird's plumage, feathers that beautify)
112: *quist* (what is right, what is just)

CHAPTER 7
Verses 32–41

Say: "Who forbids what God provides—beautifications and protections for life and wholesome provisions for sustenance—given to those who believe (to share with others) in this life, exclusively for them on the Day of Resurrection?" This is how We (God) make clear the messages for those who wish to know. Say: "My Cherisher God only forbids shameful actions and conduct, be they done openly or in secret; vices and any rebellious act without justification; any association with God without authority directed by Him and saying anything concerning God that you have no knowledge of." For every society, there is a period of performance set; when that term expires, no one can delay it by an hour or advance it.

O Children of Adam (and Eve): Whenever a Messenger from among you comes to convey My (God's) messages and guidance, whoever then becomes conscious (of their responsibilities) and acts in goodness, they will have no reason to fear nor any reason to regret, whereas those who deny Our messages and guidance out of arrogance, it is they who will face Hellfire and remain therein.

Who is more corrupt than the one who invents lies against God or denies His messages? They will face whatever their books (they follow) prescribe (for such corruption) until the Angel of Death (a messenger from God) comes to them to cause their death and asks: "Where are those that you used to call in devotion besides God?" They will reply: "These (entities) have departed us." This is how they will refute themselves and bear witness that they were not believers.

He (God) will say: "*Enter and join those nations from men and Jinn in the Hellfire.*" *Every time a new group comes in, it will blame its sister group until all of them have followed one another, and the last group will say, regarding the first group:* "*O our Sustainer, these are the ones who led us away (from Your guidance); so double the torment of fire for them.*" *God will reply:* "*It is doubled for everyone, but you do not realize that.*" *The first group will then call out to the last group:* "*You have no preference over us. Suffer then the consequence of what you have earned (just like us).*"

Those who deny God's message and behave arrogantly regarding such messages, the door of the sky will not open for them, nor will they enter Paradise until a camel can pass through the eye of a needle. This is how the guilty will be rewarded for what they earned. The Hellfire will be a bed and a covering for them; this is how the corrupt will be rewarded for what they have earned.[364]

---

[364] The choices that one should make are made very clear in these verses. Each generation of mankind must become acquainted with the guidance that came from God and use their God-given intuition, knowledge, and inner spirit to comprehend the natural order of things and the purposefulness of this life—a preponderance of goodness and humility; the absence of malice, sin, corruption, and pride; the acknowledgment of God as Creator and Sustainer; and the rejection of any false attribution to Him. Lacking such belief and conduct leads to the demise of each nation and each group at the end of their term set by God, a term sufficient to prove otherwise. Our lack of desire and will to correct ourselves and conform to the truth and the guidance in our own individual lifetime as well as the lifetime of each nation will lead to eventual consequences that are sure to come. Such eventualities have been brought to life in these verses through conversations that will take place among people, nations, Angels of death, and God Himself regarding the denial of truth and failure to accept the essential guidance from God.

REFLECTION

Belief in matters unseen such as life after death, the Day of Judgment, and Heaven and Hell, and deeper reflection on the central notion of accountability regarding our actions as individuals, groups, communities, and nations are to be taken seriously by every one of us. Those who cause injustice and those who accept such injustice are to be blamed equally and, in that sense, we are accountable not only for what we do but what we do not do. Blaming others for our failures, using unjust means to correct an injustice, expropriating wealth to a few in the name of profit, and exploiting natural resources to create imbalances in nature are becoming the mainstay of our societies—both developed and underdeveloped.

ACTION

For us not to pay attention to the Books of Revelations from God that are among us, not to listen to our inner consciousness that is already endowed with goodness and justice, not to consume natural resources in an equitable fashion among the people of the world, and so on are matters of serious concern in regard to our moral standards, ethical norms, principles of social justice, and the purposefulness of our existence as God's special creation.

Key Arabic terms

113. *fawahisha* (shameful, indecent), *bag'ye* (rebellion, unjustified chaos), *tushriku* (any divine association with God)

114. *azalun* (appointment, period of performance or test)

CHAPTER 7

Verses 42–53

Those who believe and who do good (it is all within your ability) as We do not put a burden on any soul beyond what it can bear—these are the companions of Paradise where they will reside. We will cleanse them of any ill feelings in their hearts, and water will flow beneath their feet. They will say: Thanks to God Who guided us to this (outcome)! We could not have found guidance if God had not guided us. (We knew that) the Messengers of God came with the truth from our Sustainer God. And it will be declared to them: "This is the Garden (Paradise) you have inherited by what you did (in your life on the earth)." The residents of Paradise will call out to the residents of Hellfire: "We have found the promise of our Sustainer to be true. Have you found the same to be true?" They (from Hellfire) will say: "Yes." At this point an announcer will pronounce: "The displeasure of God is on those who are evil, who take people away from God's path and distort the truth; they were truly in denial of the life after death." (God will place) a veil between them (separating Paradise and Hell).

There is a group of people, discerning and aware of all the markers of truth, but not permitted to enter Paradise yet, which they fervently hope for, who will call out to the residents in Paradise: "Greeting of peace to you all." And as they glance at the residents of Hellfire, they cry out: "Our Sustainer God, may you not place us with these evil people." Again, the people discerning and having known the markers (of those who will find themselves in Hellfire) will call out: "Your arrogance and your accumulation of wealth (and power) were of no use. Is it about these people (who are now in Paradise) that you used to swear by God that they would have no mercy (from God)?" (God will now permit them to) enter Paradise, where you will have no fear and no reason to grieve!

The residents of Hellfire will call out to the residents of Paradise: "Could you pour us some water or give any provision God had given you?" They (the residents in Paradise) will reply: "Both are denied to those who have denied faith in God—who neglected the guidance and made fun of it and were deceived by their earthly life." Therefore, this day We (God) will forsake them, as they were oblivious of this day of meeting (with their Creator), and they denied Our messages—a book that We brought to them to clarify things with knowledge, guidance, and mercy; for those who care to believe! Are they really waiting for the its finality—on the Day when it will come (all truth will become manifest), those we were unmindful of it will say: "(We do now realize) that the Messengers of God came with truth; is there anyone who can intercede on our behalf? Is there a way for us to go back so that we could do things differently than we did before?" These are the ones who have wasted their lives, and whatever errant beliefs they resorted to have failed them.[365]

---

[365] These verses offer a glimpse of life as it will unfold on the Day of Judgment so that we can visualize and perhaps develop a better appreciation for our present life and what is to come next. God starts out by saying that He never puts a task on a soul that is more than it is capable of handling or achieving, meaning that the ability to understand what is good and what is evil and to develop and sustain faith with goodness is already built into us ("*God breathed His spirit into every soul*"). Our ability to shape our lives and our societies on a path to peace and prosperity has also been motivated and guided by revelations and a constant flow of messengers throughout the ages so that we have no excuse that we did not know what to do or how to do it.

Now comes the visualization so that we can move to the future and see the state of affairs as it unfolds. Those who struggled for honor and dignity in this world through faith and good works and building societies on principles of truth, justice, and human dignity will be rewarded with Paradise, a place that each of us aspires to and strives toward. God rewards with Paradise those who have proved beyond doubt their abiding faith in God and persistent exertion to better the world—that is, those who have struggled to create a semblance of paradise on this planet will be rewarded with the real Paradise on the Day of Judgment. Then there are those who perhaps had faith, knew all the markers of good and bad, but perhaps did not do their utmost to shape their lives and societies accordingly. God will intimate to them the consequences of Paradise and Hellfire as they unfold in front of them on the Day of Judgment. As God says in chapter 102, *"They will see with their own eyes and know with certainty on a Day when they will be questioned about their lives."* (102:7-8). This is a scenario being played forward for us so that we can visualize and perceive the realities that we will come face to face with, something that we cannot avoid.

The dire condition of those who will find themselves in Hellfire is also given. Their realization of the truth and their mistakes and misdeeds will become transparent to them, but there will be no turning back.

REFLECTION

Without proper reflection and deeper contemplation, one cannot fully appreciate life and its purpose. The constant presence of prophets, messengers, and people of goodwill among us; the Books of Revelations that we can read; the constant yearning and reminders in our soul and inner consciousness about goodness and truth and the feeling and reasoning that God embedded in our physical makeup to discern evils—these all are tools and resources at our disposal given by God as manifestations of His mercy to mankind and a promise He made to Adam and Eve to protect and preserve them from the Devil and his mischief.

ACTION

Not paying attention to these realities, not using the tools at our disposal, and not being driven by godliness and goodness is a serious malaise that we cannot afford as individuals and as societies. As God said, *"We do not change the condition of a people unless they bring change in themselves."* (13:11) This is a rule that we must fully understand and implement to prove our worth as His superior creation.

CHAPTER 7

Verses 54–58

Your Sustainer God is the One Who created the universe and this planet Earth in six stages [periods, days] (see also: 41:9–12) and took control of their affairs; He lets the night overtake the day in constant pursuits; the sun, the moon, and the stars follow His commands. His is the creation, and His is the command and control (of it)—this is how Blessed and Hallowed is the Cherisher of the Universe (God)![366]

Resort to your Sustainer God in humility and in your private moments. He certainly disdains transgressions of any kind. Do not make mischief and corruption on earth after it is made to conform (to human and natural orders) and refer to God with consciousness and ardent aspirations. God's mercy and blessings are ever present to those who do good.[367]

He (God) is the One that sends the wind bearing news of His impending mercy—clouds laden (with moisture and water) and driven (by wind) to a land devoid of life and pouring down abundant water, which causes all kinds of fruits (and vegetation) to come forth. This is how We (God) extract the dead (and the living) so that you can be thoughtful and mindful. Good soil gives vegetation in abundance by the grace of its Cherisher, and the soil less fertile produces but in smaller quantity. This is how We repeat messages and change signs (in nature) that you may appreciate and become thankful.

[366] The Qur'an as a revealed book from God inspires people and educates us through two key sources: (1) the Qur'an itself as a book that contains knowledge

and guidance about our creation; our purpose; the rules of mutual conduct; the rules of spiritual, moral, ethical, financial, social, and political standards; universal norms around human equality and social justice; and so on, and (2) the universe itself, which contains our planet, the solar system, millions of sunlike stars, and the physical laws that govern such a universe, with particular attention given to the Earth itself, which is the source of our sustenance in the forms of air, water, protective atmosphere, the fertile soil with minerals and chemicals, the natural resources underground and in the oceans, and the way life and living beings evolved with extraordinary variations governed by the rhythms of life played by the constant exchange of life and death, day and night, good and evil, past and future, young and old, and so on. The instructions and wisdom contained in the Qur'an are considered signs from God for one to understand, comprehend, and act upon. In a similar manner, the universe and the natural world as we experience it from this earth are also considered signs of God and another Open Book to take lessons from and to reflect on. Our natural inclinations to love, mercy, truth, human equality, and social justice conform to the signs in the Qur'an, and our science and technological progress are nothing more than what already exists in the natural world; God is only enabling us to uncover the natural laws and nature of matter and spirits to benefit from.

367 Lessons and action should be governed by deep reflection on our lives and on the Creator Himself with a sense of humility, wonder, and genuine appreciation in our own private moments about our life and our creation and the world we live in. Preserving peace and social justice and the social and natural order of things is not only a spiritual calling but also a human responsibility. Preventing corruption from spreading; resisting any temptation to transgress against the natural order of things, be it our environment, our social order and justice, inherent human dignity and peaceful coexistence; sustaining good over evil, love over hate, and forgiveness over revenge; and so on are the real challenges and real signs of our human condition that can come from God consciousness and an ardent aspiration to be a good human being.

REFLECTION

Reflecting on and learning from what we read of revelations and our ever-expanding human knowledge, as well as our seeing and being constantly exposed to this planet Earth, with its magnificent beauty, abundance of life-giving capacity and resources, awesome variety of life and living are a true gift from God that every sensible and thoughtful human being should pay attention to and become responsible about.

ACTION

All knowledge, awareness, and deeper consciousness has to translate into meaningful action that makes our lives, our experiences, and our human existence better for all of us—this is the ultimate test of our humanity and a test that God is ever taking account of to see how we behave on this planet before we go back and meet our Creator!

Key Arabic Terms
115: *sittati iyyamin* (six days, periods, stages)
116. *astawa alal a'rsh* (took possession, power, or control of its affairs)

CHAPTER 7

Verses 59–72

We (God) sent Noah to his people, and he said to them: "O my people, serve God; you have no other deity besides Him. I worry about the consequences for you on that Day of Difficulty." The leaders of his community said: "We think he is clearly wrong." To which Noah replied: "There is no error in me, as I am the messenger sent by the Cherisher of the Universe. I deliver to you the guidance from my Sustainer, and I offer good counsel; I know from God what you do not know. Are you somewhat bewildered that a message and a reminder from your Sustainer God is being delivered by someone from among you, that I may caution you and make you conscious of your responsibility and you can be among those who are shown His mercy?" But they rejected him; so We [God] gave him and his followers in the Ark safe passage while We drowned those who denied Our Guidance. They were people who were indeed blinded (by their ignorance and arrogance)![368]

We (God) sent Hud (as a prophet) to the people of 'Ād (a descendant of Noah)—he was a member of their community, and he said: "O my people, serve God; besides Him, you have no other deity. Will you not be conscious of your responsibility?" Their leaders, who were steeped in denial, said to him: "You have foolish ideas, and you are a liar." He said: "O my people, I have no folly in me, and I am a messenger from the Cherisher of the Universe! I deliver guidance from my God, and I am here to provide counsel in good faith. Do you find it strange that your God has sent someone who is from among you so that he may caution you (in a way that you can relate to)?

*Reflect on the fact that God has established you on the land as a successor to Noah and multiplied your power and possessions. Therefore, be mindful of God's favors so that you can attain success."*³⁶⁹

His people said: "Have you come to us to tell us to worship God alone and reject others that our forefathers worshipped? You might as well bring us the consequence that you speak about, assuming you are truthful." Hud replied: "Surely evil practices (of worship of idols) and God's displeasure is already on you. Do you dispute with me about deities that you and your forefathers invented without any confirmation from God Himself? Let's then wait (for the consequences)! I too am waiting with those who wait (and have patience). We (God) saved him and those who stood by him and brought destruction (through a violent storm; see 69:7) to those who denied Our Guidance; they were not believers at all.

---

³⁶⁸ According to Islamic tradition, God sent upward of 120,000 prophets and messengers to various communities around the world, starting with Adam, as God promised to Adam and Eve prior to their life on earth. In these and other verses, the stories of Noah, Hud, and other prophets were presented from a historical perspective to lend credibility to the promise that God made to Adam and Eve that He would provide guidance to mankind so that they would be informed and counseled by their own kind and could not claim later that they were uninformed about God and the realities of life and its purpose. Such stories also assured the Prophet and his followers that history was on their side and that their cause would prevail in the long run, though there would be opposition and difficulties in the present moment. These narratives further confirm the unity of God and the unity of God's guidance throughout human history.

The stories of Noah are mentioned in twenty different places in the Qur'an, including chapter 71, which is devoted wholly to the story of Noah, while the stories of Hud appear in fourteen different places—each instance coming in a different context, with a different aspect of the story brought into focus each time, along with the repetition of the central themes of the unity of God, human consciousness, the pride and arrogance of people who deny such truth, and the humility of those who pay attention to such guidance. The ultimate success of the people of faith and goodness against the destruction of people who are arrogant and proud and deny God's grace is constantly explained so that people of all generations, no matter how trying the circumstances might be, can take a lesson, find hope, and stay focused on being just and pure. The Prophet Noah is mentioned (29:14–15) as having a long life of 950 years, and his Ark is preserved (54:9–16) to confirm his story for later generations.

369 The people of ʿĀd are known to be descendants of Aram ("Iram," 89:7), who was a grandson of Noah and preceded another group of people, the Thamud, mentioned later. In several places the ʿĀd and the Thamud are referred to in the same sentence because both were descendants of Noah and had similar social and human progress, ingenuity, and the practice of idol worship. Hud, sent to the people of ʿĀd, is known as the first Arabian prophet and could be identical to the biblical Eber, the ancestor of the Hebrews (Ibrim, Genesis 10:24–25, 11:14), who, like most of the Semitic tribes, may have originated in southern Arabia. The ancient name of Hud is still reflected in that of Jacob's son Judah (Yuhudah in Hebrew), which is perhaps the origin of the name of the Jews (Yahud in Arabic).

REFLECTION

Stories of prophets and other human beings of uncommon intellect, wisdom, and God consciousness are a reminder to all of us of our human possibilities and our human obligations to God and to one another. These stories inspire us, give us confidence, and make us aware of the higher purpose in life and how best to shape our presence on this planet.

ACTION

Human history and turns of events at various junctures of the human presence on this planet should provide us with an adequate assessment of our own condition and how to prioritize our lives in each generation. As Karen Armstrong has said, *"In Islam, Muslims have looked for God in history. Their sacred scripture, the Quran, gave them a historical mission. Their chief duty was to create a just community in which all members, even the most weak and vulnerable, was treated with absolute respect."* (*Islam: A Short History*, 2002 (preface ix, xi-xii))

CHAPTER 7

Verses 73–93

To the People of Thamud, We sent Salih, who was of them, and he said: "O my people, serve God; besides Him, you have no other deities. Your God has sent you guidance that can be easily understood. Here is a female camel, a sign (and trial, 54:27) from God; leave her alone to roam on God's earth and do her no harm, lest the evil consequence of your action touches you. Reflect how He (God) established you after 'Ād and settled you in the land, where you built castles in its valley and carved out dwellings on the mountainside. Remember such graces of God, and do not spread corruption in the land and make mischief."

Their proud leaders asked those who believed (in Salih's message) and those whom they deemed to be weaker (and less fortunate than themselves): "Do you know if Salih has been sent by his God?" They said: "We do believe in what he has been sent with." But those proud (leaders) replied: "We reject what you believe in." They then went ahead, tortured the she camel to death, revolted against guidance of God, and challenged Salih: "Bring on that punishment (evil consequence) that you warned us with if you are a messenger (from God)." The earthquake then overtook them, and they lay dead (motionless) in their own homes. So Salih moved on, saying: "O my people, I have delivered messages from my Sustainer and gave you good counsel, but you do not love such advisers (who give good advice)."[370]

(Similarly) We sent Lot, and he said to his people: "Do you commit an act so shameful that none have done this before in this world—you come on

221

to men in lust as opposed to women? You are a people who commit excess." His people had no other answer than to say: "Get him out of this town—he and his people aspire to purity!" We saved and delivered Lot and his followers, except his wife, who remained behind with others on whom We let torrents of rain descend. See then how we bring an end to those who are sinful.[371]

To the people of Midian, We sent one of them—Shuaib, who said: "O my people, worship God, besides Whom you have no other deities. Guidance has come to you from your Sustainer God; Give full measure, weigh (apportion) and give what is due to others without diminishing (by any means); do not spread corruption and mischief in the land after peace and order have been restored. This is better for you, if you care to believe. Do no put obstacles by threatening and deterring people who wish to believe in God and follow His guidance and do not attempt to distort the truth. You should remember when you were few in numbers and how God made you a larger community; you should also reflect on what happens to those who make mischief and spread corruption! Since there is a group of you who accept what I have been sent with and there is another party who does not; let's wait with patience (and give each other space to differ) until God provides His judgment between us since He is the Best of all Judges."

The leaders of his community, being arrogant and proud, said: "Shuaib, we will force you and those who believe with you from our town unless you come back to our religion." Shuaib replied: "(are you going to force us) even if we dislike it (your religion)? If we do go back to it after God has guided us, then we will be inventing a lie against God. We will not go back unless God, our Cherisher, wills as such. Our Sustainer encompasses all knowledge (so he is aware of our situation), and on Him do we rely. O our Sustainer, expose the truth between us and our community; You are the Best Exposure!"

The leaders of his community who disbelieved said (to others): "If you follow Shuaib, you will suffer losses." (Before they could carry out their threat), an earthquake (and/or volcanic eruption) overwhelmed them, and they were reduced to dead bodies, lying on the ground in their own homes. It was as if *they had never lived there; they, who called Shuaib a liar, turned out to be the real losers. As he turned away (from witnessing the calamity), he said: "O my people, I have communicated the guidance of my Sustainer God to you, and I have given you good counsel. So how can I now empathize with people who persistently deny (the truth)?"*372

370 Salih is mentioned about sixteen times in various chapters regarding his encounter with his community, Thamud, which is related to 'Ād and is descended from Aram and Noah, similar to 'Ād. The inscription of Sargon in the year 715 BC mentions the Thamud residing among the people of eastern and central Arabia. There are also mentions of the Thamud (Thamudaei, Thamudenes) in Aristo, Ptolemy, and Pliny. Rock inscriptions pertaining to their existence are still found in the region of Al-Hijr (15:80), northernmost Hijaz, and bordering Syria.

371 Lot, a nephew of the Prophet Abraham, is mentioned in greater detail in the surah *"Hud"* (11:69–83) and about twelve more times in various other places in the Qur'an, and he is also mentioned in the Bible (for example, Genesis 19:26). One of the major sins that is mentioned in relationship to Lot's people is the prevalence of coercive homosexuality, among many other corrupt social practices, false beliefs, and social injustices that the Qur'an does not go into detail about. The Qur'an also mentions that both Abraham and Lot pleaded with God for leniency, despite their transgressions, when Angels visited them regarding the future of Lot's community for their corruption and evil practices, about which the Bible contains more details. Some of the details in the Bible could be doubtful, since it also contains elements of moral lapse on the part of Lot that the Qur'an does not support or mention.

372 Shuaib is thought of as the biblical prophet Jethro, the father-in-law of Moses, also known as Reuel in the Bible (Exodus 2:18). The area of Midian (Madayin in the Qur'an) refers to areas of the present-day Gulf Coast of Aqabah and the Sinai Peninsula extending all the way to the Moab desert and mountains leading

to Dead Sea. The Qur'an brings to light a number of corrupt practices prevalent in their society:

- a lack of justice and fairness,
- defrauding people from what was justly due to them through various means (social, moral, and financial),
- the worship of multiple gods and forcing people to believe in their gods instead of One True God, and
- threating people with expulsion if they did not conform to their social and political norms, among other things.

REFLECTION

As we read the stories of various prophets and become aware of the moral, ethical, social, and financial lapses in their contemporary societies and the pride and arrogance with which these communities dealt with prophets and people who were preaching and practicing humility, social justice, and belief in One God, we have to be keenly aware of whether such practices exist in our contemporary world, perhaps in different forms and under the pretense of emerging social norms. We know and are aware of the cases of slavery on the American continent, the Holocaust in Europe, apartheid in South Africa, the atrocities of the Japanese against the Chinese, ethnic cleansing in Bosnia and Myanmar, the treatment of non-Arabs as second-class citizens in the Middle East, and the dehumanization of people in Palestine and Israel using faith as an excuse, just to name a few examples that have gained global currency. We also know of widespread political and financial corruption in many countries and in financial markets; alarming income disparities in the world; total disregard for the environment; the marginalization of human life and dignity in our political discourse, wealth propagation, and religious practices; and an unprecedented level of human anxiety at an individual level regarding terrorism and counterterrorism propagated by religious fanatics, terrorists, and civil societies alike.

ACTION

Every generation of human beings and societies will be challenged by the prevalence of corruption, moral lapses, the disturbance of human dignity, and the lack of social justice despite—or as a result of—our ever-increasing knowledge and God-given freedom of choice. At every fork of our human journey, we must make choices, individually and collectively, whether to use our collective knowledge, wisdom, and free choice to benefit humanity and our living planet or go down in history as the people who were bystanders to—or, worse still, perpetrators of—human indignity and abuse of our God-given talents and resources.

Key Arabic Terms
117. *fahishat* (despicable, shameful)

CHAPTER 7
Verses 94–102

We [God] do not send a Prophet to a land except that We make its inhabitants face misfortune and hardship (as a consequence of their conduct with respect to the prophet, his message, and social justice) so they (will have further reasons to reflect and) perhaps become humble. Then We shift their condition from difficulties to ease (and good as they perceive it) until they become affluent and self-assured and begin to convince themselves that hardship and difficulties were for previous generations only. Then We take them (to account for their conduct) by surprise while they are oblivious (to such outcome) (see also 6:41–46).

If the people of these towns believed (in God) and acted with conscience and a sense of responsibility, We would have opened up blessings from all around them—from the sky and the earth, in abundance. But they rejected (the message and did not strive to understand), and, as a result, We make them face the consequences. Do the people of these towns feel that such consequence will escape them while they sleep at night, or go on with their daily routines by day? Are they secure against what God plans (in response to their conduct)? No one should be so self-assured except those who wish to suffer losses.

Does it not occur to those who inherit the earth after its previous inhabitants that if We (God) please, We will take them to account for their sins and make their hearts incapable of comprehending (the truth)? Such were (the human conditions in those) towns whose narratives We bring to you (in the above stories). Surely such messengers came to each generation with comprehensible guidance, but they refused to accept (reconsider) what was rejected before (by their previous generations). This is how God incapacitates the hearts of those who deny the truth. We did not find in many of them a commitment to the natural order of creation (ahd—a bond with God), and we found most of them to trespass (the limits).[373]

[373] These verses draw our attention to the inevitable cycle of humanity's struggle with good and evil throughout human history. Prophets and messengers who are sent by God and other people of conscience, who come to acknowledge and act according to the realities of life and accept God's guidance as inspired by the Creator and Sustainer of mankind, bring such guidance and truth to the attention of all people in their communities and contemporary societies. The hardship, disappointments, physical ailments, loss of life and property, natural calamities, lack of control over events and outcomes, and so on are constant reminders that we are subject to a larger force and are part of a larger cosmos that we did not build, nor did we develop its inner workings. The sooner we acknowledge our origin and align ourselves with the natural order and natural bond (ahd—see term 18, volume 1) of things as they exist, the better we will be guided by God through His emissaries. The exercise of human freedom but acting with a sense of responsibility, an abundance of knowledge but putting it to useful purposes, the empowerment of individuals, communities, and nations with human capital, natural resources, intellectual prowess, and spiritual endowments—all of these can advance the causes of justice, human dignity and equality, good governance, civil society, and a sense of oneness of humanity in this global village of ours—a gift from God that should not be taken lightly.

Time and again, human societies, sometimes entirely and sometimes a group within a society, become lax to such commitments and ideals and perceive that the ease of life they master, the power they attain, and the intellect they gather as their own possessions and use them to exploit others; create social injustice and corruption; and accumulate more power and wealth through corrupt practices in governance, financial markets, business dealings, and conspiracies among the rich and the powerful. Every now and then, God restores order by overpowering one group by another and temporarily disrupting their living conditions as a consequence of their actions or lack thereof. But, more importantly, God wants us to consider the possibility that perhaps if we were to accept the natural order of things, be true to our inner compass that God has breathed into us, and genuinely endeavor to establish a society based on truth and goodness, the possibilities will be far greater than our current unjust and hasty ways to benefit a few at the expense of many.

REFLECTION

Being aware of the underlying dynamics of our society, understanding the power of faith in God and in our common humanity, and being committed to human equality and human dignity are the true drivers for human upliftment and the attainment of true purpose in life.

ACTION

As we read this book and other books of revelation and gather knowledge from all other fields of human endeavor and natural laws, we need to maintain a constant effort and vigilance in our education system, in our political environment, in our financial dealings and business activities, and in our relationships with other human beings and the natural world in which we live to be purpose driven for goodness and to improve human conditions. This is incumbent on each generation, and every one of us must play his or her unique role within his or her sphere of influence and relationships.

CHAPTER 7
Verses 103–129

(After these generations) We sent Moses to the Pharaoh and his chiefs with Our Guidance, but they rejected it; see then the end results of those who spread corruption. Moses said: "O Pharaoh, I am a messenger from the Sustainer of the Universe; I am prepared to say nothing but the truth about God. I have come with guidance from your Sustainer, and you should let the Children of Israel be free to go with me." He (the Pharaoh) replied: "Produce your evidence that you have come with if you speak the truth." Moses threw his walking stick, and it turned into a (fearsome) serpent clearly visible. He then spread his hand and it was shining (white with light) to the onlookers (see also Exodus, chapter 4).

The chiefs of the people of the Pharaoh said: "Indeed, Moses is a skilled magician, and he intends to drive us out of our land." The Pharaoh asked: "What is your advice?" They said: "Let him and his brother (Aaron) wait while we announce throughout the cities and towns and bring all skilled magicians to you." Once they all came, they asked the Pharaoh: "We sure expect a reward if we prevail over (Moses)." The Pharaoh promised: "Yes, you will be among my favored associates." They asked Moses: "Will you be the first to cast, or will we?" Moses said: "You go ahead." So they cast (their spell) and overwhelmed those in attendance with a fearsome display of sorcery and magic. We (God) inspired Moses to cast his stuff, and it overtook all that was on display of deception—thereby verifying the truth and reducing all they did to nothing. This is how they were put in their place, and they were humiliated (for their arrogance and falsehood). All the magicians prostrated (before God) and declared: "We do believe in the Sustainer of the Universe, the Sustainer of (spoken by) Moses and Aaron." The Pharaoh objected: "How did you offer such submission without my permission? I think it is a plot that you all have hatched in this city to cause commotions among people and drive them out. Be prepared then for the consequence (of such betrayal)—I will cut off your hands and your feet for your rebellion and will crucify you all together."

They all replied: "It is to our Sustainer God that we turn (for help and succor). It is because of our acceptance of the guidance of God that came to us that you now punish us. O our Sustainer God, enable us to have patience and make us approach (our impending) death with full submission (and reliance on you alone)."[374]

The chiefs among the Pharaoh's people counseled the Pharaoh: "Will you leave Moses and his people alone to cause disruption in our lands and to deny you and your gods?" The Pharaoh said: "We will kill the sons of Israelites and leave their women alone; we have power over them." Moses advised his people: "Turn to God for help and exercise patience (in this difficult time). The Earth belongs to God, and He makes among his servants whom He wills to inherit the land. In the end those who are conscious (of God) and demonstrate a sense of responsibility (to fellow humans) will have the upper hand." His people lamented: "We are being persecuted—before you came and since you have been here." Moses comforted (and cautioned) them: "It may well be that God will destroy your tormentor and give you a hand in overseeing the affairs of the land. God will see how you conduct yourselves then."[375]

---

[374] The story of Moses is repeated twenty-two times in various parts of the Qur'an, and, unlike the Torah and the Bible, which go into a lot of details as narratives, the focus of the Qur'anic narrative is always about moral of the story, lessons to be learned, and to be forward looking. The primary audience of the Qur'an at the time were Arabs who knew many of the stories of the Biblical prophets from the oral traditions of their Jewish and Christian neighbors and Christian monks who were spread in Arabian Peninsula. In a time when sorcery and magic were being practiced on a large scale and were used as instruments by the Pharaoh and his leaders to perpetuate their hegemony and false beliefs over people, God

sent Moses with capabilities that overpowered such practices in their own terms so that actual practitioners of these superstitions knew exactly that Moses came from the true God. As we know from the story of Moses, while the Pharaoh was planning to kill all the baby boys of the Israelites, God was planning to raise Moses in the household of the Pharaoh, unbeknownst to him—this is how subtle God's plan was, and He was the best of planner at the end.

375 The persecution of the people of Israel by the Pharaoh was indeed one of the worst that a community of human beings has ever endured. A similar persecution visited the Jewish people during the Holocaust in our contemporary times. The large-scale persecution of people has been witnessed in many places on earth throughout human history—the waves of Crusades by Christians against Muslims and Jews, the large-scale devastation of lands by the Mongols, the atrocities committed within European nations during World Wars I and II, the prolonged conflict between the Japanese and the Chinese, the atrocities of communist leaders against innocent citizens in Russia and China, and the history of apartheid in South Africa are examples of horrific crimes against humanity committed in the name of power and falsification of real issues and challenges. As God says elsewhere in the Qur'an, unless He empowers one group over another in turns, the human race will destroy itself and disrupt freedom to practice their faith and worship God as they see fit. As Moses alludes to in the above verses, as God makes a weaker nation to assume the upper hand, it will be watched by God to see how it behaves as it is given the opportunity to act freely, which it asked for under dire persecution and horrible human conditions. This is something that Muslims, Christians, and Jews who read the Torah, the Bible, and the Qur'an every day should pay a great deal of attention to, and they should strive to bring the world together and not split it further apart.

REFLECTION

Moses, as a great teacher and great prophet of Jewish people and of the people of Abrahamic faiths, stands as a torch bearer of human imperatives, as codified in the Ten Commandments. We all need to reflect on his teachings, his guidance, and his deep understanding of human conditions, which have been further corroborated by Jesus and Mohammad in subsequent generations.

ACTION

The time has come for us to bring unity in faith and unity in our common goodness. People of all faiths have to undertake this challenge and prove to God that given the opportunity, we will behave responsibly and not fall victim to the same immoral and unjust world that we have endured and have sought God's help to overcome.

CHAPTER 7

Verses 130–137

We overpowered the Pharaoh and his people with drought and reduction in food supply so that they might be reminded; but when good fortune came to them, they would say: "This is by us," and when any affliction came to them, they would say: "This is due to Moses and his people." (In reality) whatever befalls them, it is prescribed by God, but most of them are unaware. They refuted further: "Whatever means you (O Moses) may bring to charm us, we are not going to believe in you." So We sent widespread destruction and diseases from locusts, lice, frogs, and blood — evident manifestations (of God's displeasure) (see Exodus 7:10). Yet they responded with further arrogance; they were a people drawn to evil ways.[376]

When a plague would descend on them, they would appeal to Moses: "Pray on our behalf to your Sustainer with Whom you have a covenant (of prophethood)—if you can remove this plague, we will certainly believe in you and will let the Children of Israel go with you (O Moses)." But whenever we removed such plagues and gave them time (to make good on their promises), they failed (see Exodus 8:11). So We made them face the consequences, and We drowned them in the sea since they denied Our messages and were deliberately turning away (from such guidance).

We (God) enabled people who were considered weak (and dispossessed) to inherit the land, from its eastern side to the western side, a land We had blessed abundantly (see Genesis 17:8). It was a commitment that God fulfilled for the Children of Israel due to their patience (and perseverance) while

> *We brought down what the Pharaoh and his people accomplished and what they built.*[377]

[376] The Pharaoh and his people were tested by their wealth and power as well as by drought and shortages, in addition to the direct message and guidance brought by Moses and Aaron. As God repeated in the Qur'an, for every prophet there is an adversary, and for every nation to whom a prophet comes, there is a term set after which the matter is settled in accordance with the conduct of the people with respect to belief and the extent of their commitment to do no evil and to do good. History tells us that Moses was able to leave Egypt with the Children of Israel while the Pharaoh was drowned in the sea as he pursued Moses and his people. God mentioned in another narrative on Moses (10:90-92) that He preserved the body of the Pharaoh, which washed ashore for future generations. Egyptologists have determined that such a body was found and preserved in the Royal Mummies Chamber in Cairo Museum, Egypt. A number of movies have been made about Moses, based primarily on narratives in the Bible. The Qur'an provides the essential details needed to make the morale of the story become clear rather than dwelling on the minutiae that the previous scriptures go into, perhaps because those Biblical narratives were compiled and possibly embellished by humans. Another explanation would be that Qur'an built on the previous details preserved in the Torah and the Bible and added further clarity where warranted.

[377] The history of the Children of Israel is a prime example of how God reverses the fortune of those who are considered weak into a stronger force and gives them a chance to prove themselves in front of God and for themselves. The same situation has happened to the Christians and the Muslims throughout their histories as well. The same is true of many human communities throughout human history. The lands of present-day Palestine and Israel have been a hotbed of conflicts among these three groups, who, as the Qur'an claims, belong to the same faith—the faith of Moses, Jesus, and Mohammad, all of whom came with messages and guidance from the same God and who were given the same set of moral, ethical, and social behaviors to emulate and live up to. A new generation of Muslims, Christians, and Jews needs to come out and speak the core beliefs and social

norms of our common faith and bring an unprecedented level of human unity that mankind has not seen before—this is the test that God has presented in front of us.

REFLECTION

The story of Moses and the Children of Israel is a powerful reminder of God's grace to those who are deemed weak in the world—that they can, with faith and commitment to do good, reverse their fortune. Such conviction and belief are essential in our times today, when our individual and collective actions have created unprecedented levels of corruptions in the lands, widespread income disparities unheard of in human history, and a level of environmental pollution unseen on this planet.

ACTION

Only through faith in God and a firm belief that our futures are intimately tied together that has to be nurtured by social consciousness and respect of natural order of things that we can reverse the trends. This is an individual and a collective responsibility that we have to shoulder in the coming days for humanity to prosper.

CHAPTER 7

Verses 138–147

We (God) brought the Children of Israel across the sea, and they came upon a people (perhaps Amalekites as described in the Bible) who worshipped idols. They (the Children of Israel) said to Moses: "Set up for us a god like theirs." Moses rebuked them: "You are behaving like ignorant people. What these people are engaged in will lead them to destruction, and all they do is worthless. How shall I set up a god other than God Who has favored you above all others?" (He reminded them): "How God has delivered you from the people of the Pharaoh who imposed cruel sufferings on you—killing your sons and sparing only your women. This was an enormity of trials from your Sustainer!"[378]

We (God) appointed for Moses thirty nights (and days) and added ten more so that his engagement with his Sustainer was for forty nights (and days). Moses instructed his brother Aaron (prior to going up for his engagement): "Be my representative (during my absence) among the people, behave with righteousness, and do not follow the ways of corruption and mischief."

Moses came up for Our appointment (with God), and his Cherisher God spoke to him. He said: "My Sustainer, show me Yourself so that I might behold You." He [God] said: "You cannot see Me, but pay attention to this mountain; if it remains firm in its place, only then you can see Me." Then his Sustainer God shone His glory on the mountain and made it crumble to pieces; Moses fell down, losing his senses. When he recovered, he declared: "You are the most glorious; I turn to You, and I am the first to accept of the believers!" God said: "Moses, I have elevated you among mankind by My messages and by My words. Implement what I convey to you, and remain ever thankful. We articulated for you in the tablets guidance and exposition for all matters (of importance). So commit to these with firmness, and advise your people to follow the goodness therein. I (God) will show you the results of corruption and mischief. I will deprive of My guidance those who act with pride on this earth without justification; they will see every sign but will not accept it; they will see the means to correct themselves but will ignore them, and they will see the means to corrupt themselves and will latch onto them. Such conditions exist because they actively deny Our guidance and remain ignorant of it (see also 96:6–7). Those who reject Our guidance and Our meeting in the Afterlife, theirs is a pursuit not worth anything. How can they be rewarded except based on what they do?"

³⁷⁸ The narrative of Moses is one of the longest in the Qur'an, perhaps to emphasize its relevance to human conditions that tend to get the better of us in every generation unless we are careful about our faith in God, our mutual conduct, and our management of our communities, societal affairs, national priorities, and global peace. The tablet gifted to Moses by God contains the basic foundation of moral and ethical behaviors that all of humanity can attest to, and certainly among the Jews, Christians, and Muslims, these tablets contain guidance that is considered sacred and essential for human societies to evolve and progress. But we also know that having the knowledge and guidance is necessary but not sufficient to guide humanity unless each of us makes a conscious commitment to follow and implement them in our societal constructs. God laid out clearly some of the challenges, one of which is the willful and arrogance denial and disregard of such guidance and also the apprehension that Moses had when he instructed his brother Aaron to oversee his community in his absence since they were prone to worshipping false gods and disparaging moral boundaries, as is evident from stories in the Bible and the Torah.

REFLECTION

These stories of the prophets and their communities are living reminders for each generation to seek renewed ways to find the truth and to improve human conditions and not fall victim to the same lapses we see throughout history. For the Muslims, the early conflicts that ensued with Ali, the fourth Caliph; Aisha, the wife of the prophet; and other companions; as well as the atrocities committed by sons of Muwabia, the first ruler of the Ummayyad dynasty, which took control of the growing emergence of Muslims and Islam, are stark reminders of how human conditions degenerate rapidly if we do not have the moral courage and physical commitment to uphold truth and justice in society. The same situation continues to exist in Muslim countries where Shia-Sunni conflicts are causing the daily loss of innocent lives while each party calls themselves Muslims, where we have tolerated leaders such as Gaddafi and Saddam Hossain and let corruption overtake civil society, where cultural Islam overtakes real Islam, and where our self-proclaimed religious leaders and scholars are more interested in looking like Arabs and glorifying past generations than in speaking the Islam that is relevant today for our generation. As God said, those who have passed away will have their rewards from God, and those who are present will be accountable for their own deeds.

ACTION

Truly understanding the human guidance that God has given us and which the prophets and people of conscience have tried to implement in human societies is an obligation on each one of us. All of us will be judged based on what we do within our own community and within the sphere of influence that God has placed us in.

CHAPTER 7

Verses 148–156

After Moses (went to the mountain), his people made the body of a calf using their ornaments that produced low-pitched sounds. They took it for worship though they could see that it did not speak to them, nor did it provide any guidance; they were indeed unjust (to themselves). When they (some of them) realized their mistake and sought forgiveness, they said: "If our Sustainer God does not show mercy on us and forgive us, we will be in a state of loss."

When Moses returned, he was overcome with grief and anger and said to his people: "Evil and shameful is what you have done after me. Could you not wait until God's commands were given to you (as I was hoping to bring)?" He dropped the tablets and grabbed his brother (Aaron) by his head and pulled him toward himself. His brother said: "O Moses [son of my mother], our community considered me weak and disobeyed me. So let's not make our adversaries relish my predicament, and do not consider me as one of the unjust people." Moses regained calm: "My Sustainer God, forgive me and my brother, and consider us among those who receive Your mercy. You're the most merciful of those who show mercy."[379]

Those who took the calf (for worship), they will face God's displeasure and humiliation in this life. This is the nature of how We (God) deal with those who invent such falsehood. But to those who repent after such evil and reaffirm their faith, God is Ever Forgiving and Merciful! As Moses calmed down, he took up the tablets (to share with his people) in which the writings provided guidance and brought mercy for those who truly revered their Sustainer God. Moses chose seventy men for appointment with Us (God) and were overtaken by earthquake; Moses prayed: "If it was Your will, you could have removed them and me too already. Will you now destroy us for the acts of the fools among us? This was nothing but a serious trial from you (which we failed terribly)! You allow people to go astray as You will, and You guide people as You will. You are our Preserver; therefore, forgive us and show us (again) Your mercy, as You are the best among the Forgivers! Bless us with what is good in this world and in the life to come as we turn to You." God responded: "My displeasure touches whom I will (as deserved by them), but My mercy is spread to everyone and everything. Such is the norm for those who behave responsibly, support others from their wealth [zakat], and take Our Guidance seriously."[380]

[379] The story of the Children of Israel taking on the worship of the calf and their denial of the messages and guidance from the tablets is well documented in the Torah and the Bible. The Qur'an further reiterates the same incidents, with pertinent details (see also 20:90–97 for further details) but greater focus on the lessons learned from such incidents and from such generations who were blessed with the presence of Moses. People were impatient and could not wait for forty days until Moses could come back and provide the guidance that God had promised. Even Aaron's presence and pleading did not help the situation. Even when the message came, it was difficult for them to give up old habits and erase notions of deities other than One God. The Qur'an also refutes Exodus 32:1–5, which implies that Aaron participated in the calf worship. The Qur'an also does not confirm Exodus 32:19, which implies that the tablets were broken and had to be redone, as if there were a second appointment with God like the first (Exodus 24:1).

Now let's think of the current situation in many Muslim countries and Muslim communities where we have the Qur'an and the Prophet's teachings in front of us in full view. There are people of conscience asking questions about our failures with gender equality; social justice; corrupt practices in governing the country; religious leaders more aligned with the powerful than with the truth and the people; marginalization of the faith to mere rituals in communities, encouraged by imams and community leaders; failure to distinguish Islamic teaching from cultural norms—these situations are no less serious than what God was displeased with in Moses's time. Unless we can connect their failures with our own, take lessons from them, and do something about it as responsible human beings (*muttaquin*), the Qur'an will not help us become better people or a better person. God wills only when we will to change our condition. The current refugee crisis in Syria is a living example of our collective failure by the Syrian people themselves, the Muslims in neighboring countries, and the world at large.

³⁸⁰ The patience and perseverance that Moses demonstrated in the face of recurring moral and spiritual incursions by his generation is legendary—a lesson that we can all learn from. In our contemporary societies, we have seen people such as Martin Luther King and Nelson Mandela, who followed those footsteps in the face of enormous odds in their societies. Despite initial setbacks, the Prophet Moses gathered his people and led a collective show of repentance to God to seek His continued blessing. God affirms here that at any moment we show genuine remorse and resolve to mend our ways, God is always there to support us. God lays out a simple rule: to continue to receive His blessings, we have to (1) act responsibly, (2) be socially conscious and look at the interests of everyone, especially those who are less fortunate, and (3) show genuine commitment to understanding and implementing guidance from God to improve human conditions.

REFLECTION

The story of Moses again shows us God's continued forgiveness and blessings despite repeated failures by his community. For many communities of faithful in the world today, whether locally or nationally, similar situations exist that call for deeper reflections on the common causes.

ACTION

As we read the Qur'an, other Books of Revelations, and books on human knowledge and natural laws and discuss among ourselves the malaise and excesses of our societies, each of us has a responsibility—especially those of us who are professionals, since we have mastered certain skills and disciplines that we demonstrate in our professional lives every day—to mobilize some of our energy, skills, and precious time to make our societies and its members better, including ourselves.

CHAPTER 7

Verses 157–158

Those who follow the unlettered [Ummi] Messenger whom they find written about in the Torah and the Bible;[381] *who invites them to what is right and good and dissuades them from what is evil; who legislates for them what is pure and good and prohibits what is impure and bad; who removes from them undue burdens and constraints that have been imposed on them—and those who accept him, honor him, help him, and adhere to the light (the source of knowledge and guidance) that has been sent down to him, these are the successful ones.*

Say (O Prophet): "O Mankind! I am a Messenger to all of you from God Who has the dominion over the Universe and the Earth; there is no god but He, giving life and dispensing death (to all)." Therefore, have faith in God and in His unlettered Messenger-Prophet who believes in God and in God's words—follow him so that you can be guided.[382]

[381] The Qur'an clearly states that both the Torah and the Bible speak of the Prophet Mohammad, and some traces for such confirmation still exist in the Bible and the Torah, though many Jewish and Christian scholars and clerics have interpreted them differently in the literature authorized by established Jewish and Christian officials, who heavily edited such mentions to conform their interpretations to their theology and historical biases. One could also make the claim that Muslim scholars and historians have attempted to extract meaning and references that perhaps were not there, but the Qur'an certainly makes such claims, which is clearly evident in this verse as well as in another verse, 61:6, where Jesus is

mentioned as speaking about the Prophet Mohammad. Below are some examples of what perhaps still remains in the Torah and the Bible about references to the last Prophet.

Torah: Deuteronomy 18:15: *"The Lord thy God will raise up unto thee a prophet from the midst of thee, of thy brethren, like unto me (i.e., Moses), unto him ye shall harken."* Deuteronomy 18:18 reconfirms with direct word from God: *"I (God) will raise them up a prophet from among their brethren, like unto thee, and will put my words in his mouth; and he shall speak unto them all that I shall command him."* Deuteronomy 33:1–2: *"And this is the blessing, wherewith Moses the man of God blessed the Children of Israel before his death. And he said, The Lord came from Sinai (i.e., thru Moses), and rose from Sei'r unto them (i.e., thru Jesus); he shined from Mount Paran (i.e., thru Mohammad)"*

Gospel: John 14:16: *"And I (Jesus) will pray the Father (God), and he shall give you another Comforter that he may abide with you forever."* And then follows in John 14:26: *"But when the Comforter is come, whom I shall send unto you from the Father (God), even the spirit of truth, which proceedeth from the Father (God), he shall testify of me."* (See also John 16:7–8). John 16:12–14 add further clarity and details: *"I have yet many things to say unto you, but ye cannot hear them now. Howbeit, when he, the Spirit of Truth, is come, he will guide you into all truth; for he shall not speak of himself, but whatsoever he shall hear, that he shall speak; and he will show you all things to come. He shall glorify me."*

The English translation of *"Comforter"* comes from the Greek word *parakletos*, used in the Greek Bible. Perhaps its more accurate rendition in Greek is *periklytos* (the much praised), which is much closer to the Aramaic term *mawhamana*, Aramaic being the language that Jesus most likely spoke. *Periklytos* and mawhamana have similar implications as the dual name of the last Prophet—Mohammad and Ahmad, both derived from root words *hamd* (praise) and *hamida* (he praised). It is mentioned that in the newly discovered Gospel of St. Barnabas (translated from the Italian manuscript that exists in the imperial library at Vienna), it mentions the name of the Prophet Mohammad by its Arabic form. Such Gospel books were more in use and were read in the churches until 496 CE, when they were banned as *"heretical"* by a decree of Pope Gelasius.

The Prophet Mohammad has been declared as the Seal (Last) Prophet (33:40) as well as a prophet of mercy to all nations (21:107), whereas Jesus was sent as a prophet to the Children of Israel, as was the Prophet Moses. Matthew 25:24: *"I (Jesus) am sent but unto the lost sheep of the house of Israel."* But Jesus and his mother were declared a sign (of God) to the world (21:91).

382 The Prophet Mohammad came in the wake of Jesus and had the same continued messages brought forth by Abraham, Isaac, Ishmael, Moses, David, Solomon, and Jesus, among many other prophets, and he declared himself a Prophet to all people and the last Prophet (33:40) and a mercy to mankind (21:107). Following in the footsteps of the Prophet Mohammad is the same as following in the footsteps of Moses and Jesus. The guidance of Islam is summarized succinctly as follows:

- to encourage and establish what is good and pure and to discourage what is evil and impure,
- to legislate—that is, to put into law to practice what is good and forbid what is evil, and
- to remove unnecessary constraints and complexities that previous generations and faith groups put on themselves.

Mankind is encouraged to accept the Prophet and his teachings, to honor him, to help him, and to commit to the guidance (light) that comes from God. These commitments are essential for proper guidance and success.

REFLECTION

Time and again the Qur'an brings forth the commonality of faith and its attempt to simplify and codify the teachings of the prophets who came before the Prophet Mohammad. We need to be able to find the commonalities, which are many, and also identify the differences, which are few. Our objective understanding of these differences is essential to fully appreciate the beauty of Islamic teaching and the need for continued evolution of our thinking based on our ever-increasing knowledge of ourselves and our universe.

ACTION

Such understanding has to be translated into consensus building. We need to use democratic means to codify such affirmation into the fabric of societal norms and regulations to build a civil society and the rule of law in all matters—social, political, and financial. In the spiritual realm, we should leave it to each religious group how it wishes to pursue its spiritual development and agree to live with the theological differences that exist as a matter of human spiritual development and God-given freedom to exercise in such matters.

CHAPTER 7
Verses 159–171

From the followers of Moses, there is a community who guide themselves to truth and establish justice with such guidance. We grouped them into twelve tribes, as communities. When his people asked Moses for water, We revealed to him: "Strike the rock with your stick"; so out came twelve springs, and each community knew its source of water. We made the cloud to comfort them with shade, sent for them manna and quails, and said: "Eat of the good provisions We have provided for you." Yet, when they did make wrong choices, they did Us no harm. (Recollect) what was said to them: "Live in this town and benefit from its resources as you wish; but seek forgiveness and show humility as you enter it. We (God) will forgive your wrongs and give plenty to those who do good." But those who were prone to do evil changed the instructions for a word different from what they were told. So We sent a calamity from above on account of their evilness (see also in the Bible, Numbers 25:1–3, 8–9).

Inquire of them about the town by the sea. There they violated the spirit of the Sabbath—on the Sabbath day, fish will come to the surface, but on other days, they will not surface. This is how We (God) tried them for their repeated failures (to follow the guidance of Moses). A group among them said: "Why should we attempt to guide a people whom God will destroy or bring severe punishment?" The group (offering such guidance) replied: "To avoid the blame of not doing so in the presence of our Sustainer God and in the hope that they might become aware and responsible." So We protected those who reminded others to avoid evil and took to account those who failed to pay attention to such reminders and who were steeped in evil—an evil punishment befitting their transgression. When they persisted in doing what they were advised against, We (God) declared: "Be as apes, despised" (see also Ezekiel 22:8–15).[383]

And remember when your Sustainer announced that He will send against them, to the Day of Resurrection, people who will subject them to severe torment. Surely God is quick in taking account, but He is ever Forgiving, Merciful! We cause them to divide into groups—some of them drawn to good and some of them otherwise (to evil). We tried them with good fortune as well as misfortune to see if they would turn around.

After these people, came in their posterity another evil generation who inherited the divine revelation but opted for the vanities of life on this earth and boasted: "We will be forgiven." They were ready to do the same at the next turn of vanities (without any change of heart, despite repeated opportunities to amend). Yet a commitment was taken from them in their book (of revelation, to which they claim inheritance) that they would speak nothing about God but the truth, and they studied what was in the book. Certainly, the life after is better for those who are mindful and responsible. Do they not then understand? Those who remain true to the Book (of Revelations) and sustain devotion to God—for them, We do not waste the effort of those who continue to reform themselves. (Remember also) when We [God] shook the mountain towering over them and casting its shadow, they thought it was going to crush them. (We said): "Commit firmly what you have been given and become fully aware of what it contains, so that you can become mindful and be responsible (human beings)."[384]

---

[383] The grace of God Almighty to the followers for Moses—saving them from the tyranny of the Pharaoh and his people, bringing Moses up in the house of the Pharaoh while he was killing their sons, bringing them to the land blessed and of plenty, showering them with heavenly gifts of manna and quails, directing natural resources such as clouds and wind to provide them safety and comfort, and so on are all well documented in the Qur'an and the Bible. Even in the face of repeated lapses, God continued to shower His mercy and forgiveness.

To earn God's forgiveness and mercy, they were also subjected to a variety of trials; there were groups within the followers of Moses who always rose to the occasion, while other groups failed to uphold the teachings and guidance that Moses brought. The same turn of events is also true of the followers of Jesus and Mohammad as we review history in the twenty-first century. The devastation of the Holocaust and the Spanish Inquisition, slavery and apartheid against Africans on the American continent and southern Africa, the horrors of two world wars, and Bosnian ethnic cleansing are some examples of lapses in the followers of Jesus. The rise of religious extremism within Muslim communities such as ISIS and Al-Qaeda, unparalleled political and religious corruption in many Muslim countries, and lack of democratic governance in many Muslim communities are some of the lapses that are apparent in the followers of Mohammad. But the more appropriate analysis would be that had they been true followers of Moses, Jesus, and Mohammad, they would have never committed such crimes in the name of God.

The performance of those who advocate secular views and deny God is no better, as demonstrated in Russia and China in the name of communism and socialism. The same is true of the secular states in the West that perpetuated colonial rule over a larger part of the known world, and many of their current postures around the world and the institutions that have been built reflect the same mind-set. We all need to recognize our failures and our lapses in upholding truth and justice for mankind and work together rather than point fingers at one another.

384 The divisions among the various sects in each faith group and our inability to reconcile our differences are a continuous challenge for mankind. The continued rise of religious polarization among major faith groups and within each faith, our lack of compassion and mutual respect, our lack of ability and moral will to dispense goodness in the face of evil in all corners of the world, and our incapacity to take lessons from good times and difficult times are creating a tsunami of hatred and miscalculations leading to unparalleled discomfort among people in general about our very existence and essence as human beings and as human societies. The description in the Qur'an about our downward spiral toward evil

and divisiveness is reaching catastrophic proportions, and people of faith and good conscience have to rise to the occasion to align with those who are spoken about in the above verses *"to avoid the blame of not doing so in the presence of our Sustainer God and in the hope that they might become aware and responsible."*

REFLECTION

The rise and fall of the human condition in terms of evil and good, good fortune and difficult times, faith in God and doubts in such faith, confidence in our future and despair at our current condition are not new phenomena. These are turns of events that continually challenge us as the human race to demonstrate patience, reflect with humility, and reorient ourselves to truth and justice at every fork in the road.

ACTION

Let's take to heart the promise of God when He said: *"We do not waste the effort of those who continue to reform themselves (moslehin)."* As Jesus would have asked, Who are my helpers? Perhaps we should ask ourselves: Who are the takers, among us, of this promise from God?

Key Arabic Term
118. *moslehin* (reformers)

CHAPTER 7
Verses 172–181

*[Consider the truth] when your Sustainer God brings forth the offspring of the children of Adam, from themselves, He makes them confirm the truth about themselves: "Am I not your Sustainer God?" They say: "Yes, we do confirm." [Such is the truth], lest you say on the Day of Resurrection: "We were unaware of this," or you complain: "It was our forefathers who invented polytheism, and we are but their descendants after them. Would You then make us face the consequence of their untrue conjectures?" This is how We [God] make the guidance explicit so that you may return [to the truth].*³⁸⁵

*Relate to them the affair of him to whom We give Our Guidance, but he walks away from it so that the Devil pursues him and makes him stray in irreversible errors. If We had willed, We could have made him prosper in it but he opted for the material life and pursued his vain desires. Such a person resembles a dog that, if you pursue him, he lolls out his tongue, and if you leave him undisturbed, he lolls his tongue the same way. Such is the condition of those deny Our messages. So retell the narrative, and perhaps they will reflect. Evil is the manifestation of those who deny Our [God's] messages, and they oppress thereby none but their own souls.*³⁸⁶

*Those whom God guides are indeed guided, but whom He allows to stray, he is indeed in a state of loss. Certainly many Jinns and human beings are destined for Hell—they were gifted with a heart, but they try not to understand with it; they were given eyes, but they try not to see with them; and they have ears, but they do not listen with them—they behave like cattle, or perhaps stray further. They are making no attempt to comprehend.*³⁸⁷

God has the best attributes, so aspire to imbibe those attributes and leave alone those who disregard such attributes. They will face the consequences of what they do. (Let there be) from among Our creations a group that guides (themselves and others) to truth and pursue justice thereby.[388]

[385] The essence of human awareness about God and His attributes is fundamentally a part of our makeup, a reflection of God's breathing His essence into every human soul, a fact that constantly gets revisited in the Qur'an in the most vivid way, such as the above verse in which God affirms that every single human being is asked to confirm the Creator and we do so in the most certain way. In another verse (30:30), God says that He imparted the nature of God into the nature of each human being. Our ability to comprehend such awe-inspiring capabilities that each human being is innately endowed with and our intimate belief in the nature of the created universe are essential components for understanding ourselves, understanding God, and shaping our very existence on this planet. A testimony of such understanding is the statement of the Prophet Mohammad, who famously said: *"He who knows himself, knows God."* Every human institution, every human center of knowledge, and every sphere of our social, political, and financial endeavors has to acknowledge this truth and recognize the beauty, the dignity, and the sanctity of every human presence, without which many of current tides of racism, oppression—both political and financial—injustices, gender biases, and loss of basic human rights and dignity will remain unattended and unsolved. Even on a basic level of fairness by the Creator to His creation, He wants to make sure that we have no basis to complain or deny that we knew this primordial essence of our creation and our connection with God.

[386] Now comes the reality that if we deny such connection and lose sight of such profound basis of our creation, then we degrade ourselves to the level of an animal or even worse, where we not only not use our God-given faculties of thinking and comprehending, seeing, and hearing to aid in amplifying life, liberty, and pursuit of happiness, but some of us actively oppose such human traits to create injustice, anarchy, and loss of human dignity in our social, religious, financial, and political conduct—a trait evident far too many times in our human history.

This is a constant challenge for every generation and for every faith group as well as for people of conscience (even if they deny faith in God).

387 Now comes the call from God and an affirmation that there will always be individuals and groups within His creation who will strive to remain true to the nature of its creation, understand the attributes of God, and, by that pursuit, attain understanding of their own attributes and remain committed to truth and the cause of justice that such truth demands. All prophets of God and their followers throughout human history—the memories and teachings of Abraham, Moses, Jesus, and Mohammad are examples of such groups. The contrast of Abel and Cain, David and Goliath, British colonial rule versus the American founding fathers, slavery in American versus Martin Luther King, the Vietnam War versus Mohammad Ali, and apartheid in South Africa versus Nelson Mandela are examples of how inspired individuals and groups continue to demonstrate the best of human creation and being true to the nature in which God had created us.

388 The sublime attributes of God, as manifested in His ninety-nine names, adorn many Muslim homes but are absent from their hearts. We cannot achieve true faith and become infused with taqwa (a deep sense of personal responsibility and accountability) without subscribing the attributes of God with deep commitment and sincere devotion and morph into a community that, according to verse 7:181, lives and guides to the truth and establishes justify thereby.

REFLECTION

Here in this section God demonstrates in the most vivid way our connection with Him, cautions us about the danger of failing with our senses (heart, eyes, and ears, among others) to comprehend our own nature, reminds us of the consequences of evil and discord that come from being unfaithful to the very nature of our creation, exhorts us to reflect deeply on the attributes of God and hence on our own innate attributes, and, finally, calls us to action—there should always be individuals and groups who will rise up in every generation to keep the world on a straight course toward truth and justice.

ACTION

It would be utter folly on our part as individuals and as a community not to pay heed to such reality and such a call from the Creator Himself. What we need is not just to establish a factual understanding of our nature and the created world but to develop and nurture a deeper and intimate connection with God and the world we live in and make each and every day, each and every effort benefit our world—one person at a time, one family at a time, one institution at a time, one nation at a time, and one humanity at a time.

CHAPTER 7
Verses 182—188

Those who deny Our (God's) messages, We lead them (to their consequences) gradually, in a manner that they do not recognize that this is happening. I (God) allow them respite (to continue their denials and mischiefs), but My subtle scheme is ever effective.

Do they not reflect—this companion of theirs (Prophet Mohammad) is not under any influence; He is simply a warner, making things clear. Have they not seen the dominion of God over the Universe and the Earth and what God had created? Could it be that their own term for existence is coming to an end; what other announcement (from God) are they waiting to believe in, after this (message and the messenger)? Whoever God leaves in error, he can find no guidance. He leaves them alone to stumble around in their arrogance.[389]

They ask you about the Hour (perhaps the timing of the Day of Resurrection), when it will come about. Say: "The knowledge of it is only with my Sustainer God. None but He can me bring it about when the time is due; it will impact heavily on the heavens and the earth (in a way you cannot even imagine), and it will come but all of a sudden." They continue to ask you, as if by persistence you will gain insight into it. Repeat for them: "Such knowledge belongs to God alone, and most people do not know (about it)." Say: "I control neither benefit for nor harm to myself, except what God wills. Had I been privy to the unseen, I would have gained much good, and no harm would ever touch me. (Let me repeat), I am simply a warner and a giver of good news to those who believe."[390]

389 Recognition of the message is derived from the message itself (its content), where it comes from, whether it resonates with the realities that we see in the world around us, whether it connects with our innate understanding of who we are, and so on. Equally important is the one who delivers the message—in this case the Prophet Mohammad, with inspiration from God through Angel Gabriel, just like Jesus and Moses from the past. We are asked to understand who this person is—his character, his mannerisms, his truthfulness, his trustworthiness, and his care for people, for truth, for justice and human dignity, and the lack of any inconsistency, superstitions, or divergence in his message or in his personality. The denial of such message has its consequences, as it diminishes our human purpose and existence and leads to anarchy, oppression, and loss of human dignity at a personal level and at a societal level. It happens in a way that we might not fully understand until we are face to face with its negative manifestations, which leads us to wonder sometimes, Where does it come from? God gives us space and time to reflect and to amend ourselves as we go along our lives, and each one of us sooner or later comes to realize his or her mistakes and mischiefs in this life before moving to the Afterlife.

390 The Afterlife commences with the Day of Resurrection or the Day of Gathering or the Day of Judgment, as it has been called by various names in the Qur'an. No one knows when he or she will die, where, or in what manner—these are facts that only God knows—and this is also true of the knowledge of the Day of Resurrection. People who are in denial of such a day and of being present at the appointed meeting with God Almighty would ask, sometimes to make fun of God's messengers and people of God, when such a day will come. The prophets' answers are simple: Only God has such knowledge, and they are not privy to such matters. They are as human beings not in control of their benefits or harms except as God wills. The lapse in faith by the followers of Moses when he was in the mountain receiving God's guidance, the unjustified suffering of Jesus Christ, and the forced migration of the Prophet Mohammad are just a few examples showing that they could not control the outcome of their efforts, even as Messengers of God, except what God had planned and executed. They came to guide themselves and to provide guidance to others and to warn of the negative consequences if we do not follow the guidance or to give the news of the positive consequences if we commit to such guidance.

REFLECTION

The only way to convince ourselves of the guidance is to find meaning in the guidance, get to know the messengers, and see the nature of the created world in which we live and share space and resources with others. The Qur'an constantly calls for such reflection and deeper understanding—to see if there is any inconsistency in the Qur'an; to appreciate the character of the Prophet; to reflect on the day and night and the way they alternate, the cycle of rain and growth of vegetation, the cycle of life and death; our natural affinity to goodness and truth; the historical patterns of one group dominating another and proving or disproving their worth for such privileges, and so on.

ACTION

Death and the Afterlife are two realities that will touch each one of us. Death is the immediate reality that will put into motion the next reality of Afterlife, and we need to be prepared as best as we can during our waking moments on this planet.

CHAPTER 7

Verses 189—198

He (God) is the One who created you from a single being, from it its mate, so that he may incline to her. So when he has intimate contact with her, she conceives a weight light enough to move about with it. As it grows heavy, they both call upon God, their Sustainer: "If You bless us with a good child, we will be most grateful." But once He has given a good child, they begin to assert a partnership with God from which He has gifted them, whereas God is exalted and pure from such associations. Do they assert themselves as partners who created nothing and are themselves created? These cannot offer any help to others, nor can they help themselves.[391]

If you invite them to guidance, they will not follow you. It is the same whether you call them to guidance or remain silent. Those whom you invoke besides God are subservient to God just like you. If you feel you speak the truth, then go ahead and call upon them—see if they answer you. Do they (these idols) have feet with which they walk, or hands with which they hold, or eyes with which they see, or ears with which they hear? Say (to them, O Prophet): "Invoke your gods, try to prevail over me, and give me no concession. My friend is God Himself Who inspired this Book, and He befriends those who subscribe to goodness." Those whom you invoke besides God are not able to help you, let alone help themselves. If you invoke them for guidance, they hear you not. You might feel they are looking at you, but they see nothing.[392]

[391] The exchange of God's gift—a child is the best of all gifts—should invoke thankfulness, humility, and a willingness to fulfill our human commitment to that

child, to other human beings in general, and, in the end, to God Almighty, the Creator. Yet to the people of Arabia at the time, the birth of a son brought out pride and arrogance at its best, as if they had accomplished a great thing by themselves, forgetting that it was God Who had provided such a child, and they would prepare to assign the child its own god to worship, just as they themselves and their forefathers worshiped stones and objects and established godheads—each person and each clan would have their own set of gods to show devotion to. On the other hand, if a female child was born, they would be ashamed, as if God had humiliated them, and they would even go ahead and bury the child alive, as if to avoid the curse of a godhead. Such gender biases continue to play havoc in many Muslim societies where parents favor the son over daughters and daughters are not extended the same freedom and access to education. Daughters are being forced to marry early, offered limited voice in selecting a partner, and sometimes forced to marry cousins, a practice that continues in Arabia, Afghanistan, and Pakistan, to name a few countries. All such practices are somehow justified in the name of Islam, but no such encouragement is in the Qur'an or in the teachings of the Prophet. These are tribal cultures that persist, just as the people of Makkah did during the time of the Prophet.

392 By pointing out the basic flaws in worshiping objects that have no capability to feel, see, hear, or move, capabilities that every human being has been endowed with, God is asking us to rise to a higher level of worship, the worship of the Creator Who is infinite in knowledge, creation, and capabilities. Too often the innate nature of human beings to connect with God and to find meaning in life gets translated into worshiping false godheads, developing superstitious practices, and, in our current societal norms, a notion of spirituality that is earthbound and devoid of any divine connection and looks inward to our inner goods but fails to inquire where such goodness comes from.

REFLECTION

The search for God is innate in human nature and has been an ongoing process since the creation of human beings. As the Prophet of Islam said,

He who knows himself, knows God. It is within our ability to connect with God and to conform to the nature of things as God has created them, as has been made abundantly clear in the Books of Revelations such as the Qur'an, the Bible, and the Torah.

ACTION

Every generation has to understand its connection with God and how to shape their current practices and norms (personal and societal) in light of divine teachings and ever-compounding human knowledge, a gift from God that is limitless.

CHAPTER 7

Verses 199–206

Be true to your inner nature (nature in which God had created you), work to create goodness, and do not be influenced by those who are ignorant. If the Devil (or men of evil intent) attempts to influence you with dissention or deviation (from truth), resort to God, who is Ever Hearing and Knowing. Those who are conscious and responsible when the Devil (or men of evil intent) attempts to influence them immediately become mindful, and they can recognize (with situational awareness), whereas those who align with the Devil continue to increase in such deviation without resisting.[393]

When you do not bring them a sign (according to their desire or choice), they ask: "Why don't you demand it (from God)?" Reply to them: "I only follow what comes from my Sustainer God." This narrative is a sign and a proof, a guide and a source of mercy for those who believe. When this Qur'an is presented, pay attention to its message and reflect on its meaning (in silent contemplation) so that you can partake in its mercy. Be conscious of your Sustainer God within your inner core with awe and humility and in a voice pleasant during morning hours and evening hours, and do not allow yourself to be without such conscious mindfulness. (Think of those) who are in the presence of your Sustainer God—they are not proud to serve him, they glorify and honor him immensely, and to Him they are wholeheartedly devoted.[394]

---

[393] In the Qur'an, there is constant reference to the Devil, who tempted the first man and the first woman (Adam and Eve). God allowed the Devil to live until

the end of time (the Day of Resurrection) to continue to tempt children of Adam and Eve toward evil and falsehood. The Devil was from the Jinn, a species God mentions in the Qur'an made from fire (energy). In contrast, human beings are made from dust or mud (matter); therefore, human beings have physical presence, whereas the Devil is invisible to human eyes or senses but can influence human minds to think in ways that we do not fully understand or comprehend. Our evil thoughts and inclinations can come from within us as well as be influenced by the Devil. Any human act that is not in conformity with human nature (i.e., the nature of God) is considered an act of the Devil, and we are warned to be aware of such influence and misguidance.

[394] The question of proof has always dogged the communities of the prophets, especially those that were not inclined to believe in God or the Prophet. Moses had a walking stick that would turn into a fearsome snake, and Jesus would heal the sick, among other miracles that God empowered him with. In that vein, people would demand such miracles from the Prophet Mohammad, but he always maintained that the Qur'an itself was the proof if they would reflect on it and try to understand its content and message in the context of our own lives and our living environment. The Qur'an certainly moves the minds and hearts of millions of people who read it, think it, and put it into practice in a diverse set of communities all over the globe. The beauty of the narratives; the rhythm of its recitation, especially by trained reciters; and the reminders of its verses in the daily prayers create a powerful personal connection with God. The challenge for our generation is to comprehend its meaning and relevance to our day-to-day life and to go beyond the rituals and symbolism of faith.

REFLECTION

We are being asked to be conscious of God in our inner core with a sense of awe and humility and to be mindful of His presence and guidance on a daily basis in every aspect of our lives.

ACTION

Such mindfulness can come only if we take the message seriously, develop a deep and personal connection with God, and *"seek the truth to establish justice thereby."*

Key Concepts from Surah Al-Araf (The Elevation)

1. Embracing guidance with open arms (7:1–3)
2. All will be questioned, even the prophets (7:6–9)
3. Earth is a source of provision and a proving ground (7:10, 24–25, 27, 34)
4. The Devil's plan against human beings is all inclusive (7:11–27)
5. Adam and Eve's first repentance (7:23)
6. *Taqwa* as protection against evil (7:26, 35)
7. Genuine worship and devotion to God (7:29, 31–32, 204–206)
8. All forms of indecency are forbidden (7:33, 28)
9. Salvation is through faith in God and humility (7:40–44, 55–56)
10. The final sequel to the Qur'an (7:52–53)
11. God, the Creator Supreme and Provider (7:54–58)
12. The rule of law and tranquility (7:56)
13. Nature as a constant reminder (7:57–58)
14. The prophets as guides—Noah, Hud, Salih, Lot, and Shu'aib (7:59–93)
15. God's challenge and warning to people (7:94–99)
16. Human failure to maintain God's covenant (7:100–102)
17. Lessons from Moses (7:103–129, 148–156)
18. The Prophet Mohammad as a guide (7:157–158)
19. Moses's followers recognized (7:159)
20. Human failings and successes (7:168–170)
21. God reveals to us all (7:172–174)
22. The inability to use God-given endowments (7:179–180)
23. Seeking truth and doing justice (7:181, 159)
24. Our tendency to associate others with God (7:189–191)
25. Simple guidance of forgiveness, goodness, and knowledge (7:199)

1. Embracing guidance with open arms (7:1–3)

Many surahs in the Qur'an, especially in the middle sections and starting with this surah, make an urgent call to pay attention to the revelations and to embrace these gifts and endowments to human consciousness with an open heart, an open mind, and open arms. It forcefully argues that we not only have to pay attention but develop a detailed and nuanced understanding of what is being gifted to us from God, our Creator, but we have to act accordingly and create social, political, and financial norms in our societies accordingly. The prophet, as the first recipient of revelation, is asked to have no constraints emotionally, intellectually, or spiritually about this book that is being revealed in portions and to use this book to guide and caution those who wish to have faith and goodness in their lives. For the believers, this book serves as a reminder (*zikra*), an apt label since what these books say, and their guidance, is already built into our nature, the nature of humanity that is a true reflection of God's nature. And that is why humanity is such a precious commodity to be considered sacred—its life, its soul, its possessions, its relationships, its covenants, and all other manifestations of its existence and purpose.

Humanity is reminded that they should, as a matter of choice and not subject to any forms of coercion, strive to follow what God reveals, as He committed to Adam and Eve, and that we will be better off if we resist any temptation to follow any other deities or systems that go contrary to what the Creator revealed. That does not mean we should not compare and contrast but that we do so with objectivity, intellectual curiosity, honesty, and a genuine commitment to benefit our common humanity and not be driven by narrow self-interest, greed, lust, ignorance, arrogance, blind loyalty, and other forms of human ailments and failings.

This attitude toward revelations, which exists in its purest form in the Qur'an, is something that Muslims have to take seriously. Christians and Jews who find their Bible and Torah sometimes inconsistent and factually challenging might have a very different attitude toward scriptures. Many of us understand that such inconsistencies and factual deficiencies are man-made and have been introduced in the scriptures by their human authors, who did their best to capture the essence of what was revealed. By the same token, one has to recognize that given the ancient nature of some of the scriptures and frequent tampering by autocratic religious and political authorities, as in the case of the Bible, some aspects of divine revelations have been corrupted, and incongruent notions have been introduced and made official over time. With respect to the Bible, the establishment of the papal institution as the sole arbiter of the Bible, the role of clerics as intermediaries between layman and God, and the nature of Jesus in relation to God are some examples of why it is difficult for many faithful to have open arms to the Bible and, by implication, to any divine scriptures, including the Qur'an. I have tried to understand and explain the Qur'an as openly and as expansively as possible, and I welcome a critical assessment of my work in this series from any discerning individuals of faith and of no faith.

2. All will be questioned, even the prophets (7:6–9)

Two foundational principles of personal and communal accountability have been laid out here in its most pristine and simplest form. One is that every one of who has had the privilege of being in the presence of a messenger will be questioned about our understanding of such messages and guidance and our demonstrated commitment and follow-through on such guidance. This questioning will come from God as well as from our own selves and those we are with.

As God said in the Qur'an, a soul that question itself is at a higher level of self-consciousness and is closer to God than a soul or being that goes on with life without thoughts or self-assessment, a very human trait that is innate in our nature but needs to be nurtured and constantly revisited. Not only will each one of us will be questioned, but so will the messengers themselves as to what they conveyed, how they strived to accomplish their objectives, and the extent to which they themselves understood and realized the guidance and inspiration they received.

I also want to define what is meant by messengers (*mursalin*). In conventional and classical understanding, this relates to prophets who explicitly brought messages in the form of scriptures such as the Torah, the Bible, and the Qur'an. But in a broad sense, any good word or good act is a message and a reminder, and each of us is, at one time or another, in the presence of such a message. The one who delivers such message, be it a person, an institution, or a media outlet, to name a few, as well as the natural world we live in, constantly reminds us about our role and our responsibilities to one another. As Khalil Gibran, the Lebanese poet, reminded us – "Have you seen an apple tree that refused to give an apple to anyone who asks?"

The second aspect is that judgment from God is always just, and such just judgment is based on statistical assessment of all that we do, unless one single act is of such a proportion that it overrides all good or all evil that one had done in life. One tradition of the Prophet said that God forgave a prostitute for a single act of kindness when she used her shoe to pitch water from a well to hydrate a cat that was dying from thrust. But for most of us, our good acts and our evil acts will be out on balance, and God's justice will be dispensed in accordance with which side is heavier.

Such narratives are logical enough and resonate with our instinctive understanding of ourselves and those around us, but God goes one step further by stating that *"God relates such matters [principles and truth] to people based on knowledge, and God is never absent [distant from His creation]"* (7:7).

3. Earth is a source of provision and a proving ground (7:10, 25, 27, 34)

According to Islamic guidance (i.e., guidance from God), our lives on this planet are constructed around a few terms and provisions, such as:

- our God-given endowment of and for knowledge and free will,
- a fixed term of how long each one of us will spend a transient existence on this planet,
- our means of sustenance and provision being derived from this planet,

- our going back to our Creator God after death, in the Afterlife, and
- our being accountable for all our actions and deeds which will shape our Afterlife

A number of verses here as well as in a number of other places repeat and reinforce these terms and provision in a very forceful but empathetic way that we need to pay due attention to, because these are the ultimate realities that we are bound by and bound to. We need to keep these in perspective on a daily basis, and periodic deeper reflections are needed to keep maintaining our sense of purpose and to direct our attention to what really matters beyond our physical and animal existence.

God asserts in verse 10 that He made it possible for us to inherit this planet, and He has fitted the earth to provide our means of livelihood, which is sufficient reason to be thankful to which we perhaps fail in one way or another each day. Verse 25 reminds us that it is on this planet that we are destined to live, die, and then be raised again for the Afterlife—the first two facts are evident to all of us, while rising after death is a matter of belief that God wants us to take seriously and with the same level of certainly as our life and death, which are as evident as the rising of the sun each day.

God cautions us in verse 27 to be aware of the mechanism of the Devil and our own evil inclinations when exercising our own free will. We may take an improper turn, a turn that is contrary to our own innate sense of purpose, truth, and justice, and explicitly go against God's commands and guidance contained in the teachings from scriptures as well as of His prophets. We are reminded that we should NOT fall victim to the Devil's seduction in the way that he misled Adam and Eve, our ancestors.

Verse 34 extends these terms and provisions as listed at the beginning, applying them not only to individual human beings but also to communities, societies, and nations, as we have a collective identity and a collective personality that in many ways influence our individual identities, propensities, and choices that we can and will make. This collective and group identity and accountability also demands the imperative for organized society, building and augmenting institutional knowledge, democratic ideals, social justice, and environmental stewardship, to name a few of the major priorities of our time and our generation.

4. The Devil's plan against human beings is all inclusive (7:11–27)

The story of the Devil (Satan; *Iblis* in Arabic) in the context of Adam and Eve is pervasive in the Qur'an (see also 2:30–39), with the central theme of the Devil being the arch deceiver of human beings, whose sole purpose is to lead humanity away from God and goodness. God in return promises each and every human being that if we follow God's guidance and acknowledge God as our Creator and our Friend, the Devil will have no influence on us, but if we ignore God and goodness, the Devil will have a field day with human societies, some of which is evident in our lifetime.

The notion of conflict between the Devil and humanity starts with the story of God creating Adan and Eve and fashioning these first humans in best possible way and gifting them with best of attributes (95:4), a trait that is endowed in every human being. God endowed Adam with knowledge and free will and presented him to the Angels. All Angels did bow down to Adam except Satan, who refused out of arrogance and pride. Islamic tradition says that Satan was a Jinn (a spirit created from fire with humanlike free will) who elevated himself to an Angel for his good work and good grace from God but fell from God's grace when he refused to follow God's command with respect to Adam. Satan considered human beings the source of his fall from grace and sought permission from God to live till the Day of Judgment so that he could deceive and mislead human beings. God granted such permission to Satan, and Satan commits to every effort (7:17) to encircle each and every human being from all directions and from all vantage points to use lust and hate, jealousy and pride, poverty and wealth, injustice and oppression, lies and ignorance, false hope and despair, fake news and alternative facts to mislead and degrade human conditions on this planet.

His first attempt was to mislead Adam and Eve regarding the forbidden tree (7:19–21) by telling a lie about its fruit to instigate Adam and Eve to disobey God, as Satan himself had done before. Satan is labeled as an enemy of mankind in every sense of the word in the Qur'an, and humanity has been repeatedly cautioned not to align with Satan, an alignment that is directly opposite to God and goodness, as evidenced in 7:26–27.

5. Adam and Eve's first repentance (7:23)

Although we all know the story of Adam and Eve in the Bible and the Qur'an, there are significant differences in the narratives of the key players in this epic struggle of human consciousness and the Devil's attempt to humiliate and degrade the human condition. Biblical stories attempt to put the blame on Eve for the failure to follow God's advice not to go near the tree, display God's anger at the failure of Adam and Eve, and create the notion of original sin, which is the cause of human expulsion from Heaven onto this hostile earth, human suffering, and constant temptation from the Devil.

Qur'anic narratives, while overlapping some of the facts described in the Bible, take on a very different plane of context and understanding, with the human capacity to acknowledge failure, the resolution to do better, and God's infinite mercy and grace to His creation. The story starts by designating Adam to be a very special creation, endowed with knowledge and free will and an explicit acknowledgment from the Angels that Adam (and by implication mankind) is a superior creation whose nature is aligned with God's nature and is endowed with knowledge and free will as a reflection of a human's godly attributes. Each human being is given a soul that is the repository of such gifts, and it will continue to exist beyond our physical presence on this planet.

When Angels express misgivings about the human condition and destiny—and rightfully so, as is amply evident in our world today—God simply says that He knows better what human beings are capable of and what He designed for than what may be apparent on the surface. The Devil (a Jinn and not a fallen Angel) becomes the first casualty of the human presence and the first enemy, only to be multiplied by humans themselves, who follow the Devil's pride, ignorance, and prejudice. While the Devil deceives

Adam and Eve (the Qur'an does not corroborate the biblical story of a serpent that beguiles Eve) to lure them near the tree and eventually eat its fruit, this turn of events, instead of creating original sin, puts into motion a series of human emotions, physical awareness, and spiritual yearning (like a real child as he or she is born from the mother's womb) that paves the way for human descent to the earth and our eventual return back to God, to whom we truly belong.

Adam and Eve immediately realized their failure, became aware of their physical dimensions and attractions, and resolved to overcome their failure. This event was God's way to unleash human potential as a primordial volcanic eruption leads a beautiful island (think Hawaii) that invites all creatures to come and seek livelihood, family, and spiritual maturity. This verse articulates in the most eloquent and succinct way how a human being should react to failures and seek out God as the source of guidance, thereby epitomizing the very essence of God's design for mankind as follows:

- Adam and Eve did not blame the Devil (or worse, God) for their failure. Instead they understood that they had failed the first test of justice and truth, which is to be truly aligned with our true nature, the nature of God in which we are created. This misalignment is the source of all injustice; hence, they felt true remorse at being unjust to themselves rather than pointing fingers at others.
- Realizing their failure, they did not become despondent and desperate like the Devil when he failed the test (to bow before Adam). Instead, they were full of hope of God's mercy because they understood who God is and how His forgiveness is ever present to all who genuinely seek such forgiveness and exercise forgiveness themselves. Adam and Eve forgave each other and reflected on their own condition, vulnerabilities, and what needed to be done to recover.
- They understood that unless they course corrected and sought guidance from God, they would be in a state of constant decline, which their human nature was unwilling to accept and succumb to.

This prayer of Adam and Eve at the occurrence of their first failure (verse 23) is quintessentially human, and people of faith should take this to heart. It is not a coincidence that this prayer of Adam and Eve is a prayer that every Muslim utters during his or her daily prayer, and the very last segment of the Islamic daily prayer ends with a similar statement to keep this tradition alive: *"O God, indeed we are unjust to ourselves, oppressing our soul daily. None can forgive our failures and shortcoming but You. Therefore, shower us with forgiveness and special mercy from yourself as You are Ever Merciful and Forgiving."* This is how we connect with God and to our ancestors such as Adam and Eve.

6. *Taqwa* as protection against evil (7:26, 35)

Central to the Islamic concept of faith and goodness is personal responsibility and a genuine sense of duty to God and to fellow human beings. This is codified in the word *taqwa*, which is commonly misrepresented as simple piety and symbolized by someone who is drawn to daily prayer in the mosque, grows a beard (or wears a hijab), and perhaps wears Arab dress to show piety. This is certainly a gross mischaracterization of the what taqwa really means.

As common in all Arabic words, there is a root word consisting of three letters, and in this case, the root is *waqa*, which conveys a deep commitment to preserving, protecting, and aligning with what is the reality, the truth, the pristine state of the soul, and our human nature, which is the nature of God. Hence *wiqayah* signifies an act of preserving, restoring, and aligning with what is true and something done exceptionally well. Sometimes *taqwa* is used to signify guarding against evil in classical commentaries of the Qur'an. That is also not fully representative of what *taqwa* stands for. Google's slogan, Do No Evil, is not same as doing good, and the absence of evil does not guarantee the presence of good unless there is active imperative to do *"good."*

Taqwa represents that sense of duty and personal responsibility that draws one (as opposed to forces one) to what is good and naturally repels one from what is evil. Harnessing this instinct and being true to our human nature is what *taqwa* really implies and wishes to impart when God said that the Qur'an will act as a guide for those who have taqwa (ref 2:2), more so than who profess to be a Muslim or claim faith (*imaan*).

This verse (26) uses a simple but powerful analogy to make the same point. God gifted us with a mechanism to make clothing (after the Devil exposed Adam and Eve to their nakedness), and clothing serves several important purposes: to cover our shame (keep our evil instincts under control); to protect our physical body from heat, cold, and other hazards; and, equally important, to beautify ourselves to move us to a more aesthetically pleasing level of existence and experience. Taqwa is presented as the clothing of the soul, enabling it to fight evil, to preserve its natural state to be in conformity with God's nature, and to move to the higher spiritual ground to bring elegance and brilliance to our human condition. That is the true understanding of taqwa. You can also look in volume 1, where the glossary #9 and footnote #2 add further nuances to this very important concept and term used in the Qur'an.

7. Genuine worship and devotion to God (7:29, 31–32, 204–206)

Throughout the Qur'an, the notion of worship of God and its obligation at prescribed times such as the times of daily, weekly (Friday Mass—*Jummah*) and special prayers such as during the month of Ramadan are mentioned repeatedly as a continuous reminder. Such reminders are also accompanied by the required mind-set, spiritual predisposition, and keen awareness of our being from God and our destiny back to God. In this chapter (surah), such reminders are prominent in three different places, as listed in the verses.

The first call comes along with a command to be just and to maintain justice as a requisite as well as a result of being faithful to God and our ability and commitment to show true devotion where we reorient ourselves to God with true sincerity and commitment at each time of formal and informal prayer.

The second call comes to remind us that we should be in our best form—both physically (healthwise and aesthetically) and spiritually—at times of prayer and that we should take advantage of provisions and resources that God has gifted us with, without being driven by consumerism and wastefulness. Our commitment to God is being put on the same level with God's commitment to provide us with the good things of this world, not only in this life but in the life to come after death.

The third and last call in this chapter comes at the very end, where we are reminded that the Qur'an is a living source of God's guidance, and we should pay close attention to the Qur'an during prayer and during its reading at other times. Such reading and listening should be done with humility, consciousness, and a mindfulness that permeates our daily conduct and larger pursuits in life. We are also reminded that pride has no place in God's worship and bowing down and prostrating ourselves in front of God is the ultimate show of humility and devotion that has been made part of Islamic prayer rituals.

8. All forms of indecency are forbidden (7:33, 28)

Throughout the Qur'an a strong emphasis is placed on common human decency, and we have been warned time and again to stay away from all forms of indecency, irrespective of whether such forms of indecency are explicit or hidden from other humans. Indecencies are not only immoral and shameful acts such as indecent exposure and sexual indiscretions that are commonly associated with indecency, but, more importantly, they include any form of sinful act that is against God and against human beings. Acts of rebellion against peace and social justice, violation of all forms of human and women's rights, denying God's supremacy in our world, doing evil in the name of God, and establishing a divine partnership with God are all considered acts of indecency without any authority from God.

When a community or a nation justifies such indecencies in its individual and collective conduct and mores and then gives justification based on previous generations and, worse still, on God's command, God clearly states in verse 28 that such justifications are unacceptable and cannot be from God, since God never commands anything that comes even close to such indecency.

The key takeaway is that every generation has to revisit its social norms and continue to question what is decent and what is indecent from human and divine perspectives, rather than simply rely on the accepted norms and beliefs from previous generations, while being respectful and thoughtful about the knowledge and wisdom gathered over the generations of human understanding and experience. But it is never sufficient nor responsible behavior to perpetuate norms and practices that are incompatible with our genuine understanding of what is decent and indecent.

9. Salvation is through faith in God and humility (7:40–45, 55–56)

Salvation is a major theme in all religions, principally among the Catholics and Evangelicals of Christian faith who consider it an exclusive domain of their faith to the exclusion of others. For the better part of Christian history and the ascendency of the papal institution, Catholics have been told that only they are the ones to receive salvation though faith in God and in Jesus Christ. Many modern-day Evangelicals and people of Latter-Day Saints (i.e., Mormons) also take on this vigorous notion that only they are eligible for salvation. Some conservative Muslims and clerics, particularly from the Middle East, also expound the same notion, that they are the only ones worthy of God's grace, to the exclusion of others. Many people of Jewish faith, especially those who are Orthodox and conservative, feel that only such Jews will be favored by God to the exclusion of to others. Some of these types of mentality have led to forced conversions by the Crusaders, slavery, global conflicts, ethnic cleansing, wholesale massacre of indigenous people in the Americas, and even the current widespread sentiment about the so-called clash of civilizations, fueled by populist sentiment in the United States and Europe.

The sense of reality that we find in God's guidance and throughout the Qur'an is very different from the above sentiments and beliefs. These verses, in consonance with many other verses, in the Qur'an portray a different picture that can be summarized as follows:

- Salvation will be denied to those who deny God and reject His guidance out of arrogance, irrespective of any counterclaim perpetuated by clerics and scholars of various faiths, superficial religious affiliations, and derivation of self-serving assertions without regard to human affinity to faith and goodness.
- Unblemished faith in One God and goodness to fellow human beings are the only acceptable grounds for God's grace, and God assures us that each one of us is capable of such belief and pursuit.
- Fast-forwarding to resurrection after death, God makes it clear though storytelling and conversations among various groups of people that those who misguide people and hinder people from genuine understanding of God and cause confusion between what is good versus what is evil and who plunge into evils are the ones who will not achieve salvation. Their affiliation with a religious group will not be the deciding criteria or basis for salvation.
- Verses 55–56 add further clarity that only genuine faith, true humility, and preserving peace and harmony among people are the true attributes of seeking and hoping for God's mercy and ultimate salvation.

10. The final sequel to the Qur'an (7:52–53)

The Qur'an, as a Book of Revelations from God, is the final sequel to other Books of Revelations such as the Torah, the Bible, and other revelations of antiquity that can be attributed to biblical prophets such as Abraham and David, among others; to other historical figures such as Buddha, Confucius, and Krishna in some of the existing major religious; and spiritual teachings that continue to inspire millions of people all over the globe. The Qur'an, as well as prophetic traditions, affirms that God sent prophets over generations of human beings to every part of the planet to ensure that God's guidance would be available to all over time and distance. Some of these teachings have survived in fragments, while others have maintained their totality, in substance if not in their original forms, such as the Torah and the Bible, while the Qur'an, by all historical accounts and as affirmed by God Himself, has been and will be preserved in its entirety for all future generations. The Qur'an as such is considered the final revelation that encapsulates all of God's revelations and is declared here and in many other places as a Book that contains knowledge and guidance, and it's a source of mercy from God for all who aspire to believe as well as for those who believe.

Having said that, there continue to be doubts and misalignments with regard to the guidance contained in books such as the Qur'an and the Bible for a number of factors such as

- the lack of continued deliberations by each generation to continue to improve our understanding of the scripture and its implementation in our continually evolving social, political, and moral constructs;
- creating undue bifurcation between human sciences and scriptural guidance without open and honest conversations that focus on human upliftment rather than narrow and self-serving dogmatic views in all spheres of human knowledge, historical religious practices without proper grounding in scriptures, and doctrines and human and societal biases across nations and communities;
- the corruption of scriptures and undue control by religious authorities over how scriptures should be studied and interpreted, let alone implemented, and the outright assertion by those who lack faith in God that scriptural guidance is irrelevant and that only human knowledge, however flawed, matters; and, last but not least,
- a lack of genuine desire among various parties, communities, and religious groups to focus on our common origin, common faith in God, and common destiny that encompasses not only our presence on this planet but also the life that will continue to exist beyond our temporal life on this planet.

The Qur'an provides a framework (4:59) for addressing our issues by making reference to scripture and the teachings of prophets and community leaders; seeking input from experts in politics, human knowledge, and science; and always remaining true to our inner core of a human being, which always seeks God, truth, justice, and human dignity. Throughout human history we have seen examples of how such a framework uplifts human conditions and creates a civilization that we can be proud of. The rise of Moses and his followers against slavery in Egypt; the rise of early Christians against the Romans; the spread of Islam against the practices of polytheism, social injustice, and denial of science and human knowledge; and the American Revolution and experiment against the usurpation of power and religious corruption are some examples of large-scale successes of this framework, with the acknowledgment that even such successes had elements and periods of failure that are well documented and well known to our generation, such as the Holocaust, the Spanish Inquisition, slavery on the American continent, European colonial expansion, two world wars, widespread corruption across Muslim lands, unprecedented negligence of our environment, and alarming income disparities among people on this planet.

Verse 53 calls our attention to the fact that we will be called to account for our failures, and the final sequel to the revelations will be the revelation of God Himself, when truth will become no longer subject to denial or dispute, our intentions will made known to everyone, and we will make excuses for our failures and wish to be sent back so that we can right the wrongs we committed in our lifetime on this planet.

11. God, the Creator Supreme (7:54–58)

Unlike other Books of Revelations, the Qur'an devotes a significant part of its messages to drawing our attention to the creation of the natural world and how it is purposefully created and constructed to sustain our lives through the application of physical sciences and spiritual aspirations and how Mother Earth, with its vastness and expansive biodiversity, creates the ideal condition of fruits, vegetables, and grains growing in abundance to sustain our lives and the lives of all creatures, known and unknown.

Verse 54 reminds us that God is the Creator of the Universe and this planet of ours. He created them in a measured way and assumed full control of their existence and operation. An example of such operation is the persistent and consistent alteration of day and night that profoundly affects our lives and sense of purpose in the most elegant way conceivable. By the same token, we are told that the sun, the moon, and numerous stars are purposely driven to sustain lives, our lives. Through physical sciences we have a good grasp of how our lives depend on the sun, 93 million miles away, and how the rotation of the earth around the sun and around its own axis creates the possibility of day and night in a consistent and elegant manner, which only God can make possible. God reminds us that His is the creation and its operation, and we should acknowledge His presence and His gifts with utmost humility and a deep sense of awareness and gratitude, without which the transgression of natural laws and abuse of the natural world will take place, a situation that is far too evident already in terms of global warming, pollution of our environment, widespread income inequality, and corrupt governance all over the world, both political and financial, not to mention the moral degradation that results from such conditions.

To drive home the points made above, God reminds us to look around and see how the wind blows, drawing up moisture from oceans and rivers, forming clouds laden with His mercy, and pours down water to thirsty earth so that fruits and vegetation can grow, to the delight of all creatures, including humans; this is an apt analogy to how God will bring out the living again from the dead on the Day of Resurrection. The variety of soil and weather conditions on the earth creates varying degrees of fertility and foliage growth, reminding us once more of God's ability to sustain and constrain lives as He pleases. Our lives and our physical world are a constant reminder for each and every one of the conscious human beings to understand the essence of God's presence and purpose and to live a purposeful and thankful live. Without thankfulness and purposefulness, there can be no human development, either spiritual and physical.

12. The rule of law and tranquility (7:56)

This verse is foundational to the rule of law that God wishes and that every human society should endeavor to achieve and sustain. A call is made to each individual, especially those who believe and wish to be good human beings, that any form of mischief, be it anarchy, indecency, a violation of human dignity, injustice, income inequality, abuse of natural resources, pollution of the natural environment, or anything that we all can name and agree on, should not be a norm in one's life and in one's community, and where such a situation exists in whatever shape or form or to whatever extent, effort should be made to bring about reformation to establish the new norm (natural norm) of peace and prosperity with human freedom and allowance for equal opportunity to every human being in every part of the world.

God wants us to be mindful of Him and our responsibilities as faithful human beings to aspire to peace in the face of mischief and to fear that if we are not mindful and continuously exerting ourselves to goodness, mischief will take over even if peace is the current norm. Every generation has to aspire to peace and also fear the consequences if we are negligent so that we can be driven to be vigilant and act proactively. As the previous verse also implies, humility and quiet deliberation on matters of faith and justice are akin. Be mindful of God with humility in your private moments, not only in the public square and places of worship.

At the very end of the verse 56, God reminds us that He is always with those who wish and do good, to give us courage and confidence that the effort that we put in to curb mischief in our society and to bring about reformation of truth and justice will always win if we are genuine, thoughtful, and innovative and work collectively, because God is on our side always.

13. Nature as a constant reminder (7:57–58)

Living in the twenty-first century, many of us have become accustomed to material progress and modern infrastructure that protects us from the elements of the weather and to getting our food and other necessities from grocery stores and Amazon and have become oblivious to the direct connection with nature and our own existence. Instead of being thankful for all that God has enabled us to do and achieve through our knowledge, technology, and natural resources, some of us deny that God has any hand in our progress and our very survival on this planet.

The reality of our existence is that we are deeply and utterly dependent on this planet for our survival—in terms of food, water, and air to feed and sustain us; the natural resources we use to build our buildings, our computers, and our transportation; the cotton and synthetics for our clothing; and herbs, plants, and minerals for our medicine; and so on, to give few examples that we can readily connect to.

God reminds us that it is He who directs winds in our global weather patterns to distribute good news of His mercy in terms of rain to nourish the earth and to carry pollen to bring out fruits from trees and to distribute seed across the lands. The wind carries water vapor from oceans and rivers to form clouds and drives such water to land that needs water so that fruits and vegetables can grow to create and support our extended food chain. The emergence of such growth, its abundance, its beauty, and our freedom to cultivate and extract such nourishment should be a reminder of God, that we should be thankful in the most genuine and profound way. Also, the variations in the productivity of various lands and various climates that produce different fruits and vegetables that expansively and profoundly affect our lives and the lives of other creatures, the enormous variety of flora and fauna that are also a source of spiritual understanding of our own fragile existence, and our utter dependency on God should being a deep sense of humility and thankfulness and care for one another, as Mother Nature does without asking questions or showing any discrimination.

God repeats such natural cycles of growth and life, and our mutual dependencies to communicate and share His messages and guidance, especially for people who are tuned to thoughtfulness and purposefulness and are able to distance themselves from the day-to-day preoccupation of earning and earthly pleasure and consider it a worthy pursuit to reflect on life, its diversity, and its beauty and to connect the dots as to where it comes from, what makes life possible, and where we go from this planet after our death. Disregarding God's guidance and being overly consumed by our material progress has been one of the major shortcomings of our century, and conscientious and mindful people—young and old—have to engage to reverse such apathy and denial of God's grace to humanity.

14. The prophets as guides—Noah, Hud, Salih, Lot, Shu'aib (7:59–93)

Beginning with this chapter, the Qur'an begins to provide additional narratives on prophets—the biblical prophets mostly—with an aim to demonstrate the common thread among all prophets and the common destiny of their communities and followers. There is a common pattern of the message; the enmity that it generates among people against prophets and their followers; and the eventual outcome, where the deniers of prophets and God's messages were humbled or removed with another generation of people to come and rehash the same message, perhaps with different prophets and under different living conditions and civilizations. The overall pattern has been repeated with following key attributes:

- Prophets were raised from the communities themselves, where they spent a part of their early lives so that they would understand the social norms, existing beliefs and customs, the power dynamics, and the social structure, and they spoke their language to be effective communicators.
- These prophets were of exemplary character, and they were thoughtful individuals even before they became prophets and earned the respect of their communities for their care, concern, and humility. But once they were given prophethood and began to question their community about their false or flawed belief systems, disregarding the God Who should be worshipped, when they warned their communities about social injustice and ignorant customs and practices, when they sided with the poor and the oppressed, it generated powerful responses from the rich and powerful, from the corrupt and the morally bankrupt against such prophet's teachings and moral stance.

- In most instances fewer people followed the prophets, fearing the oppression of the powerful, expecting handouts from the rich, being ignorant of and accustomed to the existing norms and practices of their forefathers and being unable or unwilling to seek truth and justice in their lives.
- Eventually, when the lives of the faithful and the followers of the prophets were made unbearable, God always sided with them and protected them once they had proven their commitment to faith, to truth, and to justice, while He curtailed the reach and the power of the rejecters of faith through natural disaster, internal dissention, moral bankruptcy, and increasingly dysfunctional social order and practices.

The purpose of these stories is to remind future generations to take lessons and to proactively manage their affairs and safeguard faith, truth and justice in their lives and in their communal acts and practices.

15. God's challenge and warning to people (7:94–99)

God follows certain prescribed ways of nudging people toward faith and what is good, but at the end of the day, people have to demonstrate their understanding and commitment through civil discourse, reforming their lives and societies based on truth and justice, establishing rule of law that respects human freedom and dignity, and creating a social order that allows each and every human being the maximum potential to blossom into a full human being worthy of God's creation and His representation on the planet.

God has sent prophets and people of knowledge, consciousness, and goodwill in every generations in the past. And there will always be conscious human beings driven by God-given intellect, a higher vision for humanity, and a desire to right the wrongs of the day in every generation to come. As God said in the Qur'an, for every prophet there have been enemies, and so, in every generation, leaders who bring consciousness into our individual and collective conduct, call for justice in our social order, inspire knowledge over ignorance, and exhibit humility over arrogance will be faced with the forces of evil, ignorance, and arrogance, devoid of consciousness in God and in human purpose. Such affairs are part of the construct of our world, as through such means God inspires and confirms those who are committed to faithfulness and goodwill while confronting the evils of those who are creating evidence of their own wrongdoing in the process.

Human sufferings, afflictions, and even natural calamities are reminders to bring humility, patience, and conscious purposefulness into our lives, whereas sustained affluence and happiness can lead to a false sense of security and a denial of God's presence in our lives. By the same token, a reverse outcome is also a possibility. That is one of the reasons that the Prophet cautioned that sustained poverty can lead to denial of God and advised his wealthy followers not to give away all their wealth to charity but to leave some for their heirs.

God makes a conditional promise in verse 96 that if we as humanity, in any part of the world, truly believe in God and develop conscious purposefulness in our personal and communal lives, God will open up blessings and human development from all possible sources, even unknown to current generation. Throughout human history such predictions have played out. Our history has been recorded with some level of detail, and certainly our current world order reflects that reality as it continues to unfold in front of our eyes.

While God's promise for His blessing and human development is conditioned on our collective affinity to our common humanity and connection to God, we are also reminded that we do not take such blessings and prosperity for granted. Just as physical calamities and danger can appear from nowhere during any part of the day or night or from above or beneath the earth, the real danger lurks in the negligence of our soul and a diminished or lost connection with God.

16. Human failure to maintain God's covenant (7:100–102)

Human societies, from the time of Abel and Cain (the first recoded human conflict, a selfish and ungodly act recorded in the scriptures) to our modern day, continue to defy our covenant with God—sometimes with defiance and outright rejection, such as the Pharaoh, Lenin, Hitler, and Mao Ze Dung, to name a few, and at other times through deception and hypocrisy, such as corrupt practices and a lack of democratic institutions in many Muslim countries, using labels such as Islamic Republic or People's Republic; church-sponsored slavery or Crusades for Western democracies, which shows a persistent affinity for some form of racism in terms of color or national or religious affiliation in modern-day religious and atheist extremists all over the world, be it in the name of Islam (ISIS in the Middle East), Christianity (some Evangelicals and white supremacists in the United States), Hindu nationalists in India, communists in China and Russia, or corporate greed that is leading to extreme income inequality all over the world, even in the first-world countries.

As generations after generations inherit this earth, God takes stock of our conduct, our institutions, and our social constructs and afflicts us with natural consequences, as He sees it, for our evils and misdeeds (more so than as God's punishment, as some religious people would like to assert) and lets us persist in such evils with an expectation that people of conscience, godliness, and goodness will rise to the occasion and restore the balance that is very much a bedrock of human survival, success, and our savior (not Jesus, not Mohammad, but our deeds) with God.

The lack of commitment to the covenant with God is at times widespread. No generation is immune from it, but as time and again we have seen throughout history, the human condition—both material as well as spiritual—improves when we strive to be faithful to our covenant with God, which is nothing more than *"to seek the truth and to establish justice thereby"* (7:181).

17. Lessons from Moses (7:103–129, 142–156)

The stories of Moses, the Children of Israel, their sufferings, their triumphs, and their trials are mentioned in many places in the Qur'an, many of which corroborate what was already in the Torah and the Bible and, in some cases, add more color and nuance to the story and always end with a statement of lessons to be taken. In these two segments, the first segment is pre-Exodus, when Moses came back to the Pharaoh, in whose household he was raised, as a prophet of God to speak truth about God and human conditions and to rescue the Children of Israel from slavery. The second segment is post-Exodus, where the Children of Israel were secure from the Pharaoh and achieved the freedom to manage their lives, which became a trial for them when Moses went to Mount Sinai to receive the tablets of Ten Commandments and other instructions that are the basis for the Torah.

When Moses came to the Pharaoh, he had nothing with him except the endowment from God of prophethood, his intellect, his experience, his brother Aaron for company and help against a powerful king who declared himself to be God, and a group of people who were reduced to slavery and despair but sustained a deep longing to be freed and to live their lives as a community of common heritage of Israel, a lineage that goes back to Joseph, to Jacob, to Isaac, and to Abraham. Moses brought no visible hope to his people but only increased the resolve and arrogance of the Pharaoh to deny God and oppress the Children of Israel even more. In this context, the conversation noted in verse 129 between Moses and his people is worth dwelling on to deepen our understanding of human conditions and God's expectation of us. "His people lamented: 'We are being persecuted—before you came and since you are here.' Moses comforted them: 'It may well be that God will destroy your tormentor and give you a hand in overseeing the affairs of the land. God will see how you conduct yourselves then.'"

The Children of Israel were divided, as this always happens under extreme oppression and injustice. One group was in despair, as they saw that nothing had gotten better since the arrival of Moses but had only gotten worse. Another group understood that persecution would continue before things get better, as God was on their side, and they cautioned Moses and themselves not to take on the blame for the persecution and lose hope. It was to such human aspiration that Moses spoke to when he said that perhaps God would destroy their enemy and give the rule of the land to them in turn. Such a turn of events was not the end goal, as we reflect on what he said next. He said that once you get your rule and command of the land and your affairs, then God will see how you manage your freedom and your affairs, affairs that need be managed based on truth and justice.

This leads to the second segment, where Moses was in deep devotion on Mount Sinai to receive guidance from God—the Ten Commandments, which form the very foundation of evolving human societies. But his community abused their God-given freedom, created division among themselves, refused to listen to Aaron, and degraded themselves to worshipping a calf instead of God, who had saved them from the Pharaoh. This was the beginning of a series of ups and downs in Jewish history during the lifetime of Moses and afterward, as there had been repeated incursions against the covenant of God and His repeated forgiveness. In each case, a smaller group of resilient faithful always exerted themselves to bring themselves back to God's guidance and renewed their commitment to truth and justice, a legacy that was propagated by many Jewish prophets, including Jesus and finally by Mohammad, a prophet declared to be a mercy to all of mankind, and a final revelation, the Qur'an, corroborates, augments, and completes the long series of God's guidance to mankind, including the Bible and the Torah.

18. The Prophet Mohammad as a guide (7:157–158)

Aside from the confirmation that the advent of the Prophet Mohammad is mentioned in both the Torah and the Bible, which is detailed in the footnotes corresponding to verse 157, I would like to draw attention to certain attributes of the Prophet and the faithful that are really the crux of these two important verses. The following attributes of the Prophet are mentioned:

- He was an unlettered person who did not know how to read or write, but he was deeply aware of the social customs and beliefs of his people, including the few Christians and many Jews who lived in and around Makkah during his upbringing, his trade journeys to Syrian and Yemen, and his interactions with people coming to trade in Mecca during the season of pilgrimage. Some Muslim scholars would like to assert that given that he could not have read the Torah or the Bible, he must have known nothing of the Christian and Jewish faiths, while some non-Muslim scholars like to assert that he borrowed his Qur'an narratives from reading of the Torah and the Bible, thereby trying to negate the divine origin of the Qur'an. Both positions are untenable and have been refuted in the literature of the past and need no further discussion here.

- The Prophet has been characterized as someone who inspires, motivates, and provides legal frameworks for what is good and how to be good while discouraging and prohibiting all that is evil and impure—a characterization that is equally true of Moses and Jesus, but Jesus did not have the opportunity to put his teachings into practice, given the threat to his life, and Moses had repeated setbacks, as his community, time and again, deviated from his teachings even while he was with them. The followers of Mohammad demonstrated a steady resolve to adhere to his teachings and to reform societies after his prophethood and through the sixteenth century, a steady progression for almost a thousand years.
- The Prophet is characterized as liberating people from the shackles of ignorance, oppression, and superstition and enlightening them with knowledge, wisdom, and freedom to choose and make informed and responsible choices about life, liberty, and success that really matter.
- The Prophet, as declared in the Qur'an, was a teacher and messenger for all of humanity, not confined to a region or an ethnic group, and he was guided and sent by none other than the Creator of the Universe, Who is the One and Only God and Who gifts life and brings death so that we can be brought back to a new life that will be shaped by our current life.

Time and again, the Qur'an makes us take a step back and take stock of the person of Mohammad, whose life and legacy is a living memory and inspiration of what is possible when human beings put faith in God and demonstrate unfailing commitment to truth and justice.

19. Moses's followers recognized (7:159)

Throughout the Qur'an there is a persistent theme that seeking truth and establishing justice is the cornerstone of God's message to mankind. All prophets, notably the last three prophets—Moses, Jesus, and Mohammad—were inspired and instructed to deliver the same message and put their guidance into practice.

In this verse, God recognizes that a group of followers of Moses, at the time of the, Prophet, was committed to be guided by the truth and to establish justice in their communities. This has been true throughout Jewish history, even to this date, even though some Muslims and Christians might disagree. In a similar manner, there have always been groups of Christians who did the same throughout Christian history, a recent example being the founding fathers of the American Revolution, who were people of deep faith in God and demonstrated an uncompromising stance on liberty, justice, and the pursuit of human purposefulness.

In today's climate of political corruption, national isolationism, corporate greed, and religious extremism all over the world, we can take lessons from the Qur'an to have the humility and generosity to acknowledge the genuine otherness of others and their respective contributions and capacity to do good and to focus more on our collective responsibility to seek the truth and establish justice. As God said in another instance in the Qur'an (7:181), *"Let there be from among the people, a group who seek the truth and establish justice thereby"*—a call to all of humanity who wish to listen, irrespective of faith affiliation, to establish our common humanity to one another and to God, our Creator.

20. Human failings and successes (7:168–170)

There are certain human conditions that are persistent in every generation and in every geographical location but with varying levels of persistence and intensity. There are people of faith and goodwill in each, while there exist evils and evil people as well. Each group is tried with abundance, blessings, and trials of misfortunes, which affect each group differently. The intent from God is to turn evil people away from evils and toward faith and goodwill and to keep people of faith and goodwill on their path steadily.

Here attention is drawn to a generation—and this could be applied to any group from any faith, be they Muslims, Christians, Jews or other faith group—that inherited God's guidance from previous generations who were righteous and good people. This generation turned their backs to God's guidance and used God's Book to justify their evilness. The Crusades, the Spanish Inquisition, the Holocaust in Europe, and slavery on the American continent are stark reminders from the Christian group that abused their faith in exchange for evil. At the same time, the American Revolution against the British and the example of the founding fathers of Unites States of America are a shining example of those who turned misfortune and oppression into a path of righteousness and human freedom that is unparalleled in human history.

While the Prophet of Islam and his early generations of followers for a thousand years ushered in, over a vast expanse of this planet, advances in education, science and technology, the rule of law, and human freedom and justice, recent generations of Muslims, even after the experience of colonialization, have failed to bring education, human freedom, and justice to their societies and are mired in inept political leadership, widespread corruption, and abuse of Islamic laws in the name of so-called Sharia and in flagrant violation of women's rights in most of the Islamic countries.

Although the Jewish faith ushered in for the first time organized faith in One God and a community of faithful based on truth and justice, over time the rabbis and Jewish legal scholars persisted in interpreting the Torah to benefit themselves personally and brought corruption in faith and in social practices, later to be followed by the popes in the Christian faith; and their opposition to Jesus, a Jewish prophet, and the recent atrocities and massive displacement of Palestinian Muslims and Christians in the name of a Jewish state is very much contrary to the teachings of Moses. It is remarkable to reflect on the conversation that Moses had with his community at the time of their dire oppression by the Pharaoh. He said: *"Perhaps God will make you the leader of the land, and then He (God) will see how you behave."*

Perhaps it is time for all the Muslims, Jews, Christians, and people of faith all over the world to reflect on our current generation and question our individual and collective faith and our lack of alignment with truth and justice, despite enormous increases in human knowledge and human sciences. God is consistent in reiterating that any group of people who have faith, seek the truth, and establish justice will prevail in the long run on this planet and will be rewarded by God in the life to come.

When the forty-fifth president of the United States talks of faith in God on the one hand and supports white supremacists and neo-Nazis on the other hand, one can see the direct evidence of the evils that come when we allow leaders and societies to turn back on God's teachings and justify evil in the name of God and religion. We have seen this before, and we need to be ever vigilant to be successful, as God is always on the side of truth and justice, as stated in verse 170.

21. God reveals to us all (7:172–174)

The notion that God presents Himself to every newborn, the descendants of Adam and Eve, and that each one of us in every generation experiences this truth, is something that we need to reflect on deeply and treasure like no other truth and experience, yet it is hard to search and find in our memory when and how this happens or happened.

God says in this verse that He reveals Himself to every child who is born and asks him or her to assess a simple truth: Am I not your Sustainer Creator? God does not force the simple truth that He is the God; instead He gives the choice to confirm or deny that He is God, a reminder of God's commitment (and an endowment) to Adam that humans have been endowed with the unique capacity to seek, gain, and teach knowledge and the resultant freedom and responsibility to make informed choices. Every child then responds: *"Yes, I bear witness (to this fundamental truth)."* God then goes on to express the reasoning behind His desire to reveal Himself at the beginning of each child's life. There are two reasons: (1) lest we complain to God on the Day of Resurrection—on our second birth—that we were unaware and uninformed of this fundamental truth, and (2) we assert that we are not at fault for not knowing God because our forefathers denied God or were polytheists and we just followed them without proper knowledge. God then goes on to say that this Qur'an and this verse, which each one of us can touch and read, reiterates the events of God's revelation to each of us at the time of our birth so that we can remind ourselves, reflect on our lives, and subscribe to this fundamental truth about God, about faith, and about a purposeful life so that we can educate, build capacity, and demonstrate active pursuit of faith and goodness in our lives before we go back to God at the time of death and give accounts of our lives on the Day of Resurrection.

Now one of the questions we need to ponder is when such revelation of God happens to a human child—is it at the time of birth, when a child is fully formed and ready to venture out into the world, or at the first smile a baby produces, or at first sound he utters, or at the first dream she has? Or does it happen that the soul that retains that knowledge and is embedded in every child at some point between conception and birth? I am not sure that there is a scientific experiment that we can conduct to discover that moment—or it will be left to philosophers to ponder or spiritualists to try to feel in every generation. Perhaps we can look and reflect on a few human experiences and thoughts to uncover this truth about our knowledge and acknowledgment of God. Every human being, human community, culture, and civilization from the beginning till today has demonstrated a yearning for God and has instinctively tried to connect with God on two levels: (1) at a personal level at times of tragedy or elation, knowing that none seems to have capacity to remove such tragedy (e.g., death and calamity) or bring such elation (e.g., the birth of a child; life-threatening moments, once removed) in our individual or collective experience and existence, and (2) we exist as part of a larger natural world—the earth with its vast expanses and resources, the atmosphere with its protective shield, the surrounding solar system where the sun acts as the source of all energy that we need for survival—this construct, which is part of a larger construct, is beyond our human capacity to build, maintain, and organize, let alone even to fathom its underlying construct and purpose. I realize that some of my atheist and humanist friends might think otherwise.

At another level, as a scientist, technologist, entrepreneur, and, certainly, as a fellow traveler on this journey of life, I have seen time and again and have observed that in every generation throughout human history, our human capacity to think, imagine, and dream is in itself a confirmation that that thought, that imagination, that dream is real and reflects a reality that already exists, but we need to renew our feeling, our experience or rediscover that reality. The fact that every single human being has a flickering light and yearning in the depths of their soul or their thoughts or their consciousness that there is a God is itself is an affirmation of that truth about God and our existence in His creation and a consequence of that conversation between God and the human child in each one of us.

22. The inability to use God-given endowments (7:179–180)

Every human being is endowed with certain capabilities and capacities that are unique to that individual, in addition to what is given to the human species as a special endowment from God unlike what is given to other creation. Two critical endowments are our capacity to seek, learn, and teach knowledge and our freedom to make choices. To enable these endowments, we are given eyes to see; ears to hear; a heart to feel; a voice to speak and articulate with; a brain to process, retain, analyze, and decide; and a soul with consciousness to align our purpose, thoughts, and actions with what is true and just.

Having these extraordinary gifts, many of us fail to take stock of our own capabilities and capacities and thereby fall short of our human potential at personal and community levels. In this first verse (179), God points out that there are those humans and Jinns (another creation of God that the Qur'an refers to, unlike any other Books of Revelations) who fail to use their eyes to see properly and their ears to listen and internalize carefully, and their hearts are devoid of true feelings and empathy. These specific examples are a symbolism of our mental and spiritual conditions that limit our consciousness and our ability to act properly. Such conditions are like an animalistic condition, which is inferior to the human condition. We are told that these people (humans and Jinns) are like cattle, or, even more misguided than these animals, and heedless, despite the extraordinary capacity to be otherwise.

God then draws our attention to His names (attributes), which are also human attributes (30:30), and makes a call that we live and act according to these attributes and not be influenced by those humans who violate such attributes—that is, failing to honor our own better judgments and conditions, which are a reflection of what God has endowed us with, in keeping with His own attributes. We are told that those who fail in their pursuit of truth and justice will face the consequences of their failure; one such consequence is an Afterlife in Hell, as well as making our peaceful earth a hellish place for others.

23. Seeking truth and doing justice (7:181, 159)

In two instances in the same chapter, God repeats His recurring inspiration and expectations of people of faith—that truth and justice are intricately and profoundly linked, so without truth, justice cannot prevail or be restored, and without justice, truth cannot come out and be heard.

In the first instance, God proclaims that Mohammad has been sent as a Messenger to the entire world (all of humanity) by God, Whose dominion encompasses the earth and the entire universe and Who controls life and death and has no partner in His command and Glory. The attributes of this Prophet are that although he is unlettered (*ummi*), he believes in God and follows God's words. It is then imperative that those who wish to believe in God and be good should follow the lead of the Prophet. In this context God also makes reference to the fact that Moses, a prophet of God, had among his followers also a group of people who sought and guided with truth, and with such truth they established justice.

In the second instance, in the backdrop of the discussion that many people do not use their eyes to see the truth, do not use their ears to listen to the truth, and do not use their hearts to feel and align with truth, we are told that we should align ourselves with the attributes of God, which are also human attributes. From such people, God always creates a group who, just like a group of the followers of Moses, will seek and guide with truth and with such truth seek to establish justice.

Truth and justice are two fundamental aspects of our lives and are the basic foundations of human development—both material as well as spiritual. Without truth, justice cannot be found or established, and without a just society, truth is difficult to seek and find. It is a holistic circle where the pursuit of truth will always lead to justice, and pursuit of justice will always lead to truth.

24. Our tendency to associate others with God (7:189–190)

For most of us, one of the most significant events in life is the birth of a child. The process of childbirth originates from God's grace in which He created Adam and Eve and from them generations of men and women who were drawn to each other for the love, comfort, and support that create the ideal conditions to contemplate having a child. A child is conceived in the mother's womb from the union of elements from the mother and the father and progresses slowly but surely over a period of almost ten months, a consistent process that enables us to anticipate, predict, and enjoy the grace of God in creating a new human being as a gift and as a responsibility—to support in his or her growth as well as in the growth of the parents themselves, as a newborn opens up a new world of excitement and challenges in raising another human being, a process that their parents went through a generation before.

While the process of a child growing in the mother's womb follows a consistent development patterns, there are times when things can go wrong, and not all pregnancies result in a healthy child. Every expectant parent eagerly monitors and feels the growth of the child in the womb and genuinely hopes that God will grace them with a healthy baby. At times of distressing news about the baby, they fall on their knees and beg God openly, and in their private moments, they seek God's continued blessings for the child.

While God always listens to the pleas and wishes of every expectant parent, the parents and the child, as they grow together, sometimes fail to live up to their alignment with God. Their belief system is not as genuine as it should be, and they persist in giving credit to themselves and to other man-made gods for delivering them a good baby. The baby becomes a distraction from God as opposed to keeping them close to God, and they indulge themselves and their child in beliefs and practices that are contrary to true belief in One God.

This story gets repeated in every generation, and with the advance of science and technology, there is a renewed danger that we as human beings, despite knowing better, become over-reliant on our own ability. This ability continues to expand through God-given knowledge while we become unmindful to the reality that we all come from God and to Him we will eventually return, and our accountability to God is not the least bit diminished by the increase of our knowledge and ability. On the contrary, our increased capacity for knowledge, science, and exploitation of the resources at our disposal will further lend credibility to the notion that we ought to be ever more grateful, humble, and mindful of our connection to God and not use that capacity as an excuse to deny God and His grace to humanity.

25. Simple guidance of forgiveness, goodness, and knowledge (7:199)

This verse comes on the heels of discussion of and references to the human tendency to associate the One True God with other deities, persona, and natural artifacts that are nothing but created beings or things and as such should not be worshipped or invoked. The previous verses caution us against any forms of superstition or ignorant worship or bad human conduct.

While atheists deny God and His grace for humanity, humanists believe human beings and humanity are the only source of our values, aspirations, and inspiration while denying or marginalizing God as if He did not exist—or, even if He exists, He is no longer actively engaged with humanity after its creation. Polytheists, on the other hand, assume that God is not the only entity who creates, nurtures, and takes accountability but that there are other deities or creatures or persona who act with or independently of God in taking care of or punishing human beings.

The Trinity in Christianity, for example, associates Jesus and Archangel Gabriel with God as if they were a trio managing the affairs of humanity, while God is the Creator and Head of these three godheads. Unitarians reject such concepts, and there are numerous variations and nuances among numerous denominations such as Catholics, Protestants, Methodists, Lutherans, and Greek Orthodox in Europe and America, along with other variations on different continents.

Hinduism in India, while accepting Brahma as the main god, has many other deities who act like demigods, performing specific activities and/or exhibiting specific characteristic of the natural order. Some groups even worship elephants or monkeys as gods and keep a god of their choice at home to whom they show daily devotion. Some Buddhists, even though they do not believe in God, act as if Buddha is a Godhead, and many Buddhists in Thailand, for example, consider the king as Godhead.

God in this specific verse offer three pieces of advice for humanity to consider in light of their differences in understanding who God is and how God should factor into their lives and in the expression of their common humanity. First and foremost, actively engage to seek knowledge about yourself as a human being, of human societies, and of the natural world so that ignorance does not take hold of your mind and your consciousness and let your search for knowledge lead you to the Truth and to God. Second, always strive to be good and do good to others, no matter what the circumstances are and whom you are interacting with, be it a person, an animal, a tree, an insect, air, water, the world at large. Third, while disagreements among human beings and human societies are inevitable, in matters of faith as well as all matter of life, we should keep knowledge and being good at the core of our conversations and efforts to resolve such disagreements, and if we cannot resolve the differences, forgiveness is a better course than coercion or any physical violence, specifically in matters of God and faith. God says repeatedly in the Qur'an that such matters should be left to God to resolve on the Day of Judgment, and while on earth, we should respect one another's faith and customs while advocating our own point of view with wisdom and the best of manners.

GLOSSARY OF KEY ARABIC TERMS

Chapter 5: Surah Al-Maidah (The Repast)

91. **aqd** (covenant)—commitment, treaty, relationship, promises, and so on—anything that binds a human being to another human being is to be respected and carried out, and we must be faithful to it. Having faith in God has implications with regard to God and to His creations. We are to fulfill all covenants and commitments that we bound by to God, to fellow human beings, and to the natural world that is created to sustain our lives on this planet and in this universe. True faith in God as defined in the Qur'an is a profoundly expansive notion of being faithful to each and every aspect of our existence in terms of the spiritual, the mental, and the physical. We have to be true to our spirit, as God had constructed in His image. We need to be true in the mental model of the world and our existence in that we exist to serve God and to serve people. Our physical needs and the competing needs of others have to be harmonized and shared without injustice or malice.

92. **hujuan wa layiban** (mockery and sport)—the way some people who do not have faith in God regard faith with mockery and jest to trivialize such faith and to make fun of those who proclaim faith. The same is, unfortunately, true of many people who claim to have faith but make mockery of one another's faith within their own religion and at times across religions, something that we witness in every generation but more so in our current world condition, where there is a persistent effort by Muslims, Jews, and Christians, for example, to pit the faithful against one another and to make fun of one another's faith rather than uniting based on our common faith in God and the faith that Abraham professed, which we all claim to subscribe to. This notion of mockery and sport also extends to conservative people who confine themselves to rituals and literal interpretations of their faith and make fun of those who do not accept their ways; similarly, there are people

who claim faith but are not willing to commit to its tenets making fun of those who are ritual bound and unwilling to think for themselves. Such divisions have weakened the faith community in all religions and have diminished the good that comes from true faith that is steeped in humility, wisdom, and constant awareness of our responsibilities to one another and to our Creator. We are advised to steer clear of such people, no matter what faith they might claim, and not to take life as a sport without purpose or meaning, as God said (21:16): *"We did not create the sky and the earth and all in between for mere play."*

93. **esmi wal wudwan** (sin and tyranny)— Sin is a moral transgression and a transgression against divine (natural) laws, while tyranny implies trespassing against the boundaries of the rule of law in a society, denying human freedom, oppressing others without measure and with deliberation, denying human beings that which naturally belongs to them such as natural resources, income equality or fairness in income distribution, and so on. The concept of sin and what is considered tyranny is somewhat universal, in the sense that each human being is endowed with understanding and intuitively feels what these are and when such sin or tyranny occurs, although there have been arguments put forth at various times and in various societies to justify such acts. The Ten Commandments from the Old Testament, which are accepted by people of Abrahamic faiths and human societies in general, define the boundary of sins that one can commit. The acceptance and abundance of promiscuous behavior in today's world, especially in developed countries, has been identified with modernity, goes directly against the Ten Commandments, and is fundamentally at odds with the teachings found in the Bible and the Qur'an. All forms of tyranny, which deprive human beings of their rights to exercise free expression and to freely seek means for survival and income and of their rights to safety, privacy, security, social justice in the form of political will, financial dealings, and natural resources, are being perpetrated on a large scale all over the

world through corrupt rulers, the faulty pursuit of democracy, financial greed, and unholy alliances between politicians and their financiers.

The Qur'an talk about this race for sin and tyranny, which existed at the time of the Prophet and continues even today. While the new faithful have been cautioned against such acts and excesses by their predecessors, in today's world people of all faiths—Muslims, Christians, and Jews—are succumbing to the same things that Moses, Jesus, and Mohammad so adamantly cautioned against to their respective followers. The prophet in his last sermon reflected on the same themes that are in the Ten Commandments and provided further clarification regarding our relationships among human beings, trust, accountability to God and to one another, and equality of gender (see appendix B of volume 2)

94. **kaulihimul esmi wa aklihimus suhta** (uttering sinful things and amassing wealth and power through illegal means)— This is in reference to the rabbis and doctors of law in the Jewish faith at the time of the Prophet Mohammad. This was also true at the time of the Prophet Jesus, as he also encountered the corruption and tyranny of the clerics and priests and those who claimed to be in charge of the religious practices of the Jewish faith. The Prophet Moses encountered similar tendency among his people at the time of his tenure as the Prophet when he saved the Children of Israel from the tyranny of the Pharaoh.

Those of us living in the twenty-first century, looking at the history of Jewish, Christian, and Muslim successes and failures over the last three thousand years, have witnessed the excess of the clerics and so-called scholars in all three religions and of other religions as well. Reformed Judaism came about because the Jewish clerics were consolidating their hold on the masses and enforcing things in the name of the religion that did not make sense. The papal institution and its tyranny on the Catholics is well documented, and it forced Christians to divide into a large number of denominations such as Protestant, Methodist, Baptist, and so on, to name a few. The lack of transparency in the governance of the Catholic Church and control of the rigid hierarchy in priesthood had turned it into an old men's club. The endorsement of slavery, sexual abuse of minors in the churches by priests, and placing barriers between God and His worshippers are some examples of the many things that have caused many followers to turn away from Christianity.

Even though the concept of priesthood is absent in Islam, there are too many imams and so-called sheikhs (self-proclaimed religious scholars) who have carved out positions and have influence on Muslims. Some of these people encourage extremism, including endorsing terrorism, proclaiming fatwas to create rigidity in religious and social practices, and condemning anyone who challenges their hegemony and ill-informed interpretations of faith in God. There are times when they are aligned with rulers and leaders who are corrupt and aid in their corruption by saying sinful things and amassing wealth for themselves and their sponsors through illegal means to the detriment of the average citizens and followers of faith.

This is an unfortunate situation. Such excess in sinful conduct and amassing wealth is also witnessed in ideologies that are devoid of faith, such as communism, whose leaders have committed crimes against their own citizens on a large scale in China, Russia, Afghanistan, and other countries in Eastern Europe.

95. **al-adawat wal baghdhaa** (enmity and hatred)— These two words or attributes are used in two different places: 5:14 and 5:64 with respect to Christians and Jews, and they aptly apply to Muslims as well, signifying a human condition that is the result of our own actions and disposition toward one another within the same faith group and across faith groups that leads to dire consequences such as global conflicts and the deaths of untold numbers of human beings throughout the human history, more so in the recent past (the last one hundred years) than ever before. When we lose our humanity; forget where we come from; willfully neglect to follow the guidance from God, as in the Torah, the Bible, and

Glossary Of Key Arabic Terms

the Qur'an; and marginalize the voices of reason, intellect, morals, and truth, then our own evil inclinations—enmity, hatred, jealousy, greed, injustice, oppression, exploitation, and so on—take the better of us, and we see the results in large-scale colonial injustice, the practice of slavery, apartheid, world wars, ethnic cleansing, ever-expanding violence, terrorism, and counterterrorism against innocent human beings.

This is a serious situation, and it is creating havoc in world peace and the peaceful coexistence of human beings on this planet of ours. Each one of us have to reflect on his or her own actions and reactions that amplify such conditions and work individually and collectively to extinguish the wide spiral of such fire in our societies and in our world.

96. **siddiqat** (woman of great virtue and truthfulness—in reference to Mary, Mother of Jesus)— The honor and dignity conferred to Mary, mother of Jesus Christ, in Islamic faith and in the Qur'an is of towering proportions compared to other women in human history. Her chastity, dignity, faithfulness, humility, and forbearance against all claims of misdeeds by Jews of the time and the suffering that Jesus underwent for his commitment to truth and justice in the face of overwhelming injustice by religious leaders and the ruling class inspire millions of Christians and Muslims to dignify and honor Jesus and his mother.

    History also tells us that we humans, in our zeal to honor someone, can exaggerate claims of Godhead regarding human beings such as Jesus and Mary, as prevalent in certain sects of Christianity, whereas the Qur'an reminds us that they were humans who lived among humans, ate just like other humans, and died like human. Such humanity in no way diminishes their stature among the greatest of human creations by God to serve fellow human beings, to stand up for truth and justice in their own times, and to inspire generations since their times.

97. **al-khamru, al-maisiru, al-ansabu, al-ajlamu** (intoxicant, gambling, idolatrous practices, and fortune-telling)— These substances or practices, also partially mentioned in 2:219 and 5:3, are considered acts of

the Devil or evil acts that negate human intelligence and God-given faculties that should be used for personal and collective benefit. The use of any form of intoxicants such as alcohol or drugs that affect the mind and consciousness is considered unacceptable behavior. So is gambling or any gaming or decision-making based on random chance and not on the rational and deliberate use of human intelligence. And so is any kind of practice or sacrifice in the name of a false god and on an altar set aside for such gods when such sacrifice results in a lost life without any benefit to anyone. In a similar vein, any attempt to tell the future by reading someone's palm or using astrology or other types of symbols from the natural world without due reasoning is a practice of deception and conjecture.

Islam calls for the full use of one's intelligence and the exercise of full consciousness in our daily activities and in our pursuits of physical and spiritual upliftment with a full view to express thanks for our God-gifted intelligence and intuition and to make full use of the resources from the natural world for our individual and collective benefits in fair and equitable ways and by ethical means.

98. **qiyam lin nas** (support or mainstay for mankind)— The Kabah—the simple cube-shaped house of worship built by Abraham and subsequently maintained by generations of his followers and Muslims is declared a support or mainstay for mankind. The symbolism of the Kabah as a simple but grand structure, also known as the Inviolable House or the First House of Worship (some even say that it was built by Adam and Eve), without much ornamentation or pretense, is similar to the essence of God, who is grand yet invisible. His grandeur is reflected through the created world—human beings, the abundance and flora and fauna on our planet, all living beings and creatures, the wonders of nature as we see and experience them, and the vast ocean of the universe in which our planet is a tiny sand particle. The Kabah is a place that is considered sacred ground where all goods are encouraged and all evils

are forbidden, where only God is worshipped, where all creatures are safe from the harms of others, and where everyone is equal irrespective of color, race, gender, wealth, or intellectual endowment.

In a physical sense, it provides security and a means for income from trading and visitations, and it is a gathering place to reaffirm our common heritage as servants and creatures of God drawn to a common call to acknowledge Him as God and our Creator. Like all practices in Islam—whether it is daily prayer or daily work—it has a dual purpose, a physical aspect and a spiritual aspect, a duality that permeates the Kabah as it stands to support both physical and spiritual needs of those who care to come to visit and perform Hajj (pilgrimage), a one-time obligation for people who have faith in God, our Creator.

99. **wasiaat** (will)— Anyone who has a reasonable amount of wealth (perhaps according to his or her own assessment or available financial and wealth management guidelines) that will need to be distributed among heirs in an equitable manner and who wishes to bequeath a part of the wealth to general and societal benefits or to specific individuals or institutions are strongly encouraged to have a will. In the United States, less than 45 percent have wills, and among minorities, the number is much larger—less than 32 percent among African American and less than 26 percent among Hispanics, two of the largest minorities in the United States. It is remarkable that while the will is a relatively recent phenomenon and has become a recommended legal document in developed countries, Islam had such a recommendation more than 1,500 years ago, and it has been in wide practice in that society.

The reason any society or ideology gets entrenched and flourishes is because it inspires its members and followers with ideas, tools, approaches, and social norms that bring harmony and peaceful coexistence to its members and is able to secure commitment to such ideas on a larger scale than ever before, above any other societies or ideologies. That ideologies such as Islam and Christianity have a billion-plus followers and have survived and progressed over more than a thousand years and other ideologies such as communism did not survive more than a hundred years is a testimony to the enduring values in these faith ideologies and shows the moral, financial, and ethical bankruptcies of other ideologies such as communism.

Chapter 6: Surah Al-Anam (The Cattle)

100. **sur** (trumpet or event that exposes reality of Afterlife; 6:73)— Sur has traditionally been interpreted as a trumpet that can be heard over a long distance or in crowded places so that attention can be drawn over other distractions and preoccupations. In modern times, a siren is used in case of natural calamity or impending man-made destruction such as an aerial attack by enemy fighters in residential and populated areas. Traditional commentary also makes reference to the blowing of a trumpet on the eve of the annihilation of the earth as we know it to prepare for the Day of Judgment and get all dead people out of their graves and back into life (resurrection) to face the consequences of their lifelong pursuits and actions as God will take on the role of the ultimate judge, and we will lose all our previous freedom to choose or make course corrections.

    Another meaning of *sur* comes from the notion that it is the plural of *surat*, which implies forms; in other words, the reality of Afterlife that has been a cornerstone of our faith; we all will be resurrected to a second life, perhaps more in spirit or in a physical form that might be different from our current form on this planet. And this blowing of the trumpet could also mean God breathing His essence a second time to bring us back to life where reality will be apparent and all filters of the hidden realities (Al-Ghaib) will be removed. Some of the traditions (hadith—the Prophet's sayings) describe a series of trumpet blasts to unfold the reality of the Day of Judgment in a step-by-step process.

101. **takdir** (measurement, determination, outcome; 6:96)— This word occurs in multiple places in the Qur'an, and classical commentaries

have focused on two different meanings for this word, the root of which, *qdr*, implies measurements or the precision with which natural phenomena such as the germination of a seedling or the amount of rainfall or the movement of the sun, moon, and other celestial bodies, which points to the complex relationships in the natural world and the underlying natural laws while at the same time pointing to the awesome elegance of nature that God has put in place (see also 25:2, 54:49, 15:21, 23:18, 43:11).

Another meaning that has caused a significant amount of debate among Muslim scholars and various schools of thought in the past is the notion of predetermination, where all outcomes are predetermined, including one's life and its success or failure, which then leads to some unintended consequences, raising serious questions and doubts about what life is all about and its intended purpose. This concept can also lead to fatalism and resignation to one's fate as opposed to constantly striving to be better and to do good. While there is clear indication that each individual's life and its provisioning on this planet is set according to a measure as ordained by God (see also 6:60, 7:24–25), there is clear freedom of choice that one is allowed to make and shape his or her life and its conduct (see 76:3, 76:30, 10:49).

It is important to understand this difference in interpretation on this fundamental aspect of human life and the natural world we are part of. The natural world is constructed with a set of natural laws that human sciences and philosophical discourse try to uncover. While the physical sciences are more deterministic in the sense of, say, the laws of physics, where every action has an equal and opposite reaction—in other words, the current state of the universe is determined by its previous states, but given the immense scale of the universe, where billions of stars are constantly forming and evolving in a manner no different from, perhaps, the billions of cells in our bodies or the billions of neurons in our brains, there are relationships, pathways, and interactions that are deterministic on one level, like Newtonian mechanics, but they could also be undefinable under the principles of uncertainty or Brownian motion, for example, at one level, but are more definable at a macro level, which is also the case in economics. Where the microeconomic theories may have wide variations and uncertainly, the macro behavior is more predictable and has become a boon for many tech companies, and they exploit (without necessary guidance or policies) such random and micro-level behaviors to extract patterns in more macro-level behaviors.

At a spiritual level of human growth, where intent, moral judgment, the search for truth, and so on are fundamentally important and we are constantly being challenged by our consciences, societal norms, unfolding events, and deliberate actions, any form of predetermination would be fundamentally flawed and could lead to fatalism that would sometimes find a common currency across various forms of religious discourse in our rich human history.

102. **qawme yalamuna, qawme yafqahuna, qawme yu'minuna** (people of knowledge, people of insight, people of faith; 6:97–99)— The verses from 95 through 99 point to the grandeur of the world that God has created, its inner workings, and how our human lives are intertwined with its consistent, measured natural laws that govern the universe and our human lives. The germination of a seedling from an apparent lifeless seed, the emergence of life on this planet, the reproductive system and cross-pollination through which living beings and plants evolve, the cycle of life and death that we experience each day, the constant cycle of day and night, the placement of our earth and the moon in our solar system to facilitate the measurement of our lives and our day-to-day living, the stars that help us navigate, and the technological mastery that has given us ways to navigate that which was impossible in the past.

All of these poignant reminders from God are then followed by the statement in verse 97 that those who have secured knowledge, both physical and spiritual, as well as those who wish to gain knowledge, will find these aspects and workings of the natural world as definitive markers and signposts for developing faith, improving human conditions, and becoming worthy of God's creation, an opportunity and a responsibility that have been gifted to humanity.

Verse 98 then follows, with God pointing to our human existence, our creation from a single soul—Adam, and then from Adam and Eve, a reproductive process that has led to the current seven billion-plus people on this planet, which provides us sustenance, a place to work and rest, and ultimately a place to die and wait for resurrection. These realities of life and the purposefulness of our existence are exposed to people who have insight, who are thoughtful, and who wish to connect the dots and find meaning in our existence. Some of these realities we can observe as we live and some will unfold after our death, but God has given us some access through revelations such as the Qur'an, the Bible, the Torah, and so on.

Verse 99 then delves into the cycle of rain and the revival of earth with its foliage and plants—seedlings that peek their faces out of the soil, trees that sprout buds, vegetation that comes to life with its fine greenery and foliage; how God produces grains and a variety of fruits, fruits that look alike and different, how they ripen over time, and our delight at such provisions coming in abundance to support our lives and our enjoyment. These workings of God are evident in front of us and should lead us to establish our faith in God and commit to support life and its supporting natural world. Such knowledge, understanding, and insight should also continue to deepen our faith in God and our commitment to life and its purposefulness. The development of true faith only comes from a deep level of knowledge seeking, gaining insight, and a commitment to find the truth about God and our lives.

103. **mustaquarrun** (term limit) **and mustawda'un** (resting place; 6:98)—As part of the narrative defining the origin and existence of human lives that came from one single soul (i.e., Adam, and eventually from Adam and Eve), God defines two other attributes or realities that have

given rise to various interpretations or meanings over the course of Qur'anic commentaries in the past. Qur'anic text certainly added to Arabic words, advanced ideas, concepts, and realities that required discussion and interpretation among people and guidance from the Prophet himself, as some of the words were not necessarily in common use and the ideas were not in vogue or fully appreciated or acknowledged in the contemporary society and the world at large.

Mustaqarrun comes from the root *qarra*, which implies the act of settlement, coming to rest, or remaining in one place, while *mustawda'un* is derived from *wadu'a*, an act of being quiet, coming to terms, or settling or entrusting to safe custody. Another interpretation of *mustaqarrun* has been the span of a course or an activity or existence itself, implying that life has a *"fixed term limit"* as defined by God, while *mustawda'un* has been interpreted as a *"place or consignment,"* as if awaiting further processing or evaluation—that is, a place of waiting for transit or of temporary rest. Verse 11:6 is very explicit in that it declares that there is no living being on earth whose provision for life is not with God, Who knows everyone's terms of existence and final return (to God). Verse 67 in this chapter and other verses throughout the Qur'an also imply that just like individuals, every community, nation, course of human activity, and natural process has an eventual outcome or resolution that comes back to God as He wills.

104. **basaayiru** (proof, enlightenment, insight; 6:104)— This word and this verse echo the central message of revelations and the relentless effort of all the prophets and people of goodwill throughout human history. That is to comprehend and to internalize the realities of life and of our world and to act responsibly. The root word *bsr* relates to the act of seeing, comprehending, understanding insightfully, coming to informed realities of things, and so on. *Basaayiru* points to an instrument or mechanism by which one can develop deep insight, understanding, and perception of realities that are important for our existence and our sustenance, both physical and spiritual.

This word implies that the Qur'an (and by implication all Books of Revelations that have maintained the purity of their original forms and intents) contains instrument or proof or composite knowledge that has been gifted to humanity by God through the prophets. We have a responsibility to see into it or the freedom to remain blind to it, though we need to be mindful of the various consequences that result from such interest or lack thereof. We are accountable for what we do and how we see the world and the inevitable consequences that emerge. We cannot be immune to that, much as we are not immune to gravity, given our physical mass. This is part of the natural construct of our world and our human existence as God has willed, and it should not be construed as God's wrath or dislike of humanity. As the saying goes, we harvest what we sow; that is the underlying causality here.

105. **a'ridh** (turn away, unaffected; 6:106)—In contrast to the notion of coming to God, one is asked to move away from or be unaffected by any false notion of polytheism or compromising doubts about the unity of the Godhead. The root word *a'rdh* conveys various meanings ranging from widening the gap through critical examination or analysis to resisting or avoiding or remaining unaffected by something. It is a call from God that we need to harken to God, and that also implies that we need to be uncompromising against the false notion of polytheism, as God continues to affirm by the ever-present declaration in the Qur'an *"There is no god but God,"* as is evident in the natural world that we interact with every day.

106. **kitaba mufassalan** (book full of explanations, details to make distinct; 6:114)— The Qur'an here is described as a book of that which has been detailed—detailed with explanation, clarity, poignant questioning to uncover realities of the world and our own creation. The root of *mufassalan* is *fsl*, which means to set out, to separate, or to depart, while its derivative *fassala*, means detailed—detailed in explanation,

clarity, exposition with sufficiency and conclusive arguments. One of the formats used in the Qur'an is a question-and-answer session that postulates certain facts about God, realities of life, moral values, or ethical positions. It then provides answers directly by giving detailed and reasoned explanations, sometimes with a poignant question back so as to jolt the reader to dare to consider the possibilities of there being no god or a life that has no purpose or a natural world that is full of chaos or a world where there is no accountability or a life in which one is not free to choose, and so on. Sometimes there is the storytelling of prophets, historical narratives, and common observations to increase our awareness of life and to extract lessons learned.

A good portion of the Qur'an is devoted to the workings of the natural world, our own creation, and our evolution into beings from birth to death—but also the evolution of species of plants and animals to draw attention to the creative and evolutive process of the world that God has made us part of and put to us work in to understand ourselves, God, and the natural world around us with a sense of truth, justice, and accountability as part of our evolving faith in God.

Chapter 7: Surah Al-Araf (The Elevation)

107. **khalaqnakum summa sawwarnakum** (created and shaped you; 7:11)—The Qur'an has frequently added various dimensions to the very act of creation and specifically to the creation of human beings. While this particular verse mentions the fact that God created the first humans (Adam and Eve), it is immediately followed by a subsequent process or step that attests to the fact that the act of creation then led to evolutionary forms that we see in our present condition. Those who are engineers and wish a physical device or mechanism always start with an intention of what to create or make and then develop a set of functions to transform that intention. Those functions are then given physical existence in the forms of components that are integrated into a form to bring out the final product or artifact. While *khalaka*

represents the essence of creation, *sawwara* represents the transformation of that creative process into a physical form that has internal organs, arms and legs, eyes, ears, nose, and so on, aesthetically and harmoniously put together, that is at one level a physical entity while maintaining its spiritual existence as well.

In the Qur'an God expresses himself through various attributes such as the Creator, the Fashioner, the Originator, the Maker, the Shaper, the Expander, the Restorer, the Giver of Life and Death, the Enricher, the Innovator, the Teacher, and so on, pertaining to the complex art and science of His creative power and its manifested presence in our lives and in the natural world we live in. For complete list and explanations, see God's ninety-nine names in volume 1 (pages 243–268)

108. **aghwaitani** (fall from grace, life made evil, or to be disappointed; 7:16)—*Aghwa* implies falling into error or accusing someone else of your own error. In a similar vein, it could also mean to punish someone for his or her evils or failure to uphold the truth (11:34). Finally, this could also mean to be disappointed in one's failure (20:121). The current verse refers to the Devil's realization that he made a serious error in not obeying God to honor to Adam. Instead of accepting responsibility for his failure and mistake, he took God's rebuke as a form of punishment or unfair treatment to him and vowed instead to do further harm to Adam and Eve.

To that end he sought God's permission to allow him to continue to deceive and mislead human beings while being invisible or visible to human beings, as stated in the following verse (7:17). While God has made human beings with the sublime nature of God, the Devil's presence also makes us vulnerable, and his persistent and hidden attempts to lead us from the sublime nature of God is something we need to be constantly aware of and guard against. Otherwise we will continue to fall prey to his machinations, as did our first parents—Adam and Eve. As some say, the Devil is in all of us, and this is literally true if we reflect on verse 17, and we should set up barriers in our minds, in our psyches and in our consciousnesses against the Devil, as he will tempt us on our good days and on our bad days as an equal opportunist.

Too many people also act like the Devil while they sow dissent among people; do evil; justify the evil acts of others; and perpetuate corruption, mischief, and anarchy in our societies instead of accepting temporary failure and correcting their conduct for the future. To commit more evils in the face of first evil is the Devil's way, whereas God wants us to reflect, repent, and correct our behavior so that we can improve our lives and the lives of others while securing God's forgiveness and mercy, which is ever present.

109. **Sawatihima** (of their shame or nakedness; 7:20)—*"Sawat"* implies a sense of shame as it pertains to certain parts of the body, but it could also mean acts or conduct that if exposed might be shameful or any evil act, custom, or practice that might be contrary to social, ethical, or moral norms and God's guidance. In this instance, the Devil through deception was able to persuade Adam and Eve to act contrary to God's guidance and eat from the forbidden tree. As a consequence, instead of finding immortality and becoming Angels, they suddenly realized their own sense of shame in their failure to follow God's command and came to realize their need and urge to cover their physical bodies and were suddenly aware of the evil potential that resided in them, all of which they had been unaware of.

As also stated in 20:121, their failure was the beginning of their mindfulness for differentiating good from evil, realizing the purity as well as the ugliness of their physical bodies and the potential to do evil and good. This realization also propelled them to seek forgiveness, unlike the Devil, and to develop means of knowledge, awareness, and tools to fight evil and move toward good and God. In verse 7:76 God gives an example of such effort—of clothing for human beings (see key concept note 112 below).

110. **khasirin** (loser or be lost; 7:23)—This verse is the famous prayer of Adam and Eve on the event of their first failure to be truthful to their own nature (i.e., the nature of God) by ignoring God's guidance and being deceived by the Devil with an enticement that was not true. In their repentance and affirmation of their true human character, they turned to God over and over again, which I am sure they did throughout their long lives on this planet, constantly being deceived by the Devil and helping their children and grandchildren stay true to the course of going back to God. The root *khsr* implies to lose, to suffer loss or damage, to lose direction, to be cheated. The moment they realized that they had disobeyed God by eating from the forbidden tree, they became immediately awareness of their own failure and shortcoming, evil inclinations, and disregard for God's directives. Their awareness was also aided by their sudden recognition of their own nakedness which was unknown to them prior to their disobedience to God. They first and foremost acknowledged that they had done wrong to themselves instead of wasting time blaming the Devil as the Devil had done when he disobeyed God (i.e, showed arrogance and tried to claim his superiority over Adam), and their second thought was to turn to God and plead for His forgiveness and mercy so that they would not lose their way and diminish their human stature in the eyes of God and in their own eyes.

This is a classic case of how one should deal with failure—a lifelong lesson that is pertinent to every human being, since we all are subject to failure at one time or another in our lives, without exception. Step number one of is to recognize the failure, analyze the root causes, and take personal responsibility. Step number two is to chalk out a path of recovery and exert yourself with due earnestness while seeking God's forgiveness and mercy so that you can overcome the loss of dignity, character, and negative physical and spiritual consequences, which are part of the natural laws of cause and effect in a world governed by God, Who wants us to seek the truth and establish justice for all.

111. **rishan** (bird's plumage, feathers that beautify; 7:26)— This word is part of an expression of the purpose of clothing in a physical sense and in a spiritual sense. God sent down clothing—in other words, gave humanity the ability to find materials and make clothing, first to cover their shame in a physical sense. The second purpose of clothing is compared to the feathers or plumage of birds (*rish*), which exhibits exquisite beauty, such as that of the peacock, the puffin, and almost all birds such that human beings also use clothing to beautify and to symbolize richness or abundance.

    The Qur'an then continues to define another type of clothing that is spiritual in nature and is about this human sense of responsibility (*taqwa*), which is a fundamental part of our alliance with God and our stewardship of our natural world (especially the earth that we inhabit). This spiritual clothing is declared to be best form of clothing that we should aspire to while making good and appropriate use of our physical clothing. This fundamental attribute of a responsible human being who seeks truth and strives to bring justice is like an invisible cloth that protects our dignity, our sustainability as a human race, and our relationship with our Creator.

112. **quist** (what is right, what is just; 7:29)— The root word *qst* appears in the Qur'an multiple times to denote a sense of intense *"fairness and justice"* in the way the world is created and the way the world operates. Fairness and justice require a system that is based on truth, that establishes rule of law, and that encourages equitable treatment of all. This implies balance and a system in which all parts are consonant with one another, and the human race is part of that larger whole—the earth, the universe, the rubrics of life. This also applies to our own bodies and existence; every cell in a person's body has to find its unique role and be in harmony with every other cell, and every one of us has to find his or her unique role and be in harmony with every other human being.

This verse asks the Prophet to declare that God commands that justice and fairness should spread and prevail as the foundation of our existence, that we be committed and constant to fairness and justice, and that we demonstrate genuineness in our conviction of fairness and justice. The sentence ends with a reminder that God is the Creator, and God will gather us back to Him to take account of how we demonstrated our commitment to this fundamental aspect of our life and our existence.

113. **fawahisha** (shameful, indecent), **bag'ye** (rebellion, unjustified chaos), **tushriku** (any divine association with God; 7:33)— Whereas in verse 29 God issues commands about justice and fairness (*quist*), here God commands against three things that we see happening in regular frequency in the world today. The first is all types of acts or social norms that are indecent, such as corruption; morally and ethically inappropriate conduct at the personal and social levels; acts of persistent injustice to individuals and groups of people; structural income inequality; racism; misogyny; religious persecution; and coercion and gross negligence to the health and well-being of our air, water, and soil, which then impacts our own health. Second is any type of anarchy or rebellion in societies where peaceful and amicable means are not given priority and expressions such as the proliferation of weapons of mass destruction, frequent terror attacks, unjustified counterterrorism that adds fuel to the fire, wanton disregard of human dignity and human rights, large-scale exploitation of natural resources, and corporate profiteering by a few people at the expense of many that disrupts the natural order of things in human societies and in our natural world.

Lastly, failing to acknowledge God and His guidance for human societies creates a vacuum that is filled by corrupt leaders and self-serving clerics, unjust systems of governance, deviant ethical and moral standards, and constantly changing rules of games that favor a few at the expense of many.

114. **ajalun** (appointment, period of performance or test; 7:34)— The root word *ajal* refers to postponement or delays, whereas *ajalun* here indicates an appointment, a time when certain things will happen or when a certain outcome will manifest itself or a term or period of performance in which one has to demonstrate certain commitments and achievements. We all are very familiar with such events as the birth of child about ten months after conception, the life span of a person at about sixty to eighty years, the life span of a tree or a bird, as well as other natural phenomena. In our daily lives and professional lives, we have annual plans to be achieved, payments to be made, houses to build—all with a timeline that we set ourselves or are imposed by others.

This particular verse states that God defines certain timelines for every group of people (*ummah*—a community or group of people with certain unified affiliations, be it ethnic, religious, political, or social— however it is defined) in which they are given opportunity and leeway to pursue their goals and objectives as they see fit, whether influenced by God's guidance or not. We are bound by those terms and timing, whether we like it or not, and whether we are prepared or not, God will bring those outcomes at such appropriate times as part of the natural order of things.

We certainly do not know exactly what those term limits might be, but it is important to recognize such realities and prepare ourselves to do our best to do the right things, have the right thoughts, and aim for the right goals in our pursuits to improve our human conditions and our human existence before death comes to each one of us or large scale extinction comes to our own species.

115. **sittati iyyamin** (six days, periods, stages; 7:54)— The notion of the creation of the solar system (Heaven) and the earth in six days or periods or stages is repeated several times in the Qur'an (41:9–12, 10:3, 13:2, 25:59, 32:4, 57:4) and also corroborated in the Bible and the Torah. *Iyyam* is the plural of *yoom*, which means a day. Sometimes this word is used to imply a particular day or any moment in time (1:3, 55:29), and at other times, it implies a span of time or a stage of

a certain process (70:4, 32:5) where a day in the measure of God is considered fifty thousand years or a thousand years of earthly days.

As we know now from Einstein's explanation of time and space, time is relative and not constant, and days have different lengths, depending on where we are in the solar system. A day on the moon is different from a day on Mars, and so on. Even a day on our own planet has different meanings if you are in Japan versus the United States; between the two countries, there is a fourteen-hour time difference. So if a child is born on Sunday at 2:00 a.m. in Japan, it will be noon Saturday in the United States—not Sunday yet.

We do not even know if the notion of a day makes any sense outside the solar system with respect to other such systems in our enormous Milky Way galaxy and how time is measured from different points in our universe. The Qur'an was revealed about 1,500 years ago, when our understanding of the solar system and natural laws were limited; yet ideas about natural phenomena and the evolution of our earth and solar system had to be expressed in a way that were comprehensible at that time, and the fundamental ideas expressed have to continue to be consistent with our expanding, but not perfect or complete, understanding of our world in the twenty-first century. As the Qur'an says, if all the oceans of the earth were to turn into ink and all the trees into pens, they could not exhaust writing about God—or, in other words, gain full knowledge of the universe. So the Qur'an used simpler but conceptual notions of how the earth evolved and how life evolved on it in verses such as these and others sprinkled throughout the Qur'an to confirm our faith in God and purposefulness of our existence.

116. **astawa alal a'rsh** (took possession, power or control of its affairs; 7:54)— Following the conversation about the creation of our solar system (Heaven) and the earth in it and before giving some of its implications that manifest themselves in the constant alternation of day and night, the sun, the stars, and the moon being bound to one

another and to the natural laws created by God, God mentions that He not only created these celestial bodies and the living beings that inhabit planets such as Earth, but He established (*astawa*) His Seat of Eminence (*arsh*), which in classical Qur'anic commentaries has been described as the *"Throne of Power,"* drawing a parallel to the court and seat of a king or emperor.

There are a number of instances where the Qur'an repeats this statement (10:3, 13:2, 20:5, 25:59, 32:4–5, 57:4) using same or similar language, each time adding further nuances and elaborations to the concept of active control of the world and its affairs by God. Some of these verses draw attention to the fact that the earth is in place and steady without any visible support that eyes can see; there are on it mountains and oceans to benefit mankind; there is not a leaf that falls but God does not know about it; the sun, the moon, and the stars are subservient to God's will and laws, and, by implication, human beings are given knowledge and capabilities to extract benefit, but this is to be done in a measured and fair way without being arrogant or extravagant; and that God regulates the water, the wind, life, and death to remind people of their vulnerabilities and limitations.

The notion of God's Seat of Eminence (a metaphor for God's encompassing presence in the universe, exercising active control and regulation) is further corroborated in verses 40:15 and 40:7, where Angels and spirits are considered participants in celebrating God's eminence and control and selected human beings (spirits, prophets and God's messengers, endowed humans) are given the light as He pleases so that they can in turn can remind us (the rest of humanity) what purpose we need to fulfill.

117. **fahishat** (despicable, shameful; 7:80)—The word *fahish* implies a sense of excess, something out of the norm, shameful, and detestable. The word is used in the context of Lot and his visitors (who were Angels), who were being forced to engage in homosexual conduct without their consent or acceptance of such conduct. To the Prophet Lot, it was

unacceptable that a male should have lust for another man instead of a woman, especially when such an act was forced, without mutual consent. The first impulse of lust toward a man by a man was not normal, as the verse explains that this was never done before his time, and the second impulse of coercion and a general societal acceptance of such coercion was strongly condemned by the Prophet Lot. He was a man of impeccable character, although the biblical narratives imply some flaws in him that are unacceptable by the Qur'anic standard of a prophet's moral and social conduct.

Our understanding of homosexual behavior has evolved over time, to the extent that some men or women being attracted to their own gender for lust or sex as a biological predisposition and that a person's sexual orientation is different from his or her physical orientation are things that we are uncovering as a society. While we may not agree with this orientation as a societal norm and may even find such acts unacceptable, the universal notion of human freedom to choose and act as granted by God and accepted by all human societies dictates that we do not discriminate against anyone of the basis of such conduct as long as it is done without any coercion and with mutual consent. Some clerics, imams, and rabbis have taken strong positions in opposing such conduct based on stories from the Qur'an, the Bible, and the Torah, which is understandable, but to condemn such people to Hell fire and to incite physical violence against them is without any justification. In the same vein, our political, legal, and financial systems should not discriminate people based on such orientation and should not interfere with their rights to exercise their freedom as long as it does not violate the freedom of others.

The Qur'an also condemns acts of adultery and fornication even if they are done with mutual consent and prescribes moral and, if needed, legal deterrents. Through the stories of the Prophet Lot, homosexuality was also condemned, as it was against the prevailing social norm, but more due to its coercive nature of compelling people and travelers throughout the land without their consent or safely or morality and justice. It was this widespread corruption of morality, human freedom, safe passage for strangers, and scorn for moral purity, justice, and truth that were behind the strong opposition by the Prophet Lot to such conducts rather than the mere display of homosexual behavior among the population, as evidenced from several verses in the Qur'an - 7:81—social excess in their conduct and behavior has been questioned and warned against; 11:77, 29:33—the inability of the Prophet Lot to protect his visitors and give them safe passage; 15:68–72—imposing on Lot who can entertain or not, and their frenzy in satisfying their lust without respecting other people's choices and freedom; 21:74, 51:34—committing evils and transgressions against God's guidance; 26:167—threatening Lot with exile if he does not conform to their ways; 25:56—threatening Lot's followers with driving them out from their land for their adherence to truth and moral purity; 37:137–138, 11:69–83—making their case an example for future generations as to why excess leads to destruction [as a natural course of event and as God wills]; 54:33, 66:10—ignored all guidance and did not take the warning seriously for evils, demonstrated treacherous behavior, etc.

118. **muslehin** (reformers; 7:170)—The root world *salah* implies goodness, purity, proper order, peacefulness, and making amends, and the word *muslehin* refers to someone who strives to bring peace, purity in conduct, order, and the rule of law into society—that is , a reformer, a doer of good, one who encourages what is right and just and strives against all that is evil and unjust. This verse appears in the context of a discussion of the followers of Prophet Moses, who went through many trials at the time of the Prophet and afterward for their own doings. This verse reminds them as well as the current readers of all Books of Revelations that if they were to follow the guidance given in the Book (the Torah) and remain faithful to God, God would reward them, as He does not waste the work of any reformer for truth and justice in any generation or any faith group.

This verse has semblance to verse 2:2, where it is categorically stated that the book of God (the Qur'an, the Bible, the Torah) will be useful only to those who are constantly striving to achieve and practice *taqwa*, which is a constant reformation of our beings to be aligned with God and to restore our pristine state as beings whose nature parallels God's nature, to uphold truth and justice (7:181), and to fight against evil and injustice (3:110)—that is, we need to reform from inside and to the outside.

Reformation starts with pure and deliberate intentions, which become the driver for reformation. And then persistent and consistent follow-through using the guidance of God and our own best and informed understanding of how things work and how to propagate and encourage truth and justice in society. The outcome of our reformation is based on our intention and our exertion. As God said: *"Mankind can have only what s/he strives for"* (53:39).

APPENDIX A: FIVE PILLARS OF FAITH

As I am completing volume 3 and as I listen to many voices during our book discussions and in social media, especially those of younger generations, some of whom are getting turned off by the overemphasis on these rituals without their underlying spiritual roots, I feel it is time for us to take a fresh look at the Five Pillars of Faith (commonly known as Five Pillars of Islam), to challenge our conventional thinking about these five very important manifestations and demonstrations of our faith-based rituals. They inspired early adopters of the faith, the followers of the Prophet Mohammad, for generations to become better human beings and to change the social order of their own time and for future generations. Many Islamic centers in the West and the madrassa-based religious education in most Muslim countries emphasize these rituals with a singular focus on the Afterlife while remaining unconcerned about and uncommitted to social justice, unwilling to have open discourse and debate about faith and reasoning, and giving lip service to gender equality.

I have chosen to call these five Islamic practices the **Five Pillars of Faith,** as opposed to the common name Five Pillars of Islam, since Islam calls for faith in God and active engagement in good works, principally for truth and justice in our world. These Pillars provide the support system, say, for the house of Islam. But the house is there to provide safety, security, and the ability to think and act in a safe and free environment so that life can become meaningful and purposeful, without which the Pillars alone cannot benefit us and cannot manifest their true potential. I have traveled around Muslim countries, and I see mosques full of worshippers. During the month of Ramadan, the countries are transformed into a festive mood, and zakat is being doled out to feed and clothe the poor. But I also see widespread corruption, a lack of civil society, absence of social safety network to give dignity and empowerment to the poor; women are not given freedom and support to become educated, self-empowered, and be a full partner in family and public life – all these point to the fact that the leadership as well as the general public are not benefiting from these rituals other than feeling good about themselves, and they are not being inspired to transform their lives and their societies toward truth and justice, without which faith cannot exist and thrive and human dignity cannot find its proper footing.

Here are these five Pillars—to remind ourselves, and also for those who might not be familiar with them:

1. A formal declaration of faith known as **Shahada** *(delcaration, confirmation, testimony, witness),*
2. Daily worship and prayer known as **Salat** *(worship, communion, mindfulness, supplication, blessings)*
3. Annual fasting during the month of Ramadan, known as **Sawm** *(abstinence, mind over matter, emotional intelligence)*
4. Pilgrimage to Makkah (once in a lifetime), known as **Hajj** *(travel – physically and spiritually),* and
5. Annual obligatory charity designating 2.5 percent of one's accumulated wealth and resources for social welfare, known as **Zakat** *(purification, increase)*

Paralleling human existence on a dual plane, Islamic guidance and rituals put equal emphasis on physical as well as spiritual upliftment of our being and our spirit. The Qur'an repeats time and again that success and purposefulness depend on **Faith in God** and **Goodness to Humanity** as manifested in this verse as well as many others: "*Surely, those who believe (meaning Muslims), and those who are Jews, Christians, and Sabians—whoever believes in God and the Last Day (Day of Judgment) and does good (to humanity and to the world), they will have their reward from their Sustainer God; there is no fear for them, and they will have no regrets*" ("The Cow," 2:62).

The real intent of the Five Pillars of Faith is to bring out personal commitment and practices to build a relationship with our Creator; shape our character through emotional and moral maturity; be inspired to share our resources with others, especially the poor and the vulnerable; and build relationships with other human beings to bring harmony at personal and social levels across the globe. Let me repeat: I have been to many Muslim countries, and the mosques are full of worshippers, but at the same time, there is widespread corruption, where party loyalty supersedes loyalty to truth and justice and civil discourse and rule of law are widely absent. How could that be if prayers and worship of God were meaningfully adhered to? Did not God say in the Qur'an: *"Indeed, worship and prayer (Salat) protects from evils and shamefulness"* ("The Spider," 29:45) and *"God commands acts of justice, goodness, and generosity to fellow human beings, and He forbids any and all that is indecent and shameful, socially and morally undesirable, and disapproved of and acts of anarchy and endangerment of public safety"* ("The Bee," 16:90); these are the verses that are routinely being recited in every Friday prayer sermon in the mosques, but with no effect. Why is it so? Because we are too busy making these Five Pillars as mere rituals and have forgotten in the process what Islam is.

This appendix is meant to encourage us to rethink what these Five Pillars of Faith are meant to be, according to my understanding and to spur meaningful dialogue among people, especially the young, as they challenge their faith and make a renewed commitment to faith and goodness based on intense debate, discussion, and consensus building. Such rethinking is not needed in Islam and among Muslims only. It appears to me that every major faith group and ideology in the world today could reflect on the mindless rituals that are being propagated and practiced in places of worship or work, where loyalty to clerics is superseding loyalty to God (e.g., the Catholic Church), where religious intolerance is causing death to human life that has been mads sacred by God (e.g., Buddhists in Myanmar), where poverty is becoming widespread and income inequality is reaching a breaking point (e.g., capitalistic creeds and free markets), where speaking the truth and bringing social consciousness is being trampled by the far right and religious fundamentalists while freedom and human dignity are supposed to be the cornerstone of all major religions and ideologies.

Since I've discussed those who claim faith but fail to live up to the tenets of faith in terms of truth and social justice, let also be mindful that societies in countries such as China and Russia, who have reneged on faith in the name of atheism and class warfare, have done far worse in terms of destroying human life and dignity, denying people the right to practice their faith and suppressing freedom of expression and the rule of just law. People all over the world are suffocating from the combined weight of the religious right, the communist-atheists, and unencumbered corporate greed that favors capital owners at the expense of those who provide labor and intelligence to make the capital bear fruits. People who genuinely believe in God and in human goodness, irrespective of religious affiliation, and those who believe in human goodness while unsure of their faith all have a collective responsibility to make this world a better place—a world devoid of division, racism, gender inequality, and poverty and where truth and justice prevail for everyone, in every corner of this planet.

Declaration of Faith (Shahada)

The Declaration of Faith is known as the First Pillar. Early followers of the Prophet Mohammad were required to make this a private and eventually a public declaration as the first step toward faith and goodness and to change their lives for the better, not only for themselves but for their society and for the whole world at large.

The real intent of this declaration (*Shahada* actually means an act of witnessing) is to bring simple but deepening clarity around our nature and our relationship with God, the Creator—we are His creation, made in His nature and bound by His cosmic, moral, and social laws, and prophets such as Mohammad, Jesus, Moses, and Abraham, among many others, came to communicate such understanding and to gain commitments in human terms. Every faith demands such clarity, but most have fallen short, including today's Muslims. Judaism has marginalized its relationship with God and accountability before God and revolted against prophets time and again, even with Moses or with Jesus, which is well known and documented. Some sects in Christianity, in their excess of love and adoration for Jesus and Mary, have positioned God Almighty as one of the three rather than the only God and have imposed celibacy, monastery, papal hegemony, and so on, on people which were not in accordance with the teachings of Jesus. Muslims, despite spectacular success during their first millennium (600 AD to 1600 AD) in all spheres of human endeavor—godliness, moral clarity, social consciousness, science and technology, governance—have fallen behind most developed countries despite adherence to rituals and Qur'anic memorization by one part of the society, while the other part has marginalized the faith, and both parties only give lip service to God's guidance toward truth and justice.

Deeper understanding of and relationships with God, of the role of prophets and spiritual leaders, of the harmony of the spiritual and material worlds, of human existence and the natural world, are becoming less of a norm, whereas Shahada was meant to bring out such awareness and help develop a deeper understanding and realization of a genuine commitment to make our lives and our societies purposeful and beneficial to all of God's creation, not just for humans. Even there, we are falling short.

It is a standard practice for new Muslims to publicly make this declaration in a religious gathering in a mosque to initiate the journey into faith. In reality any place will do, and a couple of witnesses to the declaration should be sufficient. Many of the Prophet's early followers took Shahada in the fields, in homes, and in the precinct of the Kabah—wherever the Prophet was available at the time of such events or where he wished to perform such an event as planned. Muslim children who are born into the faith are never required to take the Shahada, and if today's world is any guide, there is no assurance that a person born in faith understands the real meaning of faith, can demonstrate real commitment to faith, and attain the natural follow-through to practice goodness to humanity.

Perhaps, therefore, it is time to make Shahada a requirement for all who wish to take this journey into faith and make a real commitment rather than make an empty appearance. All young children born to faith between the ages of fifteen and eighteen, as well as those who wish to come to faith, should undergo a personal preparation for such an event, and the community needs to provide the space and forum to help them engage in debates about faith, study the Qur'an and other Books of Revelations, educate themselves in human sciences, and question and seek meaningful answers to attain clarity before taking the Shahada. While it should be the norm that children born into the faith take the Shahada between the ages of fifteen and eighteen, no one should be forced against their free will to take it until such a time when they feel ready and when they have come to an understanding that such commitment is what they aspire to. We may also want to expand the basic declaration with additional commitments pertaining to the generation one belongs to and the challenges of the day. Here is an example for our generation:

Primary Declaration: I bear witness that there is no god but God, the One God Who has no associates. I further bear witness that Mohammad, Jesus, Moses, and Abraham are prophets of God among many others whom God has sent to humanity throughout our existence on this planet.

Supplemental Declaration: My faith in God and in the guidance of the prophets demands, and I do commit to, the following:

- to seek and gain knowledge from revelations and from human sciences and humanities as the first family (Adam and Eve) were taught by God and by each other,
- to seek and gain a profession to gain financial independence and not compromise my faith for material or personal gains or seek compensation for sharing faith with others,
- to commit to serving the community, irrespective of faith, through honest work, generosity to fellow human beings, finding the truth and realities of our world, and establishing a just society,
- to fight against evil and disharmony to give truth and justice a firm footing,
- to keep the natural order of this planet and be a responsible steward of this planet and all that exists, over which we have been gifted control and understanding by God and our collective efforts, and
- to sustain a fervent aspiration to be Godlike in all our personal pursuits and human activities so that in our Afterlife we can be with God.

As seen from the above, this act of Shahada has three different parts:

- Part one is about God and our relationship with God, the spiritual.
- Part two is about the prophets, their guidance, and their role in shaping our physical and social life, the physical.
- Part three is a personal and social commitment to harmonizing our spiritual and physical dimensions. This last part is really important as a tradition of the Prophet himself—when he administered such an oath (Shahada) to his early followers, he would invoke a set of social behaviors

such as not to lie or steal or be unjust and to remain committed to truth and justice as part of the oath.

This act of Shahada is manifested in all creations and in all stages of our evolution, as the Qur'an makes references to such witnessing and conversations between God and His creation. Here are few examples from the Qur'an:

> *[Consider the truth] when your Sustainer God brings forth offspring of the children of Adam, from themselves, He makes them confirm the truth about themselves: "Am I not your Sustainer God?" They say: "Yes, we do confirm." [Such is the truth], lest you say on the Day of Resurrection: "We were unaware of this" or you complain: "It was our forefathers who invented polytheism, and we are but their descendants after them. Would You then make us face the consequences of their untrue conjectures?" This is how We [God] make the guidance explicit so that you may return [to the truth].* ("The Higher Elevation," 7:172)
>
> *(Reflect) when the earth will be violently shaken, and it will expose its secrets and people will say: "What is the matter with her?" On that occasion, the earth will tell her story, as inspired by her Sustainer God. On that occasion, people will come out individually so that their life's worth can be shown to them—one who did an atom's worth of good work will see it, and one who did an atom's worth of evil work will see it.* ("The Shaking," 99:1–5)
>
> *Are you not aware that all that is in the universe and on earth bows down and acknowledges God—the sun, the moon, the stars, the mountains, the trees, and many human beings, while many human beings will face negative consequences (due to their own conduct). Anyone whom God brings to shame (due to their own conduct), none can bring honor to them.* ("The Pilgrimage," 22:18)
>
> *With Him [God] are the keys to the world beyond human perception and cognition. None knows them but He. He knows what is on the land and what is in the sea. Not a leaf falls but He knows; nor is there a grain in the deepest darkness of earth that he does not know; nor is anyone dead or alive—all is recorded in a book manifest (to Him). He is the One Who causes*

you to be like dead at night (in your sleep), and He knows what you earn by daytime. He brings you back to life each day so that a term set (for you) may be fulfilled. Eventually you must return to Him, and He will make you understand all that you were doing (in your life). ("The Cattle," 6:59–62)

We [God] offer this trust (knowledge and freedom of choice) to the Universe, the earth, and the mountains, but they (all) were afraid to accept it (such a responsibility), but human beings accepted and proved to be unfaithful and ignorant (even after knowledge and guidance). ("The Allies," 33:72)

Say: "Do you deny Him Who evolved the earth in two eons [days], and do you claim that there are others equal to Him? Such is the Cherisher of the Universe, as He established mountains on it (rising high) above its surface, blessed them, and ordained food for all who wish to seek such provisions over four eons [days] with equal right to access. Then He applied himself to the heavens, which was like smoke, and said to it and to the earth: 'Come into a system together, willingly or unwillingly.' They both said: 'We come willingly.' So He arranged them into seven heavens in two eons and revealed to each Heaven its affairs and functions. We beautified the lower Heaven with lights and made it a protective shield. Such is the way with the Mighty, the All-Knowing." ("The Plain Text," 41:9–12)

The Worship of God (Salat)

The Worship of God is meant to align us with the spiritual and to continually renew our commitment to expanding what is good and diminishing what is evil. As the Qur'an says, the Salat should keep you away from evils and from shameful acts; yet I have seen too many worshippers and too much corruption coexisting in many religious communities and nations. Some Muslim countries and many Muslim communities are no exception.

Five times daily to commit to the worship of God is a unique contribution of Islam to human development. It constantly reminds us of who we are, what our purpose in life is, and where we go back to at the end of our journey in this life. We are asked to do this on a daily basis. For early Muslims, the passion and devotion to prayer was a clear demonstration of their faith in God and a spiritual preparation to engage in goodness in the world for the benefit of all humanity. Prayer awakened the true nature of their beings and the nature of God in which all human beings are created, and it was an opportunity on a daily basis to renew the vow of faith and goodness and extend an opportunity to retire from daily preoccupations to establish a sanctuary of tranquility, reflection, and assessment of where we are on this infinite scale and potential to achieve clarity with faith and commitment to do good.

The Qur'an has many verses describing and encouraging the requirements and expectations for prayer, the timing for prayers, and the purpose of prayer, which was further corroborated and demonstrated by the Prophet and his followers for all future generations of believers and people of understanding, reasoning, and goodness. Formal and obligatory (*fardh*) Islamic daily worship is clearly established in the Qur'an, and, through the tradition of the Prophet, it is to take place at following times:

1. Morning Prayer (*Fajr*), before sunrise (starting at the time the daylight becomes discernable or visible till sunrise),
2. Noon Prayer (*Zuhr*), immediately after noon and till the early part of afternoon,
3. Afternoon Prayer (*Asr*), the later part of afternoon, prior to sunset,
4. Sunset Prayer (*Maghrib*), immediately after sunset, and, lastly,
5. Night Prayer (*Isha*), an hour after sunset and till midnight.

The Qur'an encourages the faithful to do these obligatory prayers at the mosque, to build a sense of community, but these prayers can be done individually, with family and in small groups at any place at the appropriate times.

On Fridays, the Noon Prayer (*zuhr*) is replaced by the Prayer of Gathering (*Jumua'h*, or Mass), which is similar in tradition to Sunday Mass for Christians and Saturday Sabath for Jews. During this prayer there is a formal sermon (*khuthab*) by the leader of the prayer (typically known as the imam but more appropriately an informed community leader who is from the community, has a good reputation and good understanding of faith, Islam, and contemporary social constructs). In many Islamic centers in the United States and other

Western countries, imams educated in madrassas are brought in from overseas, and they have very little understanding of the social and cultural norms of the society they are supposed to live in and guide the people in. This is creating a greater divide among many Muslims who are more committed to reasoning and having discussions about their faith and rituals, versus these imams and overly religious community members who are committed to simple memorization of the Qur'an, focused on rituals, prefer preaching over reasoning and discussions, and favor traditional gender inequality practiced in many Middle Eastern Muslim countries.

Besides the formal and obligatory daily and weekly worship and services, there is a prophetic tradition of Late-Night Prayer known as *Tahajjud*, which the Prophet Mohammad did regularly, but it has not been made obligatory. There are other types of prayer, such as short formal worship (*zanazah*) for the dead before burial, which is a requirement, and there are traditions of worship to overcome difficulty (*ishigfar*) or to help make the right decisions (*ishtikhara*) or to seek sincere repentance and make a commitment not to do it again (*tawba*), and so on.

The formal worship is both a physical act and a spiritual act of cleansing, recitation, and reminders from the Qur'an; a reflection on life and God; and a renewed commitment and vow to worship God and to serve humanity, to avoid all forms of evil and injustice, and to commit to truth and justice for all. Without such awareness and commitment, prayer will not be useful or meaningful. To a large extent, that is evident all over the world; where such prayers (in all faith) have been marginalized, they have lost their deeper meaning and inspiration. Among some people, spirituality has become a form of mindfulness (e.g., yoga exercise) without any real connection to God and to our soul/spirit, which originates from God.

The details of the prayer in terms of physical cleansing (ablution, or *wudu*) with water or symbolic wudu (also known as *tayammum*), as a prerequisite before initiating formal worship and the process of bowing down, prostration, and the required recitations from the Qur'an and other utterances, commitment, and vows, are all explained in English in volume 2 and can also be found in many books on Islamic prayer as well as on the internet, though one needs to be careful of the commentary that goes with such sources, especially on the internet since there are many sites infused with extreme views and rigid (fundamentalist) rituals that do not adequately explain the purpose and reasoning behind such forms of worship.

One of the important traditions and issues during Islamic prayer is the recitation of the Qur'an as part of the daily and weekly ritual prayers so that we can be mindful of what God says in the Qur'an. The Qur'an is God's revelation to and conversation with humanity in every generation and with the faithful in particular. I am not sure how many of you can teach a subject in a school when you speak in a language that the students don't understand. I suspect you will not have a teaching job if you can't teach in the language of the students. In a similar vein, how good would it be for you to address an audience in a language that they do not understand, only to irritate them and abuse their time and presence? Yet, in the name of tradition and without fulfilling the real intent of Islamic prayer, which is to be in God's presence, to communicate with God in a meaningful and purposeful way in the language that one can converse in, most of our imams and Islamic scholars are unwilling to accept or even discuss the need for such revision in our ritual prayers. It becomes more acute during the month of Ramadan, when we are required to recite, remember, and reflect on the entire the Qur'an; yet the imams, with their Arabic recitations of the Qur'an, leave us standing and unable to remind, reinvigorate, and reignite our understanding of God's message every year. This is an aspect of our worship that needs urgent and vigorous discussion with open mindedness and focused attention to the intent rather than the pure rituals.

Below is a sample of verses from the Qur'an that provides different aspects of this daily worship in Islam:

"Worship of God [Salat] has been prescribed for the faithful at fixed times (of the day)." ("The Women," 4:103)

"Encourage worship of God [Salat] on your followers and let them be committed to it…" ("Ta Ha," 20:132)

"So be patient about what they (your adversaries) say and praise the Glory of your Sustainer God before the rising of the sun, before its setting, and during the hours of the night and parts of the day so that you may be content" ("Ta Ha," 20:130)

"When this Qur'an is presented (recited), pay attention to its message and reflect on its meaning (in silent contemplation) so that you can partake in its mercy. Be conscious of your Sustainer God within your inner core with awe and humility and in a voice pleasant during morning hours and evening hours, and do not allow yourself to be without such conscious mindfulness. (Think of those) who are in the presence of your Sustainer God—they are not too proud to serve Him; they glorify and honor Him immensely and to Him they are wholeheartedly devoted." ("The Elevation," 7:204–206)

"Stand up to worship God [Salat] from the declining of the sun till the darkness of the night and the recital (of the Qur'an) at dawn; such recital at dawn is always witnessed. And during a part of the night (latter part) stay awake [in tahajjud prayer] beyond what is obligatory on you. Perhaps your Sustainer God will (help you) rise to great eminence!" ("The Night Journey," 17:78–79)

"When you travel through the earth, there is no blame if you shorten your worship; also, if you fear that the deniers of faith (anyone else) will cause you trouble." ("The Women," 4:101)

"And when We [God] bless a human being, he becomes unmindful and withdraws (thinking that he is self-sufficient) until an evil (adversity) touches, then he is full of prolong supplications." ("Ha Mim," 41:51)

"Woe to those worshippers who are not mindful in their worship, wish only to be seen, and refuse to perform any kind acts." ("Kind Acts," 107:4–5)

"Be mindful of your worship [Salat], worship that is balanced and stand before God as truly devoted." ("The Cow," 2:238)

As part of Islamic worship, after the formal rituals, recitations, and vows, which include many supplicatory recitations and commitments, a personal or community supplication is traditionally done at the end of the worship in most cases, but not by all. There are beautiful examples of supplications in the Qur'an that pertain to Adam and Eve; to prophets such as Abraham, Moses, and Jesus, among others; and supplications of other historical figures mentioned in the Qur'an, as well as the rich tradition of the Prophet Mohammad as recorded in his life story and the formal collection of his sayings and activities (*Hadith*). Here are some examples:

> "All praises belong to God, who is the Cherisher of the Universe. He is the most Merciful, and He instills mercy in all His creatures. He is the Arbiter for Judgment Day. Our God, it is You that we (strive to) serve, and it is You that we ask for help (in serving others). Our God, guide us to the right guidance, the guidance followed by those whom You bless and not the guidance of those who earn Your displeasure by deviating from Your guidance" ("The Opening," 1:1–7; the supplication that is repeated each day in Muslim Prayer; see volume 1 for details, pages 1–7).

> "We believe in the Book (the Qur'an), that it is all from our God. None minds expect those who understand. O our Sustainer God, may you not make our hearts deviate after You have guided us. May you bless us since you are the most generous of all. O our Sustainer God, You are the gatherer of people on the Day of Judgment, about which there is no doubt. You surely do not fail in Your promises" ("The Family of Amran," 3:8; the supplication of people of knowledge who accept divine guidance and revelations).

> "Our Sustainer God, We believe in You, so count us among those who also believe and give witness. What reason do we have not to believe in God and the truth that has come to us, while we sincerely desire for guidance that Our God will help us to be with those who are righteous people?" ("The Repast," 5:83–84; the Prayer of Negus - the Christian king of Ethiopia, who sheltered early Muslims who were persecuted and sought refuge in his kingdom)

> "O our Sustainer God, grant us good in this world, grant us good in the life to come, and protect us from the evils of the Fire" ("The Cow," 2:201, seeking goodness and protection in this life and the life to come, a supplication that is recommended for all faithful).

> "O my Sustainer God, if You had willed, you would have them perished and me too. Will you now destroy us for the acts of the fools among us? This is nothing but a trial from You. You cause some to perish as You will, and

You guide others as You please. You are our Protector, so forgive us and have mercy on us; You are the Best of those who forgive. Ordain for us what is good in this worldly life and in the Hereafter since we turn back to You and repent (wholeheartedly)" ("The Elevation," 7:155–156; the prayer of Moses for his people).

"Say: 'My Sustainer God, increase me in knowledge'" ("Ta Ha," 20:114; seeking knowledge and gaining better understanding of divine texts and worldly affairs).

"O our Sustainer God, accept from us our work; surely You hear and You know. Our God, make us both align with You and bring from our children a nation that is aligned with You. Show us our ways of devotion to You and bless us. You are Ever Forgiving and Merciful" ("The Cow," 2:127–129; the prayer by Abraham and Ishmael on the occasion of rebuilding the Kabah, the place of worship that all Muslims turn to during daily Salat and congregate at during the annual pilgrimage).

Before we finish this short discussion and understanding of the Second Pillar of our Faith, let us be reminded of what God said in the Qur'an about the language in which it was revealed—not because something was special about the Arabic language (though many Muslims, imams, and Muslim scholars will argue otherwise), but because that was the language of the people to whom a prophet was sent from among themselves, a prophet who spoke Arabic as his native tongue with unmatched eloquence and impact. Without getting into arguments and counterarguments in this volume, I would encourage strong debates and discussions in our living rooms, Islamic centers, and public square on this important aspect of our prayer if we are to make daily, weekly, and annual prayers impactful and mindful, as was intended and as was demonstrated by Muslims for centuries until we fell into mindless rituals and forgot their real purpose and benefit. It is, in my opinion, difficult to make the prayers impactful if most of the prayers, including the recitation of the Qur'an, is done in Arabic when the majority of the Muslims today do not speak the language and when we select imams based on their ability to recite the Qur'an but not on the depth of their understanding of the Qur'an and their ability to effectively engage the congregation on how to perform this important ritual that inspires us rather than makes us fearful of God.

> "We [God] never sent a prophet except with the language of the people, so that he could explain clearly to them (Our Guidance and messages). Then God allows some to remain in error (and continue erroneous practices) while He guides others as He will. God is Powerful, Wise!" ("Abraham," 14:4)
>
> "These are the verses (guidance and messages) of the Book [Qur'an] that makes (matters and affairs) manifest. We [God] have revealed it—an Arabic Qur'an, so that you (who speak the language) may understand. We narrate and expose to you the best of narratives in this Qur'an, though before this (revelation), you were uninformed and unmindful" ("Joseph," 12:1-3; also see 41:3).
>
> "If We [God] had prepared this Qur'an in a foreign language (to the immediate audience, who were Arabs), they would have said (in surprise and disbelief): 'Why have its messages not been made clear to us—a foreign tongue and an Arab (messenger)?' Say: 'It is sent to those who believe a guidance and accept its healing'; but for those who lack belief, there is deafness in their ears, and it remains unreachable for them. (It is as if) they are being called from a far-away place (they can hear but can't understand what is being said)'" ("Ha Mim," 41:44).

These verses should be sufficient to start a vigorous dialogue among ourselves to reflect on our daily, weekly, and annual prayers and how we need to make these important and powerful rituals more understandable, meaningful, and relevant to our generation.

Fasting during the month of Ramadan (Sawm)
Fasting as a way to develop self-discipline, train one's mind and body to deal with deprivation, and deny instant gratification and mindless consumerism, while focusing on the spirit and temporarily forgoing the materials aspects of our lives is an important pillar of human development and spiritual awaking. Yet many of us, as the Prophet had warned, only experience hunger but do not

gain the spiritual upliftment, as it was meant be. Fasting is no different from the daily worship (Salat), which is meant to develop consciousness and natural affinity to be good and to do good. In many religious communities, ritual prayer and fasting have become a source of showmanship and arrogance and to hide their evil deeds. In a similar vein, many leaders in communities and nations use prayer and fasting to fool citizens as to their godliness and to mask their evils.

A month-long fasting during the month of Ramadan was formally made an obligation by the Qur'anic verses 2:183–185 and established the following:

- It is a formal obligation that was also prescribed for other people of faith in the past (fasting is very common in all religious faiths, even outside the Abrahamic faith group).
- It is meant to practice and develop our individual and collective sense of human responsibility to God and to fellow human beings (*taqwa*).
- It builds self-discipline, denies instant gratification, and helps us to practice generosity, align ourselves with those who are less fortunate, and build character imbued with self-sacrifice, empathy, and a keen awareness of our own physical limitations and spiritual possibilities.

While fasting can be done at any time, the formal fasting during the month of Ramadan has certain characteristics that are unique in Islamic rituals. It is an obligation and expression of faith to

- fast during the entire month of Ramadan, from sunrise to sunset each day, for twenty-nine to thirty days, depending on the length of the lunar month, but the daily fasting in reality starts a bit earlier than sunrise since one is expected to take a meal or breakfast based on personal preference early enough so that that person can also perform Morning Prayer before sunrise;
- abstain from any food or drink, sexual activity, profanity, all forms of evils and injustice, and any form of bad acts;

- actively pursue goodness, generosity, active reflection on life, spirituality, God, and human conditions;
- attend special Nightly Prayer (*Taraweeh*) and read/recite the entire Qur'an to be mindful of its entire guidance and spiritual instructions; and
- undergo a month-long training with a deliberate intention to sustain this wholesome mind-set, physical exertion, and a renewed learning and awareness for the rest of the year, only to be further invigorated by the next Ramadan fasting.

God says repeatedly in the Qur'an—and the teachings of the Prophet emphasize this point—that the real purpose of fasting (during Ramadan and at other times) is not just the physical hunger and deprivation, but to build a deep sense of responsibility (*taqwa*) regarding our human condition and human purpose, so that we become better people because of fasting and can relate to our fellow beings, especially those who are vulnerable, who are exploited, and who lack food and shelter, a condition that is much wider and more entrenched today than ever before.

The month of Ramadan culminates in a festive celebration known as Eid-ul-Fitr (Festival of Breaking Fast) at the end of the month-long fasting, the following morning a special celebratory and communal prayer is held, and people visit one another and distribute gifts among family and friends. This celebration is preceded by giving a special charity (Zakat ul Fitr), which needs to be distributed prior to the Eid morning so that needy people and families can also join in the festivity.

One of the significant endeavors during the Month of Fasting is the nightly special prayer known as *Taraweeh*, as mentioned earlier. The tradition is to recite the entire Qur'an during such prayers, reciting one-thirtieth of the Qur'an each night during the eight to twenty *rakah* of congregational prayers. Since the Qur'an is in Arabic and majority of the Muslims today do not speak or understand Arabic, the tradition of reciting the Qur'an in Arabic during Salat reduces the impact of such recitation, since we should know what we are saying, and the benefit of the annual reminder of the Qur'anic message is compromised. A simple solution would be to recite the Qur'an in Arabic and also in the native language of the congregation, such as English in America and Malay in Malaysia, for example. There is no religious reason why this could not and should not be done.

During Ramadan, given the length of the *Taraweeh* prayer, to do so both in Arabic and say in English would be burdensome on the imam as well as on the congregation. My strong recommendation is that to receive the full impact of the Qur'anic remembrance during the month of Ramadan, the recitation be done in English in America. This will help the congregation, during the lengthy Taraweeh prayer, to be mindful and experience the Qur'an in a way that will improve their understanding, help them pay attention during the prayer as they can focus on the meaning, and be more mindful in God's presence, which is the real intent of such prayers. Again, I would hope that we discuss such ideas among ourselves, listen to people, and see what makes our prayer effective, not only in terms of ritual prayer but its impact on us in our day-to-day living, as well as the longer-term prospect of being more effective human beings in terms of faith and goodness. I would also encourage our religious leaders, imams, and scholars not to bring fear, blind imitation of tradition, and inhibition of discussions—all of these are contrary to the teachings of the Prophet who brought hope, challenged the traditions of his contemporary society, and encouraged discussion to bring people closer to God, to truth and to justice.

Here are verses 2:183–185, which give definitive instruction about fasting during the month of Ramadan:

> *For People of Faith [Mo'men], fasting has been mandated as it was mandated for previous generations, for a certain number of days so that one may become responsible (through sustained God consciousness, Taqwa). But whoever is sick or on a journey should make up that number of days later. Also, those who find it extremely difficult (to fast) can compensate by feeding a person in need (instead). Whoever does good work with deliberation, it is better, and you should know that fasting is good for you.*
>
> *Ramadan is the month in which the Qur'an was revealed as guidance for mankind and as proof of the guidance (itself), as well as a means of*

differentiation (between good and evil, right and wrong). Therefore, whoever is present in (or witnesses) this month shall fast (during the month). (Again), if one is sick or on a journey, one should fast an equal number of days (later). God wishes ease for you and not hardship. You should complete the number (of days of fasting) and glorify His Greatness for guiding you and as a means to thank Him.

Fasting for reasons other than the obligation of the month of Ramadan is mentioned in a number of places in the Qur'an, primarily as a means to repent, reflect, and take personal responsibility for mistakes made, commitments broken, and harm done to others unjustifiably, and to do so on a voluntary basis. Such fasting should provide the time and the spiritual backdrop to reflect on our failings and to make promises to ourselves (besides promises to God) to avoid such mistakes. Such fasting should also be accompanied by increased generosity to fellow human beings, whether in need of help or justice or just plain human courtesy. The confluence of such sheer spiritual beauty that can radiate from fasting is the true essence of fasting, and it can only happen if we are mindful and thoughtful about why and how we fast.

Annual obligatory charity (Zakat)
Islam made charity a form of commitment to acknowledge that all the resources (wealth, intellect, good health, businesses, natural resources, sources of labor, etc.) that we gain or take control of are a gift and a trust from God, and unless we dedicate a portion of that to better the lives of the less fortunate, we cannot claim to be worthy of God's creation or to be beneficiaries of His grace. This is distinct from regular or voluntary charity (*sadaqah*) and is more of a community and institutional commitment based on a collective and purposeful undertaking. I see in many Muslim countries political and community leaders and wealthy individuals go on charity shows to distribute clothing and food to the poor but fail to institutionalize improving the conditions of the less fortunate citizens through legislative mandates such as free education, job creation, social security, and block and entitlement grants, which I have seen in the United States. There is a separate agency called the Agency for Children and Families (ACF) under US Health

and Human Services (HHS—the largest agency in terms of money allocated in the US budget), for example, to take care of orphans, single mothers, vulnerable children, the old, the handicapped, and so on in a way that helps them to rebuild their lives and maintain their human dignity. ACF also put in place performance measures and the monitoring of activities, and they applied statistical means to calculate needs and future trends as part of the congressional mandate that these resources are used in a responsible way and generate the benefits they are meant to create.

Zakat is a unique form of charity through self-imposed taxation, where every person/family of faith is required to allocate a minimum of 2.5 percent of their accumulated wealth (cash, savings, inventory, personal property, harvest, etc.) to the benefit of others in the form of organized charity, where the collective resources are dedicated not only to feed and clothe the needy but to build societal capacity and institutions to reduce poverty and vulnerability and to restore health, education, and freedom of choice through human development in a holistic manner and thoughtful longer-term social strategy.

For many immigrant Muslims in the United States and Europe, a tradition has evolved to send money back home through family and friends to feed and clothe the poor and donate to orphanages as part of the zakat commitment. While this is commendable, it lacks the collective power and intent of this organized charity and also ignores the needs of the local community where they live and thrive. It should include all people who are in need rather than only Muslims back home. There needs to be a resurgence of charity using zakat, and we need to explore ways to create sustainable and long-term local projects, pool our collective zakat charity at various levels—the local community, districts/provinces, nations, and globally. Think strategically/globally how this vast resource can be used to improve health, education, and the social empowerment of needy human beings, the number of which is increasing at an alarming rate as the divide between the poor and wealthy increases and wealth is getting accumulated by fewer and fewer people all over the world.

Such issues are also becoming apparent since 2016 election in the US where rich and incompetent people are being put in charge of government institutions and there has been a giveaway to the rich in terms of significant tax cut for big corporation and wealthy individuals. The backlash is percolating among the population and specially among he Democrats where a number of representatives and presidential candidates are pushing ideas on a wealth tax on the rich (above certain threshold of wealth) around two to three percent, not unlike the concept of Zakat but to be made mandatory under the law and tax code.

The Qur'an provides specific and expansive guidance on the purpose of this special social charity in several verses (listed below), and we should expand on this guidance in the context of our time and our social and current human needs and wants. Worship (*Salat*) and charity (*zakat*) are mentioned repeatedly and together in the Qur'an, just as faith and good actions (*imaan* and *aamal*) are repeated together throughout the Qur'an.

> *"Establish worship [Salat] and pay your designated charity [zakat]. Whatever good you do and send ahead of yourself, you will find these with God. God sees and is fully aware of what you do"* ("The Cow," 2:110).
>
> *"Righteousness is not that you turn your face east or west, but the (truly) righteous are those who (1) believe in God, the Last Day, the Angels, the Book (of Revelations), and the prophets, (2) give away wealth for the love of God to relatives, orphans, the needy, travelers, and those who seek help, (3) free people out of bondage (e.g., slavery, debt, imprisonment without cause, etc.), (4) maintain worship [Salat], (5) pay obligatory charity [zakat], (6) keep promises when they make promises, and (7) act with patience in times of distress, affliction, and conflict. These are the ones who are truthful and act with a sense of responsibility [taqwa]"* (2:177).
>
> *"Charity (zakat) should be directed to the poor and the needy, those employed to administer it, and those who are inclined to faith and goodness, to free captives, those in debt, those who commit their time to godly purpose, and those who are on a journey (away from home and in need of support)—an obligation prescribed from God. God is indeed Aware and Wise!"* ("The Proclamation of Immunity," 9:60)
>
> *"A kind word with forgiveness is better than charity that causes harm. God is Independent and Forbearing. O People of Faith, do not make your charity worthless by claiming credit and causing harm like the person who*

spends his wealth to be seen of men and who does not believe in God (goodness) and the Last Day (accountability)" (2:263–264).

"O People of Faith, give charity from good things that you earn and things that We [God] bring for you from the earth (and the natural world—harvest, fish, water, air, natural resources, discoveries, inventions, etc.). Do not aim at the least valuable to spend (for others) while you would not take it for yourself, without being hypocritical. You should know that God is Independent and Worthy of Praise! It is the Devil (and your own selfishness) that causes fear of poverty and encourages niggardliness, whereas God promises for you forgiveness and abundance. God is Generous and Aware!" (2:267–268)

"We [God and Moses] made a covenant with the Children of Israel—you should worship none but God; be good to your parents; take care of your kin and neighbors, the orphans and the needy; speak and do good to all men; establish worship [Salat]; and pay designated charity [zakat]" (2:83).

Once-in-a-lifetime pilgrimage (Hajj)

The once-in-a-lifetime pilgrimage to Makkah, the place where the Kabah is situated, is meant to draw people of faith, irrespective of wealth, status, color, race, gender, age, and so on, on an equal and universal footing of our common humanity, to come to God with a penitent mind and a purposeful mind to reflect on our past; seek God's forgiveness and grace in the midst of millions of other faithful; to reenact the footsteps of the Prophet Abraham, his wife, Hagar, and his son, Ishmael, to rebuild the first house of worship and to dedicate it for the benefit of mankind; to remind us of our perpetual quest to serve God and our fellow human beings; and to renew our commitment to lead a socially purposeful life when we go back to our respective communities after Hajj. Yet this great institution of godliness and equality is a source of corruption when one sees the disparity in the ways the poor and the rich are given accommodations for Hajj; how the leaders segregate themselves from the masses when performing Hajj; how one adds titles to one's name, such as Al-Hajj, after Hajj; how one becomes arrogant, feeling that one is better than those who did not perform Hajj; how rich people perform multiple Hajjes while neglecting what is due to their poor neighbors or their employees; how they feel freer to commit more sins and corruption and then perform another Hajj to cleanse themselves, and so on.

Hajj is a seven-to-ten-day affair to visit the Kabah and Makkah, in which a set of well-defined set of rituals, visitations, reflections, and supplications to God is made along with fellow brothers and sisters of faith. If one adds the travel time and the personal obligation one feels to visit Medina and the Prophet's Mosque, it is a significant commitment to two to three weeks of time and financial resources. While Hajj during the Arabic month of Jul-Hijja (two months after Ramadan) is a once-in-a-lifetime requirement, the lesser Hajj, known as Umrah, can be performed at any time and as often as one pleases and can afford.

The rituals of Hajj are simple yet profound in their implications. First and foremost, it is an annual gathering for people of faith and a place to share their common faith, renew their vows to God, declare their aversion to the Devil (Shaitan) and his evil ways, and to make sacrifices during the Hajj to glorify God and to help the needy. Here is a summary of basic steps (for specific details consult any reliable source on the internet, and also confirm with fellow Muslims and Muslim community centers and groups that organize Hajj travel each year from your area):

UMRAH:

1. Intention (*Niyyah*) and Putting On Simple Garb (*Ihram*): Once you arrive on the grounds close to Mecca and prior to approaching the Kabah, you have to declare your intention to do Hajj (or Hajj combined with Umrah) and put on simple garb of two white, unstitched sheets to wrap around your body for males and unassuming and modest clothing for females that covers the body. But, as general guidance, you can expose your feet, hands, and face.
2. Declare: God, I Am Here (*Talbiyah*): As you approach certain entry points to Mecca and the Kabah, you declare your desire to come to God in a state of mental and physical purity by reciting loudly (the words of Talbiyah): *"I am, O Allah, here. Here I am, and I declare that You have no*

associate. Here I am. All praise, grace, and sovereignty are yours. You have no associate or partner."

3. Approach the Kabah: As you approach the Kabah and see it for the first time, declare *"God is Great"* three times, followed by *"There is no god but God,"* and offer supplication for the Prophet and a general prayer for all people of faith and for all humanity. Also, feel free to recite any particular part of the Qur'an that resonates with you on this auspicious moment.

4. Circle Around the Kabah (*Tawaf*): Get ready to perform the ritual of going around the Kabab (Tawaf) in a counterclockwise direction to get to the eastern corner, where the *"Blackstone"* is located. Legend says that it was a precious stone brought to earth from Heaven by Adam and Eve. Declare your intention for Tawaf in the Umrah: *"O Allah, I am ready to perform this Umrah and Tawaf to please you. May you make it easy for me and accept it from me, by Your grace."* As you come close to the Blackstone, attempt to get close, kiss it as per tradition of the Prophet or touch it with your hand or face it at a distance, and praise God: *"In the name of God, God is Great, God has all the praises."* From this point onward, make seven circles around the Kabah, being aware each time you come to the Blackstone to face it, and then continue circling, being mindful of God and your fellow beings and reciting prayers seeking God's blessings, mercy, and forgiveness. This tawaf is also the ritual walk in the footsteps of the Prophets Abraham, Ishmael, and Mohammad.

5. Walk Between Safa and Marwah (*Say'e*): The next step is the ritual walk (Say'e) between two small hills known as Safa and Marwah. Starting from Safa, you walk seven times back and forth to Marwah. To start from Safa, you declare your intention: *"O Allah! I intend to perform seven rounds of Say'e between Safa and Marwah to please You. May You make it easy for me and accept it from me."* At this time, also face the Kabah, repeat *"God is great"* three times, and offer any prayers that resonate with you before proceeding toward Marwah. During your walk, continue to beseech God: *"God is Glorious; all praises belong to God; God is Great;*

Appendix A: Five Pillars of Faith

He has no partners; and there is no real power without God." When you get to Marwah, face the Kabah and say, *"God is Great"* three times, say any prayer that resonates with you, and go back toward Safa. Carry on this process seven times and finish at Marwah. These steps back and forth also symbolize walking in the footsteps of Hagar, the mother of the Prophet Ishmael, who was looking for water for her infant child in this desolate and remote place when they were left behind by the Prophet Abraham as per God's will.

At this time, one should shave (men) or trim his or her hair (men and women); delay it if you are planning on continuing for Hajj. These steps complete your Umrah rituals and requirements and begin the process for Hajj. You can also remove your ihram (the simple garb for men) if you have couple of days in between your Umrah and Hajj, depending on the logistics and timeline for your travel and plan for Umrah and Hajj.

HAJJ:

6. Ihram and Intention For Hajj: Once you are ready to resume for Hajj, put back on your simple garb, if you have taken them off, and establish your intention: *"O Allah, I am ready to perform this Hajj, as you have commanded, to please you. May you make it easy for me and accept it from me, by Your grace."* Repeat Talbiya three times as in Umrah (step two) and proceed to Mina on the eighth day of Jul-Hijja. Hajj is performed over a period of five days, from the eighth to the twelfth day of the month.

7. Day 1 (The Eighth Day of Jul-Hijja)—Travel To Mina: Mina is just outside Makkah, and there are accommodations of tents for pilgrims. In the morning, depart for Mina. You have the whole day to spend here until the next morning. The primary purpose is to mentally prepare for the Hajj rituals, spend the day in prayer and reflection, and take in the moment and the occasion of Hajj as it begins, being ever closer to God in mindfulness, purity of thought, and worship.

8. Day 2 (Ninth Day of Jul-Hijja)—Move To Arafah And Engage In Deep And Devoted Remebrance of God (*Wakuf*): On the second morning,

prepare to depart and arrive at Mount Arafah by noon so that you can join everyone in an intense and heartfelt vigil (*wakuf*) of supplication, prayer, and reflection about God and our life on this planet. This vigil starts as the sun begins to decline from high noon and continues until the sun sets completely.

9. Day 2—Perform Sunset (*Maghrib*) Prayer In Muzdalifah: After the vigil on Mount Arafah, at sunset, move to Muzdalifah, a place between Mount Arafah and Mina, to perform Maghrib prayer and spend the night under the open sky without the benefit of any dwelling so that you are exposed to the elements and have no barrier between God and you, as if you have submitted completely to God and are under his direct view.

10. Day 3 (Tenth Day of Jul-Hijja)—Perform the Ritual of Stoning the Devil (*Ramy*): On the third morning, collect seven pebbles and move back to Mina to perform the ritual of *Ramy* at a stone monument known as Jamrat at Aqabah. Here you throw stones at the monument to symbolize your effort and resolve to deny the Devil any temptation and your commitment to do no evil. This place gets very crowded and has had safety lapses, so one needs to be careful and respectful of others and perform this ritual in a safe manner. It is better for the elderly, children, and the physically weak or handicapped to avoid the crowd and perform this with gestures rather than actual stone throwing or to have someone else perform on their behalf.

11. Day 3—Offering of Sacrifice: After the performance of Ramy, one is required to perform the ceremony of sacrifice with an animal (a lamb, camel, etc.) that is locally available, which symbolizes the sacrifice that the Prophet Abraham offered in place of his son Ishmael and to donate the meat to the poor and the needy. Today, third parties (rather than the pilgrims themselves) perform this on the pilgrims' behalf, and the meat is presumed to be distributed all over the world to feed the needy. This sacrifice can take place at any time during the third through the fifth day, but it is better to do it sooner so that you can then perform the remaining rites of Tawaf and Say'e.

12. Days 3–5—Perform *Tawaf* and *Say'e*: This is essentially the same as what was performed during Umrah as described in steps four and five. After shaving or trimming your hair, the formal part of Hajj is complete, and you can return to normal clothing and daily activity.

Many people go back to Mina and spend time supplicating, reflecting, and just being in the moment of the grand presence of the Kabah with people from all over the world and being in the footsteps of the prophets. Some people repeat the ritual of Ramy by throwing stones to two other stone monuments known as the First Jamrat (Jamrat Oolah) and the Middle Jamrat (Jamrat Wasatan), in addition to the Main Jamrat (Jamrat Aqabah), which was previously completed in step ten. This Ramy can be repeated on day five, as desired, but it is not required as part of Hajj.

At the end of the Hajj journey to Makkah, everyone prefers to perform a last rite of Tawaf around the Kabah to bring the Hajj to a close and prepare to depart for home or to visit Madinah and spend time at the Mosque of the Prophet, which is also his burial ground, to see some of the historical sites of Islam and reflect on the life of the prophet, his struggles for this community and humanity at large, as he was *"a mercy to mankind."*

Below are couple of verses from the Qur'an that define the purpose and rituals of Hajj. The details of the Hajj rituals are further elaborated and established by the examples of the prophetic traditions and practices of early Muslims.

"The first house established for humanity is the one at Bakkah (in the city of Makkah), fully blessed and serving as a guidance to the world. In it is clear testimony—the presence [makam—station] of Abraham (his legacy) and established security for whoever enters. Pilgrimage to this house [Hajj] is a human responsibility to God—whoever can find and afford the journey. As for those who deny (such faith and responsibility), God is above the need from this world." ("The Family of Amran," 3:96–97; see also "Al-Hajj," 22:26–28)

"Perform the pilgrimage (Hajj) and the visitation (Umrah) for the sake of God, but if you are prevented, then use whatever offering is easy to obtain and do not shave your head until the offering reaches its destination (completion). Now, if one of you is sick or has an ailment of the head, then fasting, alms, or sacrifice will be acceptable (as a substitute). And when (if) you are secure, combine the visitation (Umrah) with the pilgrimage (Hajj) and take whatever offering is easy to secure. But whoever cannot afford it, he should fast for three days during the pilgrimage and for seven days upon his return—these ten days will complete (the offering). This exception is for those whose families do not reside in (the vicinity of) the Sacred Mosque (Ka'bah). Keep your duty to God, and be cognizant that God is committed to making you face the consequence of your conduct.

"The months of pilgrimage are well known. Then, whoever intends to perform Hajj in those months should refrain from (1) indecent speech, (2) abusing others, and (3) fighting (verbally or physically); God knows whenever you do any good. Take provisions for yourselves while knowing that the best provision is your sense of responsibility (to God and to your fellow men). Therefore, be mindful of your duty to Me (God), O people with understanding. ("The Cow," 2:196–197; see further through verse 203)

"The Safa and Marwah (the two hills in the compound of the Ka'bah) are among the symbols of God, and for whoever makes the pilgrimage (Hajj) or pays a visit (Umrah) to the House of God, there is no blame if he steps back and forth between these two (hills). (For) whoever does good out of his or her own volition, then God is ever Responsive to gratitude, and He is All Knowing." ("The Cow," 2:158)

"O People of Faith, be faithful to your covenants. Lawful to you are all beasts similar to cattle, except any specific mentions (as unacceptable), and do not hunt when you are in the state of pilgrimage. God prescribes according to His will. Do not violate the symbols set up by God (or of God), or the Sacred Month, or the offerings for sacrifice marked as such, or those who flock to the Inviolable Mosque seeking God's pleasure and grace. Only after your pilgrimage can you hunt.

> *"Never let your hatred of a people who may hinder you from the Inviolable House of Worship lead you to an act of aggression. Rather, help one another to advance virtue and increase your (collective) sense of responsibility (to God and to fellow humans). And do not help one another to further evil and enmity. Be conscious of God and know that God is fully committed to retribution (for good and evil)!"* ("The Repast," 5:2)

Concluding comments

I have summarized in this appendix the basic and often-repeated Pillars of Faith, to make the point that as important as each pillar is, they themselves can become devoid of life and meaning unless one is consciousness of the essence of faith and its implications in our lives. Similarly, when one looks at the all guidance (legal, moral, and social) that is contained in the Qur'an and the teachings of the Prophet Mohammad, which build on top of all teachings contained in other Books of Revelations and propagated by other prophets, this guidance is broad and constitutional, and it builds a framework for practical implementation. When specifics are given, they are meant as examples to help us understand the meaning and how to put such guidance into practice. The specifics are never meant to confine the meaning or to deprive continuing generations from applying their God-given intellect and evolving human knowledge to continually reflect on the guidance in the context of time, situation, and the complexities that will inevitably arise. Hence the reason why some verses and prophetic traditions state that when guidance is given, one should take it in the broadest meaning and not try to confine or unduly specify its meaning and application so that it becomes burdensome, loses its essence over time, and leads people to question faith and become disengaged, which is contrary to its enunciation in the first place.

Many Muslim scholars and clerics have contributed much to the multitude of rituals and mundane details while neglecting the essence that the Islamic faith, its Pillars, its guidance, and its rules and regulations are derived from. Verse 3:7, as explained in greater detail in volume 2, points to the same thing when it categorically states that the broad guidance given in the Qur'an is foundational in nature and that specifics are examples to be used for further elucidation by each generation with due scholarship and collective discussions and debates, a tradition that has been lost and needs to be brought back.

Faith and goodness go together, just as our physical and spiritual aspects coexist, and we need to have harmony between the two. There can be no faith without goodness, and faith will have no breathing room if there is evil and injustice and the absence of truth in societies. The following verse from the Qur'an makes the point very forcefully: *"What kind of faith is it that permits you (worse, commands you) to do evil?"* ("The Cow," 2:93). Too often faith is narrowly defined and confined to mere rituals, and religious clerics use these rituals to rule over the masses and pass judgment on who goes to Hell or Heaven while they ignore the greater goal of establishing truth and justice in human societies and in our personal conduct.

This is an ever-increasing divergence, and some of the organized Islamic centers, many imams, and some Islamic scholars define Islam in terms of the Five Pillars, thereby minimizing the major thrust of Islam to seek truth and to establish justice and peace in the world. There are others who aspire to seek truth and justice but fail to build real affinity for faith (hence a deeper and personal connection with God), which leads to lack of deep commitment, frustration, and frequent compromises that take them away from truth and justice.

This makes both sides equally incompetent in organizing their lives and their communities and in establishing truth and justice in societies. This leads to widespread corruption in the mosques and religious institutions as well as wider corruption in the government and other social and political institutions. Such a situation has been exemplified in the way the military government and Islamist party behaved in Egypt after the Arab Spring, when each party was given a chance to rule, to make amends. Both have failed to make the lives of ordinary Egyptians better, the major aspiration of Arab Spring.

Such drama is playing out in the majority of Muslim countries as we speak, and it is showing some of its ugly heads in some Western countries in the form of anti-immigrant sentiment and the emergence of nationalism and the religious right, despite their deep roots in Christianity and Judaism. Other countries are not immune, as we see in frequent religious riots against Muslims and the persecution of lower-caste Hindus in India; in Burma's Buddhists' ethnic cleansing of Rohingya minorities; and in communist countries such as China and Russia, where religious minorities such as Muslims, Christians, and Tibetan Buddhists are persecuted in China, while Russia is exploiting Orthodox Christians to support state-sponsored corrupt practices and their ethnic cleansing in Chechnya and Afghanistan. One-party rule is also becoming standard practice in China and Russia, denying their citizens the freedom of expression and equal opportunity to all religious and ethnic groups. The ever-widening crisis in the Catholic Church, where clerics have abused children for sexual purposes and where there has been a lack of moral clarity and transparency in dealing with this abuse within the papal institution, is another sign of how religious dogma has taken over basic human decency and the upholding of human dignity, which is one of the fundamental tenets of what God demands of the faithful.

There is a real danger that if we do not fully comprehend the real intent of faith and instead create religious dogma that is contrary to faith and develop practices and rules in the name of rituals and traditions but not in accordance with seeking truth and justice, we will create a world order that is full of conflicts among nations and communities of the world and fail in being good stewards of ourselves, our species and our own planet.

With God is the knowledge of what is unknown—none knows but He. He knows what is in the land and what is in the sea. Not a leaf falls but He knows, nor is there a grain in the deep darkness of the earth or a thing green or dry; all are clearly defined and documented. He is the One Who takes your soul away as you sleep at night, and He knows what you accomplish during the day. He lets you rise each day so that your appointed term for life can be completed. Eventually all of you will gather back to God, and He will inform you the end results of your lifelong pursuits.

—"The Cattle," 6:59–60

Say: "Have you considered this possibility—If God were to take away your hearing and your sight and harden your heart, who is there besides God that can bring these back to you?" This is how We [God] expound the message in different ways, yet they walk away in arrogance.

—"The Cattle," 6:46

There are no animals on earth nor birds that fly on two wings but that are creatures and communities like yourself. [See] We [God] have not neglected anything in this book [the Qur'an]. Eventually to your Sustainer all will be gathered."

—"The Cattle," 6:38

ABOUT THE AUTHOR

RASHED HASAN HAS A DEEP faith in God and shares a deepening concern about the welfare of the human race. He was born in a third-world Muslim country but was fortunate to be educated in some of the finest institutions in the Western world. As he traveled throughout Muslim lands, he saw poverty, a lack of education, a rise in conservative thinking, and a lack of empowerment and self-governance on large scales. Yet he was fascinated by the humility and God consciousness of the average person. As he traveled around the Western world, he witnessed vigorous intellectual discourses, unprecedented economic well-being, and awesome technological innovations. But he was dismayed by the absence of humility, the lack of respect for human equality, the reappearance of far-right groups and racism, and the alarmingly sharp rise of income disparity.

Rashed has had a long career in industry, management consulting, and technology entrepreneurship. He worked for premier management consulting firms such as Booz Allen Hamilton and Ernst & Young. He worked for and consulted with major global corporations in the automotive industry, health care, energy, media, pharmaceuticals, transportation, building materials, and so on, including companies such as the Ford Motor Company, Alyeska Pipeline, Pfizer, Lucas Aerospace, CNN, Monsanto, Westinghouse, GAF, and others. He cofounded several technology companies in health-care informatics and big-data analytics. He has also established social ventures in Bangladesh in software and health care.

Along the way he also founded and led a number of faith-based grassroots political youth leadership and immigrant advocacy organizations in the United States, in collaboration with the US Department of Justice, the Pennsylvania

Department of Health, the Jewish Healthcare Foundation, the Heinz Endowment, and other philanthropic groups. He also worked with multinational donor agencies such as the United States Agency for International Development, the Swedish Development Fund, IFC, Abu Dhabi Development fund, and so on for social ventures and nonprofit initiatives.

Rashed lives in Alexandria, Virginia, a town known for its historical connection to the American Revolution and George Washington. He devotes part of his time to building a technology consulting company and is actively involved in community dialogue and building relationships at professional, personal, and community levels, with special attention to and interest in young people who question the world as it is and aspire to change the world to be a better place. While not working, he can be found reading books, traveling, cooking a meal, and gardening (with limited success) with his wife, to whom plants are no less dear than her own children.

Rashed earned a bachelor of science and a master of science in mechanical engineering from the Massachusetts Institute of Technology in Cambridge, Massachusetts, and a master of business administration in finance and operations from the Wharton School of the University of Pennsylvania in Philadelphia. He also teaches as an adjunct faculty member at George Mason University's School of Business in Fairfax, Virginia. He also founded and is the executive director of a nonprofit, MyLLife Inc. (www.myllife.org), in Alexandria, Virginia. Further information on the book and the author can be found at www.rashedhasan.com.

www.ingramcontent.com/pod-product-compliance
Lightning Source LLC
Chambersburg PA
CBHW051032160426
43193CB00010B/921